Thank you
Alis

ATTACHMENT AND PERSONALITY IN CLINICAL SETTINGS

ASSESSMENT AND TREATMENT ISSUES

Adriana Lis, Claudia Mazzeschi,
Silvia Salcuni & Daniela Di Riso
Editors

ATTACHMENT AND PERSONALITY IN CLINICAL SETTINGS

ASSESSMENT AND TREATMENT ISSUES

Psimática

© 2008 Psimática

First Edition: July 2008

Editorial Psimática
Modesto Lafuente, 5, Bajo 1
ES-28010, Madrid, Spain
Tf. +34 914 475 052
www.psimatica.com
psimatica@psimatica.com

Cover design: Juan Esbert Lilienfeld
Layout: Agustín Sanz
Printed and bound by Publidisa

ISBN: 978-84-88909-22-0
Depósito Legal: SE-3858-2008, U.E.

TABLE OF CONTENTS

FOREWORD

In clinical settings psychological tests can help us access the inner worlds of the confused and distressed people who seek our help. In this way, we are able to understand these clients' internal dilemmas, which can help them and the people close to them find new compassion for their struggles and new ways of moving forward. To use psychological tests in this way, clinicians must be well informed about psychological theory and research and how these relate to the tests they use. In this volume, Lis, Mazzeschi, Salcuni, and Di Riso enhance our ability to understand our clients by elucidating attachment theory and its relationship to psychopathology and the major personality assessment instruments in current use. To my knowledge, this ambitious undertaking is the first of its kind, and the amount of information the authors have compiled in one place is remarkable.

The book begins with a concise and readable synopsis of Bowlby's attachment theory and a summary of the research relating attachment status to psychopathology. I have almost never seen a clearer depiction of Bowlby's basic concepts. Next, Lis and colleagues examine the two major methods of assessing attachment status, the Adult Attachment Interview (AAI) and the Adult Attachment Projective (AAP). Clinicians unfamiliar with these techniques will come away with a good basic understanding of how they work and they relate to each other. Then, the authors review the two most widely used personality assessment instruments--the MMPI/MMPI-2 and the Rorschach inkblots (as scored and interpreted by Exner's Comprehensive System)—and discuss how these tests relate to the concepts of attachment. While much of the research they review is still in its infancy, the authors valiantly pull together a number of studies and discuss their implications for clinical use.

The latter third of the book consists of five case studies in which the authors illuminate the lives of clients from different clinical settings, using the assessment techniques reviewed earlier in the book, and paying particular attention to attachment concepts and how they help us understand these clients' difficulties. This was my favorite section of the book, and I enjoyed seeing the careful integration of the different sources of information, and how the authors resolved apparent discrepancies between the different tests. One of the cases involved a collaborative assessment of a 20-year-old woman, and I appreciated the opportunity to read actual passages from the authors' feedback letter to this client. The letter used the client's AAP stories to help her understand the internal dilemmas she faced, and I am certain that it helped her feel less ashamed and more accepting of her difficulties.

In closing, this book is a gift, and Lis, Mazzeschi, Salcuni, and Di Riso have had courage to tackle a daunting task not yet attempted by others. I appreciate their efforts and am sure you will too.

Stephen E. Finn
Center for Therapeutic Assessment, Austin, TX

INTRODUCTION

A.Lis, C. Mazzeschi, S. Salcuni, D. Di Riso

Attachment theory as developed by John Bowlby (1969, 1973, 1980) and Mary Ainsworth (1978) postulates that people who experience parenting which adequately meet their emotional or physical needs, will develop internal representations of self and others as safe and available. In the child, the *attachment control system* is activated by a perceived dangerous situation, which generates in the infant a feeling of vulnerability and the consequent search for an attachment figure and the activation of attachment behaviors (calling, smiling, crying ....). The attachment figure's tasks include availability, responsiveness and to offer proximity and contact. In the course of development, based on these experiences of attachment relationships in early childhood - particularly relationships with early caregivers - individuals develop internal representations of themselves and others which forecast and organize subsequent interpersonal behavior (George & West, 2001). Ainsworth first described three major attachment styles based on infant responses to the *Strange Situation*: secure, avoidant/dismissing, preoccupied/ambivalent-resistant. Main and Solomon (1990) added a fourth attachment style called disorganized/unresolved. This fourth attachment classification is an important marker for developmental risk (see Lyons-Ruth & Jacobvitz, 1999, for review; Solomon & George, 1999b). Therefore, there are now four classification groups of attachment: secure, avoidant/dismissing, preoccupied/ambivalent-resistant, and disorganized/unresolved (Ainsworth, Blehar, Waters, & Wall, 1978; Main & Solomon, 1990).

Numerous research studies have demonstrated a few correlations between attachment relationships and other kinds of relationships the individual is involved with during the course of his or her development; such as friendship, love relations. However, attachment is not love, friendship, romance, empathy, attunement, emotion regulation, inter-subjectivity or theory of mind (George, 2005).

Attachment theory is well known not only for its theoretical importance, but also for its methodological contributions to attachment research. Among others, contributions include devising specific instruments that measure attachment patterns (developmental approach) and attachment styles (socio-cognitive approach). There is a close relationship between theoretical approaches to attachment and measures of the different kinds of attachment identified above. The Adult Attachment Interview (AAI, George, Kaplan, & Main, 1984, 1985, 1996) was the first attachment theory-based measure developed to assess adult attachment. Over the course of the two past decades, the AAI has become the *gold standard* adult attachment assessment to assess attachment status as defined by the Bowlby-Ainsworth construct. More recently a new tool has been devised to assess attachment status; the Adult Attachment Projective System Picture (AAP, George & West, 1997). Besides the AAI and AAP an increasing number of researchers have come to use self-report adult attachment questionnaires (see Crowell & Treboux, 1995, for a comprehensive comparison of the AAI with self-report measures).

Attachment studies have been often accused of being carried out without non-clinical versus clinical samples. In our book, we will present the increasing literature which shows connections between attachment and psychopathology and analyses shortcomings.

However, attachment theory is a theoretical model currently used to explain normal development and adaptation and psychopathology and normality versus psychopathology. Different meta-analyses carried out on the distribution of attachment in a non-clinical population have showed the following percentages: 58% Secure, 24% Dismissing, 18% Preoccupied and 19% Unresolved (van Ijzendoorn & Bakermans-Kranenburg, 1996). In other words, a large part of non clinical individuals are insecure. So, an important question about attachment concerns patterns of attachment and psychopathology. For example, is insecurity equal to psychopathology or does it indicate a less profound liability and is unresolved/ disorganized attachment a major indicator of psychopathology and, if so, what kind of psychopathology?

Numerous studies have sought to explore the effect of attachment security on the normal and abnormal personality functioning of children and adults. Several important questions about attachment can be formulated as follows: do attachment patterns and/or styles represent a personality dimension; how and how much this dimension is connected or interwoven with other personality dimensions, and how and how much should a clinician relay on attachment theory to complete their picture of the patient's personality function?

These broad questions can be approached by different theoretical and methodological viewpoints. Many papers, for instance, have been written about possible relationship among psychoanalytic theories of personality and attachment theories. Also many papers have been written about a relationship between family-therapy approaches and attachment theory. However, the aim of this book is not to examine all the research of possible theoretical or methodological relationships among attachment and personality theories.

Instead, an aim is to focus on instruments used to assess personality dimensions and attachment. An indicator of recent interest in the relationship between projective methods and attachment is demonstrated by the fact that a new projective method has been devised: the Adult Attachment Projective (AAP, George & West, 2001).

This book focuses on several specific instruments: Rorschach, MMPI, AAI and AAP. The first three instruments are the three most used and studied personality and attachment pattern assessment tools. The last one is a new instrument which assesses attachment and, therefore, we think that its inclusion in this book would be useful for clinicians and researchers.

Assessment tools of attachment, the Rorschach and the MMPI will be included in a multi-method approach of personality assessment. Every day clinicians try to integrate the results from different assessment methods that often seem contradictory. Integrating these, at least, apparent contradictions is often very fruitful. *Multi-method assessment*, a strategy increasingly used by clinicians around the world, is more and more the focus of validity research (Funder, 1997; Meyer, 1996b; Meyer et al. (2001), Ozer, 1999). Although, different methods of assessment provide largely unique information about a person's personality and functioning, no single assessment measure is sufficiently comprehensive on its own to provide a comprehensive picture of personality, unambiguous information about overt behaviour, or reasonable, individualized predictions (Meyer et al., 2001, Gacono, 2001). A number of researchers (e.g. Meyer et al., 1998, Meyer et al., 2001, Gacono et al., 2001) have emphasized the importance of using a number of different assessment methods when examining a client-multi-method assessment (Mattlar, 2003; Meyer et al., 1998; 2001). Also, the *incremental validity*, i.e. additional information different methods contribute increases the validity of the evaluation, and has recently become the focus of validity research.

In this book, the multi-method approach will be explained using clinical cases and measures of attachment status will be described together with other assessment methods.

This book was developed with several purposes in mind. First, give a general description of attachment theory and its connection with personality functioning. Second, describe the state of the art of some specific measures that have been and continue to be used in the assessment of attachment and psychotherapy. In this book, two measures of attachment status, AAI and AAP, were chosen for study as well as two measures of personality assessment: the MMPI and the Rorschach test scored by Comprehensive System. Finally, clinical cases are used to demonstrate how attachment theory, is useful for the clinician. Future developments will be described in the conclusive chapter.

The first part of this book includes two chapters. The first chapter is devoted to a review of Bowlby's original contribution to the understanding of personality functioning as described in Bowlby's *trilogy*. Special attention is given to the organizing role attachment has in the dynamic function of personality structure. The second chapter is devoted to a review of the most recent thinking about attachment and personality, post Bowlby. This review briefly includes: (a) personality structure and attachment; (b) psychopathology and attachment; (c) attachment and its importance in psychotherapy, and psychotherapy progress.

Research studies on attachment and personality using the personality assessment tools that are described earlier are in the second part of this book). One chapter is devoted each to the AAI and the AAP. Then, one chapter each describes the latest and best of the published studies on MMPI assessment and Attachment, and on the Rorschach assessment and Attachment.

The third part of this book features the AAP, the Rorschach and the MMPI assessments measures can be used in clinical practice, and together provide a more integrated picture of personality than using them assessment separately.

PART I

ATTACHMENT, PERSONALITY AND PSYCHOPATHOLOGY

1 THE ATTACHMENT THEORY: THE THEORETICAL BACKGROUND

C. Mazzeschi, L., Laghezza, D. Di Riso, Chiara Napoli

1.1 Introduction

Attachment theory is specifically focused on the role that relationships play in human development, from the cradle to the grave. From infancy to adulthood, along all the course of the life span, mental health seems to be closely tied to relationships with attachment figures who provide emotional support and protection. These basic principles are the legacy of John Bowlby's work, the father of the attachment theory.

Attachment theory is the combined work of John Bowlby and Mary Ainsworth (Ainsworth & Bowlby, 1991) who worked together to explain and empirically support how relationships are important for the well being of human beings. Drawing on concepts from ethnology, cybernetics, information processing, developmental psychology, and psychoanalysis, Bowlby formulated the basic tenets of his theory. He revolutionized modern thinking about a child's tie to the mother and its disruption through separation, deprivation, and bereavement. Mary Ainsworth's innovative methodology not only made it possible to test some of Bowlby's ideas empirically but also helped to expand the theory itself. Her work is responsible for some of the new directions in attachment theory. One Ainsworth contribution was the concept of the attachment figure as a secure base from which an infant can explore the world. In addition, she formulated the concept of maternal sensitivity to infant signals and its role in the development of infant-mother attachment patterns. The ideas now guiding attachment theory have a long developmental history. Although Bowlby and Ainsworth worked independently of each other during their early careers, both were influenced by Freud and other psychoanalytic thinkers-directly in Bowlby's case, indirectly in Ainsworth's. Bowlby's first formal statement of attachment theory, building on concepts from ethnologic and developmental psychology, was presented to the British Psychoanalytic Society in London in three now classic papers: *The Nature of the Child's Tie to His Mother* (1958), *Separation Anxiety* (1959), and *Grief and Mourning in Infancy and Early Childhood* (1960). By 1962, Bowlby had completed two further papers (never published; 1962 a and b) on defensive processes related to mourning. These five papers represent the first basic blueprint of attachment theory. In the meanwhile, Mary Ainsworth conducted two groundbreaking projects: the Ganda Project (Ainsworth, 1963, 1967) and the Baltimore Project (Ainsworth, 1978).

1.2 The attachment Trilogy. Attachment, Separation and Loss

The best way to illustrate Bowlby's theory is to follow historically the development of this theory as it is explained in the three volumes of the trilogy: *Attachment, Separation and Loss* (1969, 1973, 1980).

1.2.1 The first volume: Attachment

In *Attachment* (Bowlby, 1969) Bowlby developed a new theory of motivation and behavior control. Bowlby began by defining attachment behavior as a behavior that has proximity to an attachment figure, has a predictable outcome and whose evolutionary function is the infant's protection from danger. In defining this new motivational-behavior system, Bowlby distinguished three concepts of attachment (Cassidy, 1999): 1) attachment behavior 2) attachment behavioral system and 3) attachment bond. *Attachment behavior* is the behavior that promotes proximity to the attachment figure. The *attachment behavioral system* essentially *asks* the following fundamental question: is the attachment figure nearby, accessible, and attentive? If the child perceives the answer to this question to be yes, he or she feels secure, confident and is likely to actively explore his or her environment, play with others, and be sociable. If, however, the child perceives the answer to this question to be no, the child experiences anxiety and is likely to exhibit attachment behaviors ranging from simple visual searching on the low extreme to active following and vocal signaling on the other. These behaviors continue until either the child is able to reestablish a desirable level of physical or psychological proximity to the attachment figure or until the child *wears down*, as may happen in the context of a prolonged separation or loss. In such cases of helplessness, Bowlby believed the child experiences despair and depression.

The attachment behavioral system monitors the physical proximity and psychological availability of a stronger and wiser attachment figure and activates and regulates attachment behavior directed toward that figure. The attachment behavioral system is the organization of attachment behaviors within the individual. From the perspective of attachment, attachment behaviour can be seen in isolation from other behaviours since each form of behaviour (attachment, exploratory, caretaking, sexual, food-seeking, etc.) is seen to exist as a separate behaviour system in competition with other behavioural systems. These behaviour systems are deemed separate, biologically, genetically determined, evolutionary adaptations serving species preservation.

The *attachment bond* is an affection tie. According to Ainsworth, this bond has an individual characteristic: it is not something between two people because a person can be attached to another who is not, in turn, attached to him or her. Attachment as a bond is part of a larger range of affective bonds that a person develops during the lifespan. According to Ainsworth "…an affection bond is persistent…involves a specific person who is not interchangeable with anyone else…the relationship is emotionally significant..the individual whishes to maintain proximity to or contact with the person…the individual feels distress at involuntary separation from the person or, in case of voluntary separation, he or she experiences distress when proximity is prevented…and – this is the specificity of attachment bond – the individual seek security and comfort in the relationship with the person…" (Cassidy, 1999, pg. 12). The presence or the absence of attachment behaviors does not demonstrate the existence of an attachment bond. Even if a child does not show attachment behavior to the parent, the child is still attached. While attachment behaviors are largely situational, the attachment bond exists consistently over time, whether or not attachment behavior is present. The behavioral systems, proposed by Bowlby, can provide insight in individuals that have progressed an ability to construct internal working models of the environment and of their own actions in it (Craik, 1943, J. Young, 1964). The more adequate is an organism's internal working model, the more accurate the organism can predict the future. However, adds Bowlby, if working models of the environment and self are out of date or are only half revised after drastic environmental change, pathological functioning may ensue.

1.2.2 The second volume: Separation

In *Separation* (Bowlby, 1973) devised a new approach and described an epigenetic model of personality development inspired by Waddington's (1957) theory of

developmental pathways. In this volume, studying fear in children, Bowlby assert-
ed that two distinct sets of stimuli elicit fear: the presence of unlearned and later of
culturally acquired clues to danger and/or the absence of an attachment figure.
Although escape from danger and to an attachment figure commonly occurs together, these two classes of behavior are governed by separate control systems (observable when a hostile dog comes between a mother and her young child). Even if
conceptually distinct, Bowlby considers both as members of a larger family of
stress-reducing and safety-promoting behavioral systems whose more general function is maintaining an organism within a defined relationship to his or her environment. Rather than striving for stimulus absence, as Freud had suggested, Bowlby
posits that humans are motivated to maintain a dynamic balance between familiar-
ity-preserving, stress-reducing behaviors (attachment to protective individuals and
to familiar home sites, retreat from the strange and novel) and antithetical exploratory and information-seeking behaviors.

In *Separation,* he expands on the ideas proposed in *Attachment* by suggesting that, within an individual's internal working model of the world, working models of self and attachment figure are especially salient. In this volume, Bowlby also
elucidates the role of internal working models in the intergenerational transmission
of attachment patterns. Individuals who grow up to become relatively stable and
self-reliant, he postulates, normally have parents who are supportive when called
upon, but who also permit and encourage autonomy. Such parents tend not only
to engage in fairly frank communication of their own working models of self, of
their child, and of others, but also indicate to the child that these working models
are open to questioning and revision. For this reason, says Bowlby, the inheritance
of mental health and of ill health through the family micro-culture is no less important, and may well be far more important, than is genetic inheritance (Bowlby,
1973, p. 323).

The internal working models (IWM)

The idea of an internal working model, appeared – as we have seen - in the volume Attachment, came to Bowlby from the work of Kenneth Craik who proposed
in 1943 that organisms are capable of forming complex "internal working models"
of their environment and this capacity improve their chance of survival by making
their behaviors more flexible and adaptive. At the same time, Bowlby was very
familiar with the Freud's thinking about the inner or representational world and
with the ideas of internalized relationships (Klein, 1932; Winnicott, 1958). The general conception of an internal working model can be applied to all the kind of representations. However, Bowlby (1969/1982) used the concept of "inner working
models" to describe specifically the processes involved in the internalization and
continuing influence of *attachment-related* experiences beyond childhood and adolescence.

The working models of self and attachment figure

According to Bowlby (1973), adult personality is a product of the interaction that the individual had with a very important caregiving figure, as an attachment figure.

Bowlby shared Waddington's hypothesis that the psychological processes that produce the personality structure is very sensitive to the environment and specifically to the family. A good environment produces an adaptive development. One of the most important aspects that seems to influence personality development, are familiar experiences. This means that relationships are fundamental from the beginning of life till the interaction with mother in adolescence, when individual interacts with both parents. The child builds an IWM of the attachment figure. The IWM are representations of the general behaviour that parents have in different situations and they guide the child's expectances in the life.

A person who grew in a *good enough* family, with loving parents, largely had experiences with supportive and protective significant others. These positive experiences allowed him to have the stable and positive expectances towards others which are often confirmed during his lifespan. In challenging situations he felt to have at his disposal an available and protective person. On the other hand, the absence of a figure able to give protection and security to the child produces individuals who have a vision of the world as uncontrolled or/and desolated. They don't have a representation of the other as a secure base. This type of adult thinks that there isn't a figure very available to ask for comfort and protection. There are different experiences that can modified the normal and adaptive development. For example, separation, loss or abandonment experiences seriously can undermine development.

There are also people with less extreme experiences, but they have precise expectances regarding the other and the world. For example, there are people that have learned during infancy that they can produce a reaction in the other only if they follow rules. The rules can be moderate: in this case the person has faith that he can ask help in a difficult moment but if the rules are inflexible and punishments are very hard, the person lacks faith in others. These experiences produce an adult with fear to be alone, to be abandoned and with a tendency to react to new situations with fear.

We can define a mature individual as a person who has faith in others and in the world and has the capacity to ask for support and help from others. An immature person is always anxious and always in need of help or is a type of person that never needs an other.

Following this idea, beyond infancy, attachment relations come to be governed by internal working models that young individuals construct from the experienced interaction patterns with their principal attachment figures.

The function of the IWM

As already seen, repeated interactions with caregivers set the foundation for infants to develop 'internal working models' of self and other (Bowlby, 1982; Bretherton, 1985). These models are 'dynamic internalized representations of relationships that are comprised of both cognitive and affective components' (Pipp, Easterbrooks & Harmon, 1992, p. 738). According to each of these views, the emergence of the self from intimate caregiving relationships is expected.

Attachment's IWM serve to regulate, interpret and predict both the attachment figure's and the self's attachment-related behavior, thoughts and feelings. If appropriately revised, in line with developmental and environmental changes, an IWM enables reflection and communication about past and future attachment situations and relationships; thus facilitating the creation of joint plans for proximity regulation and the resolution of relationship conflicts. Moreover, an individual who can count on an attachment figure's responsiveness, support and protection is free to give full attention to other concerns, such as exploration and or companion interaction.

According to Bowlby, early successful attachment becomes organized into an array of complex social behaviors and, by extension, the capacity for a wide range of successful relationships. With successful early attachment to one person, an individual learns to tune her behavior to the subtle social cues of others. This tuning, in turn, transforms, via development and experience, into the ability to engage in social relationships, to make friends and to eventually attain physical intimacy. Attachment theory perceives that the development of these structures is influenced by both an inner and outer world (Eagle, 1997; Harris, 2004). Currently, Schore (2003a) is elucidating how this perspective is also supported by neurobiology.

Bowlby stated that "in the working model of the self that anyone builds, a key feature is his notion of how acceptable or unacceptable he himself is in the eyes of his attachment figure" (1973, p. 203). Through exchanges of positive affect sharing or negative affect regulation within relationships, infants learn about their care giving partners from early in infancy, as well as their own effectiveness in the social world (Sroufe & Fleeson, 1986). What begins as an infant–parent partnership becomes internalized in the *self*.

According to attachment theory (Bretherton, 1985, 1991) multiple aspects of the self emerge, including affective (e.g. self-worth), behavioral (e.g. agency), and cognitive (e.g. expectations) (Sroufe, 1989). As we will see later, some of these are dimension that can be assessed by specific tools (AAP).

IWM's characteristics

Since they derive from the internalization of the interaction with attachment figures, the IWM of self and of the attachment figures are complementary. An IWM of self as valued and competent is the product of a context of parents as emotionally available. Conversely, an IWM of self as devalued and incompetent is the counterpart of a working model of parents as rejecting. If the attachment figure has acknowledged the infant's needs for comfort and protection while simultaneously respecting the infant's need for independent exploration of the environment, the child is likely to develop an internal working model of self as valued and reliable. Conversely, if the parent has frequently rejected the infant's bids for comfort or for exploration, the child is likely to construct an internal working model of self as unworthy or incompetent. With the aid of working models, children predict the attachment figure's likely behavior and plan their own responses. What type of model they construct is, therefore, of great consequence.

Bowlby advocated that an IWM will change developmentally. If a sense of security is given to an infant from the availability of the mother, with the growing mastery of cognition and verbal communication, children become increasingly able to rely on internal working models to feel secure even when the attachment figures is not physically present. Growing, children learn that their attachment figure's goals and motives can differ from their own, resulting in the *goal-corrected partnership*, a notion recently supported by research (Wellman, 1990).

Internal working models tend to be stable and have some resistance to change. This characteristic has opened the question on the continuity versus discontinuity in development, a topic that will be explored later in this book.

Another aspect connected with IWM characteristics is their organization in light of defensive process. In the third volume of the Trilogy (Loss, 1980, see later) Bowlby proposed a different model to understand the consequences of the loss of the mother based on cognitive psychology and on the theory of information processing.

As will be explained later, we consider this a central hypothesis of attachment theory, specifically in understanding mental functioning; even if it hasn't been sufficiently taken into account by attachment scholars. This hypothesis will be considered especially from a clinical point of view.

Attachment classification in adulthood and the Adult Attachment Interview, AAI

The origin of AAI. In the 1980s, the field of adult attachment began to evolve. As seen above, a child's pattern of attachment is the product of the complex dynamics of the caregiver-child relationship. Until 1985, attachment classification was based only on observational data (Chapter 19). In 1985, Main, Kaplan and Kassidy with the paper *Security in infancy, childhood and adulthood: A move to level of representation* made a crucial shift in the field of attachment research.

Until that time, research on attachment was focused on the non-verbal behaviors of parents/mother that could be observed and that were correlated to the SS material (also observational). But, at that time, it became apparent that the possible mediator of the differences in care-giving behavior, that respond to different patterns of attachment in children could be representational processes. George, Kaplan and Main (1984, 1985, 1996) devised the Adult Attachment Interview (AAI), a narrative tool able to assess the state of mind of a parent with respect of attachment. The first research using this tool showed that this dimension was related to the infant's response to the parent in the Strange Situation and many studies were then conducted in this field. One of the major results of that research was that an attachment status of a parent would predict the attachment status of their child: with as high as 80 percent predictability (van Ijzendoorn, 1995). This was also called the intergenerational transmission of attachment.

So from the beginning, adult attachment was considered as a dimension of parenting. The introduction of the construct of adult attachment in the field of developmental research will be a continuing significant contribution.

The adult classification system. There are two main adult categories: Secure *versus* Insecure (Dismissing, Preoccupied plus Disorganized), (the last category needs a deeper explanation; see later in this chapter). Following AAI coding system, a person can be assigned to one of the three/four major adult attachment classifications: Secure/Autonomous (*F*), Dismissing (*DS*), Preoccupied/Entangled (*E*) and Unresolved/Disorganized (*U*). The *U* classification especially measures with respect to loss and abuse. In the AAI coding system, this category is assigned in conjunction with a best-fitting alternative adult category (for a more detailed explanation of the AAI categorization, see Chapter III).

These four categories can be grouped in two main categories: Secure *versus* Insecure (Avoidant plus Resistant); the fourth classification – Disorganized – the last one conceptualized by scholars - is treated as something different. It was derived from its association with parent's Unresolved classification and is explained later in this book.

1.2.3 The third volume: *Loss*

The third volume of the Trilogy, *Loss* (Bowlby, 1980) explores the way in which young children respond to a temporary or permanent loss of mother-figure and its implication for the psychology and psychopathology of personality. The third volume is also devoted to the understanding of the origins of adult psychopathology in the light of the experience of childhood. Quoting Bowlby: "...at the beginning of the enquiry, psychoanalysis was the only science that was giving systematic attention to ... affection bonds, separation anxiety, grief and mourning, unconscious mental process, defense, trauma, sensitive period in early life...my theory differs from the classical theories advanced by Freud...I have drawn heavily on findings and ideas of two disciplines, ethnology and control theory...moreover, I draw on recent work in cognitive psychology and human information processing in attempt to clarify problem of defense. As a result, the frame of reference now offered for understanding personality development and psychopathology amounts to a new paradigm and is thus alien to clinicians long used to thinking on other ways..." (Bowlby, 1980, pg. 2).

A model for the mental apparatus

With regarding the historical period, one of the most original ideas proposed in this volume is Bowlby's conceptualization of the mental apparatus. In this model Bowlby adopts the notion of representation and he conceives the mind as made up of different mental models. These ideas came to Bowlby from the information processing theory that - in the 1970s and early 1980s, many researchers were studying and demonstrating. But, as Bretherton said (Bretherton, 2005), "...Bowlby adopts the notion of representation as mental models before empirical support for this speculative idea became available..." (pg. 16). However, Bowlby had known the idea of a working model from the work of Craik as he was quoted in Attachment. According to Bowlby, the concept of an internal working model is general and can be applied to all the kind of representation. Every situation we meet, he says, is constructed in terms of the representational models we have of the world about us and ourselves and the information that reaches us is selected and interpreted in terms of those models.

Bowlby hypothesizes that in the working model of the world a key feature is the notion of who attachment figures are, where they may be found and how they may be expected to respond and he refers to it as attachment internal working model. This model is the one that the assessment tools are supposed to assess. Already in this book – as later in the course of the attachment studies – the way in which these models are connected, is still not completely explored (Bretherton, 2005). According to Bowlby, the mental apparatus is made up of a large number of complex control systems organized in a hierarchical way and they operate with a network of two-way communications between them. At the top of the mental apparatus there is the Principal Systems; its nature is representational even if based on physiological mechanisms. Its construction is important in the role of learning experiences because experiences that begin during the first year of life are repeated almost daily throughout childhood and adolescence. Like physical skills, the cognitive and the action components of attachment representational models become over-learned and they operate automatically and outside awareness.

This model of mental apparatus provides a revision of the previous concept of self and Bowlby began to speak about one self or more selves. Bowlby refers to the two ways of storing information - the episodic and semantic storage- as a distinction that "...may have very significant implications for psychopathology..." (Bowlby, 1980, pg. 61). In the episodic storage, information is stored in terms of temporally dated episodes or events and of temporal - spatial relations between events; in the semantic type, information exists as generalized information about the world, derived from a person's own experience, from what he has learned from others or from some combination of the two. This is very important for Bowlby because he suggests that the construction of mental representations could be very connected to what the child has been told from the parents. Inflow into the semantic memory system is always referred to as an existing cognitive structure. This possible distinction could be the ground for the genesis of emotional and cognitive conflict.

Discrepancies between the information in one type of storage and that in another is because there being a difference in the source from which each derives the dominant proportion of its information. The episodic storage derives information from what the person himself perceives and, in part, also from what he may be told about the episode; the semantic storage derives information from what he is told being dominant over what himself might think. Regarding this issue with respect of the question of self, Bowlby says that: "…in most individuals there is a unified Principal System that is capable of self-reflection but has more or less ready access to all information in long term store, irrespective of its source, of how it is encoded and in which type of storage it may be held…but there are also individuals in whom the Principal System are not unified so that, while one such System might have ready access to information held in one type of storage but little or no access to information held in another, the information to which another Principal System has, access might be in many respect complementary. The two systems would then differ in regards to what each perceived and how each interpreted and appraised events…in so far as communication between systems is restricted they can be described as segregated" (pg. 63-64).

The idea of defense

In the revision of the current theory of defense, Bowlby proposed two major defensive strategies: a) the defensive exclusion and b) the segregation of principal systems.

a) The defensive exclusion. Regarding the first type, following the idea of the selective exclusion - a conscious process aimed to not overloaded and not distracted the person's capacities- Bowlby postulates the existence of *defensive exclusion*, a process that differs from the other in the *nature* of the information that is excluded.

Defensive exclusion arises "…when an individual has developed two inconsistent working models of the same relationship, but only one of dominant in consciousness while the other is repressed or suppressed" (Bretherton, 2005, pag. 18). When Bowlby made a theory for this defense, he followed Peter Freund ideas (1971). Freund thought that the information likely to be defensively excluded is of a kind that, when accepted for processing in the past, has led the person to suffer more or less severely. There are a number of possible reasons why incoming information of certain kinds could, if accepted, lead the person to suffer. With respect of attachment, for example, it could happen that a child's attachment behavior is strongly aroused but, for some reason, it is not responded to. If this situation recurs frequently and for long periods – especially during the early years of life – the system controlling that behavior becomes deactivated. There are consequences when information - because of its significance to the individual - is defensively excluded. Also, the deactivation can be partial or complete. A behavioral system becomes active when the necessary combination of inflows reaches it. When such inflows are excluded, the system must be immobilized, together with the thoughts and feelings to which such inflows give rise. The traditional term for this situation is repression. We may also say that this deactivation is due to certain of the information being significant to the individual. Like repression, defensive exclusion is regarded as being the heart of psychopathology. In such a case, fragments of the information defensively excluded seep through so that fragments of the behavioral defensively deactivated becomes visible; or feeling and other products of processing related to the behavior reach consciousness. In traditional psychoanalytic theory this concept is similar to the dynamic unconscious and the return of the repressed.

The effect magnitude on personality functioning of a behavioral system being deactivated will depend on the status of the system within the personality. If the system is of marginal importance, the absence of the behavior from the personal repertoire may be of no great consequence. If, however, a behavioral system – or a set of behavioral systems – is central for personality functioning, as the set controlling attachment behavior, the effects are likely to be extensive. Many of the patterns of behaviors, thought and feeling considered by clinicians to be defensive can be understood as alternatives to the behavior, thought and feeling that have disappeared following deactivation. They seem not to be merely alternatives but to play a diversionary role.

One or a set of responses a person makes may become *disconnected cognitively* from the interpersonal situation that is eliciting it, leaving him unaware of why he is responding as he is.

The activation of a system mediating attachment behavior - thought and feeling - appears to be achieved by a more or less complete defensive exclusion of sensory inflow of any kind that might activate attachment behavior and feeling. The resulting state is one of emotional detachment which can be either partial or complete. It is when the person is a child that he is especially prone to react in this way particularly during the second half of the first year of life because attachment behavior is most readily elicited and continues to be so at high intensity and for long periods which leads to great suffering if no one is available to give comfort. Also another class of conflict with parents accounts for defensive exclusion. It is when a child observes features of a parent's behavior that the parent wishes he should not know. This emerges in the therapeutic work when a person maintains consciously a favorable image of a parent but, at a less conscious level, he has a contrasting image. Defensive exclusion originates when during earliest childhood or also during later childhood, adolescence and adulthood: 1) the vulnerability to conditions initiating defensive exclusion is at a maximum during the early years of life (the first three); 2) a person's vulnerability seems to diminish during childhood but remains comparatively high throughout the childhood and adolescence and 3) there is no age at which a human being ceases to be vulnerable to factors that maintain or increase defensive exclusion already established.

The effects of defensive exclusion are important for the development of the person. We can say that while defensive exclusion has got benefit, it has also got important consequences that can result in certain not good adaption. Those people in whom defensive exclusion plays an important role are handicapped in their dealing with other people and they are more prone to suffer breakdowns in functioning.

b) The segregation of principal systems and the concept of *Segregated System.* Segregation of principal systems occurs when two or more selves are segregated from each other, each having access to its own sectionalized memory store or working model (Bretherton, 2005, pg. 19). Segregated systems describe a mental state in which painful attachment-related memories are isolated and blocked from conscious thought. This material is likely to be rooted in experiences of trauma or loss through death (Bowlby, 1980; e.g., death of an attachment figure or family member – especially in childhood; physical, sexual, or emotional abuse; abandonment). Thus, the concept of a segregated system seems to be useful for understanding cases of prolonged absence of mourning, cases of compulsive self-reliance and compulsive care giving. This kind of defense is similar to dissociative processes.

The concept of Segregated System is proposed by Bowlby when referring to the case of Geraldine (Volume 3, pg 338) - a case of disordered mourning. Geraldine was a patient seen in therapy and described as "composed and self-assured...aloof..." in the first couple of years of therapy. Geraldine, after several years of therapy, after describing the pain experienced at the time of her mother's death, became intensely attached to the therapist. In this paper, Geraldine is described as having two selves, governed by two different systems. "During the first two years the governing system, the one having free access to consciousness, was a system from which almost every element of attachment behavior was excluded". But coexistent with this Principal System, there was another System, *segregated* from it and unconscious, in which belonged all the missing elements...the autobiographical ones" (Bowlby, 1980, pg. 345). This segregated system was in a state of deactivation but it occasionally found expression. When a segregated system becomes in some degree active, its elements become evident and the system becomes disorganized and dysfunctional.

Bowlby's idea was that two principal systems of behavior, thought, feeling and memory are present but segregated. On the one hand, one system governs the everyday life. On the other hand, there is a system that – like a black box inside the mind – normally is deactivated and has only marginal access to consciousness and because of its state it provides only fragmentary evidence of its existence. According to Bowlby, a segregated system is organized and it is self-consistent (in this sense, it is not different from the one that has access to consciousness), it is mental, characterized by cognitive and affective elements, desires, thought, feeling and memory. "...when the *SS* takes control of behavior, the segregated system shows itself to be so organized with reference to persons and objects in the environment that it is capable of framing plans and execute them, albeit in rather ineffective ways...and the intensity of its feelings is important..."(Bowlby, pg. 348). A segregated system is deactivated by the means of the defensive exclusion. But, according to Bowlby, the opening of the segregated system is not an issue of quantity or intensity pressure of feelings inside it. There are others features of the system being kept segregated "...patterns of behavior that go to make up attachment behavior together with the desires, thoughts, working models and personal memories integral to them", (pg. 348). The segregated system has a structure. However, as Bowlby says, we can also have personality in which the two segregated systems are organized on opposite premises yet both of them are active and conscious.

1.2.4 The role of attachment in the development: a look to the longitudinal studies

Bowlby (1973) stressed the importance of a life-span perspective in the attachment field. In the Epilogue of *Loss*, Bowlby underlined the importance of attachment by saying: "Intimate attachments to other human beings are the hub around which a person's life revolves, not only when he is an infant or a toddler or a schoolchild but throughout his adolescence and his years of maturity as well, and on into old age." (Bowlby, 1980, pg. 442). According to Bowlby, the quality, nature, and effectiveness of the infant– caregiver behavioural organization would forecast the infant's later evolving, complex organization that we know as personality.

From these theoretical considerations, the attachment field has been characterized by research in which attachment theory itself has been more and more considered from a developmental point of view. Attachment research in the Bowlby-Ainsworth tradition has shown itself to be one of the richest longitudinal studies traditions in the developmental domain.

The longitudinal view of studies on attachment has at least two pathways. The first one regards if attachment, once established in infancy, changes in the course of life or if it remains stable. This is known as the question on stability or continuity in attachment. The second one regards the role of attachment in the development of other dimensions of personality functioning along the course of life. We proceed with some consideration regarding the complexity of the second topic by referring to one of the most important follow up studies ever conducted, the *Minnesota Longitudinal Study* (Sroufe, Egeland, Carlson and Collins, 2005).

1.2.5 The role of attachment in the development of personality functioning

The *Minnesota Longitudinal Study* highlights the place of attachment in developmental processes by using primarily the examples of peer and romantic relationships.

The first assessment phase, conducted using the Strange Situation (at 12-18 months) and some observational sessions focused on how parents supported the child's first movements towards autonomy and self-regulation. They, also, collected comprehensive school assessments. When the subjects were 13 years old, parent-child interactions were videotaped in order to study some "attachment variables", such as affective components, conflict negotiation or resolution or possible parent-child boundary violations (Sroufe, 1991). In adulthood, participants were administered the AAI and CRI in order to assess adult romantic relationships. One of the questions addressed in this study was the role of peer relationships as a developmental construct from preschool age to adolescence. The authors suggested that competencies at each phase draw upon competencies from each previous phase. As a consequence, adult romantic relationships draw upon this entire history of interactive and emotional experiences with peers. At the same time, effectiveness with peers is supported in part by experiences in the family, including early attachment experiences. In general, attachment security provided the basis for later effectiveness with peers. Major findings showed that being engaged in a secure relationship during the infant period allows the individual to acquire the attitudes that support engagement with peers. Moreover, peer relationships are predicted by attachment history from preschool to early adulthood. This allows one to suggest that attachment history is a fundamental aspect of individual functioning in life span. However, the most interesting result comes when we consider how attachment experiences work together with other aspects of experience. For example, when the authors evaluated the relationship between early attachment pattern and couple conflict resolution in young adults, they found that the impact of attachment seemed largely mediated through other variables (e.g dyadic balance at 13 years). In conclusion, although attachment seemed to strongly predict adult functioning, when attachment history is combined with others variables, predictions of later outcomes are enhanced.

1.2.6 The development of the field of adult attachment

Despite a common theoretical foundation in attachment theory (Bowlby, 1969), two relatively independent lines of research have emerged in the area of adult attachment with each using a different type of measurement (Crowell, Fraley, & Shaver, 1999; Shaver, Belsky, & Brennan, 2000; Shaver & Mikulincer, 2002).

Primarily, narrative measures, such as the Adult Attachment Interview (AAI; George, Kaplan, & Main, 1984), have typically been used in the study of parent–child relationships. On the other hand, self-report measures have been used in the domain of romantic and marital relationships from the tradition of the social perspective. This second perspective – the social one - arises on the assumption that attachment is an important component of romantic love. In this sense, attachment represents an important issue for marriage engagement along the topic of security. The origin of this line of research is based on the assumption that romantic relationships qualified as attachment bonds and, for this reason, constitute the appropriate context in which adult attachment phenomena can be investigated (Hazan and Zeifman, 1999). According to these authors, it was from early 1980 that Bowlby argued for the relevance of attachment principles to adults' close relationships by comparing the state of desperation of widows with the one of children when they were separated from their mothers. Even though there are important differences in the quality of the bond – specifically due to the asymmetry in the adult relationships, the reciprocity and the role of sexual component – (Weiss, 1982; West, Sheldon-Keller, 1994) couple relationships has become conceptualized in terms of the attachment theory.

At the end of the 1980s, using this perspective, Hazan and Shaver (1987), following Ainsworth's three patterns for children, described three analogous adult attachment styles in couple relationships by using a categorical measure called style of attachment. As we will see later in this book, much research has been conducted using this conceptual framework of attachment (Mikulincer and Shaver, 2003; Steven Rholes and Simpson, 2004) and bringing this original construct to other fields of attachment research.

For our purpose, we want to emphasize that from a methodological point of view, the authors belonging to this field of adult attachment use self-report measures that start from the assumption that people can accurately describe some of their thoughts, feelings and behaviors in romantic attachment relationships. Researchers using questionnaires identified *attachment styles* defined it to be akin to a personality trait. There is a debate of construct equivalence between *attachment pattern* (measuring attachment status) and *attachment styles* (measured by self-report measures). First, many studies have failed to demonstrate a reliable correspondence between attachment style (self-report) and attachment status (AAI) (Crowell & Treboux, 1995). Instead, a reliable correspondence was found between AAI and AAP (George, et al, 1997). But it mainly appears that these two forms of assessment (interview and projective measure vs. self-report measures) may not be tapping the same theoretical construct. Attachment style data appears to be assessing social-cognitive or self-attribution constructs rather than developmental attachment security. The classification outcome using both methods involves both conscious and unconscious mental processing of attachment-related experience and affect. There is an important distinction, however, in how judgments regarding an individual's attachment classifications are derived. Classification using an interview or a projective protocol is based on the evaluation of unconscious defensive processes. This essential dimension is lost in self-report methodology. The items that are or are not endorsed are likely to reflect conscious self-evaluation and/or how the individual wishes to represent him- or herself to others The outcome of self-report items (i.e., the items endorsed or not endorsed) is the product of thoughts about attachment that ultimately must enter conscious thought. (Crowell & Treboux, 1995; George & West, 1999).

Another problem in self-measures of attachment styles versus attachment status is related to the theoretical conceptualization of individual differences in attachment. The vast majority of studies of adult attachment using self-report measures continue to use the traditional 3-category model, based on Ainsworth's original categories: secure (B), avoidant (A), and ambivalent (C) (see Hazan & Shaver,1987). Further, despite the availability of a 4-category self-report measure (Bartholomew & Horowitz, 1991), research suggests that classification based on this measure is not equivalent to the unresolved status as measured by developmentally- based attachment assessments (AAP and AAI – see George & West, 1999). The processes related to "unresolved" adult attachment include experiences of the individual's failure to find solace and care in the fact of traumatic attachment events, such as loss, sexual trauma, parental psychopathology and/or alcoholism (Carlson, Cicchetti, Barnett, & Braunwald, 1989; O'Connor, Sigman, & Brill, 1987; Teti, Gelfand, Messinger, & Isabella, 1995) intimate partner abuse (George & West, 1999; Lyons-Ruth & Jacobvitz, 1999; West & George, 1998). The failure to integrate the disorganized/unresolved attachment group into research ought to result in confusion in theory-building theory and intervention program design that require clear articulation of the ethnology, correlates, and sequel of attachment disorganization and the lack of resolution of loss or trauma (Solomon & George, 1999b).

2 ATTACHMENT, PSYCHOPATHOLOGY PSYCHOTHERAPY OUTCOME

C. Mazzeschi, L., Laghezza, D. Di Riso

2.1 Bowlby and psychopatology

In his formulation of attachment theory, Bowlby (1973, 1980, 1982, 1986) postulated that experiences of insecurity with primary caregivers in infancy establish patterns of social interaction and emotional regulation that may be the basis of some adult psychopathology.

Bowlby (1969/1982, 1973, 1980) provided a model of development with specific implications for psychopathology. The child's negative representation of self and others seems to compromise normal functioning in processing attachment-related thoughts and feelings. In general, specific attachment-related events in childhood as trauma or early and long-lasting separations from parents, could be associated to different kind of adult psychopathology (Warren, Huston, Egeland and Sroufe, 1997).

The impact of an individual's early interpersonal experience is never lost but structured and interpreted in later mental representations of attachment, the work of Bowlby (1973, 1988) can be considered a starting point for a truly developmental perspective of psychopathology (Carlson & Sroufe, 1995; Cicchetti & Cohen, 1995).

Over the last two decades, research carried out within the framework of attachment theory has generated a rapidly growing body of findings on the importance of early caring experience in the development of psychopathology and in the promotion of adaptation (Main, 1995). Attachment theory, in particular, states that the modality in which the individual's personal expectations, feelings and defences are organized – the mental representations of attachment – is central to the understanding of many psychopathological disorders (Cicchetti, Cummings, Greenberg, & Marvin, 1990; Sroufe, 1995). In this context the following relevant questions can be outlined: (a) How individual differences in attachment are rooted in patterns of early dyadic regulation, (b) How these patterns provide the basis for individual differences in the emerging self and, finally, (c) Which implications such early differences have on the development of patterns of more or less adaptive self-regulation in later development (Sroufe, 1995).

It is within this theoretical context that the importance of the clinical application of attachment theory can be appreciated; indeed, it allows us to obtain essential information in order to identify risk or protective mechanisms associated with development (Sameroff & Emde, 1989). If it is true that negative childhood events are considered risk factors for psychopathology because of their frequency, their severity or their cumulative effects, it is also crucial to consider their potential translation into stable representations (i.e., states of mind concerning attachment), and how these may be associated with specific psychological conditions. From this perspective, developmental mechanisms shed light on some crucial clinical issues, viewing adaptive and maladaptive patterns of personality as emerging from the reorganization of previous patterns, structures and competencies (Crittenden, 1998; Rosenstein & Horowitz, 1996).

To begin this chapter, we would like to report Van IJzendoorn and Bakermans-Kranenburg's (1996) meta-analysis on 33 studies, including more than 2,000 Adult Attachment Interview (AAI) classifications. The study examined the distributions of AAI classifications in samples of non clinical fathers and mothers, in adolescents, in samples from different cultures, and in clinical groups. Fathers, adolescents, and participants from different countries show about the same distribution of AAI classifications as non clinical mothers do. The distribution of non clinical mothers is as follows: 24% dismissing, 58% autonomous, and 18% preoccupied mothers. About 19% of the non clinical mothers are unresolved with respect to loss or trauma of other kinds. Mothers from low socioeconomic status show more often dismissing attachment representations and unresolved loss or trauma. Autonomous women and autonomous men are more often married to each other than can be expected by chance, and the same goes for unresolved men and women. Clinical participants show highly deviating distributions of AAI classifications, with a strong overrepresentation of insecure attachment representations. The effect size discriminating non-clinical versus clinical groups (d = 1.03) was found to be strong. Ultimately, in a four-way analysis, only 8% of members of clinical samples were judged secure. But systematic relations between clinical diagnosis and type of insecurity were absent.

A number of studies in the 1990s (Adam, Sheldon-Keller, & West, 1996; Allen, Hauser, & Borman-Spurrel, 1996; Fonagy, Leigh, Steele et al., 1996; Patrick, Hobson, Castle, Howard, & Maughan, 1994; Rosenstein & Horowitz, 1996) established the validity of using of the AAI in adults and adolescents with a wide range of psychopathology.

Patrick, Hobson, Castle, Howard, and Maughan (1994) administered the AAI and the Parental Bonding Instrument (PBI; Parker, Thupling, & Brown, 1979) to 12 dysthymic and 12 borderline patients, matched for age, educational achievement, and socioeconomic status. They found that 10 of 12 (88%) of the borderline patients were classified as "fearfully preoccupied by trauma or loss" (E3). In this study, 75% of the borderline patients were classified as *unresolved*. Moreover they found that the borderline group reported lower maternal care and higher maternal overprotection on the PBI.

Fonagy's et al. (1996) examined the relation of patterns of attachment and psychiatric status in 82 non psychotic inpatients and 85 case-matched controls using the AAI. Psychiatric patients were diagnosed with the Structured Clinical Interview for *Diagnostic and Statistical Manual of Mental Disorders* (3rd ed., rev.) There was a highly significant difference between the psychiatric and control groups in the three-way distribution of attachment pattern as well as for the four-way attachment distribution. Psychiatric patients' narratives of their childhoods could be readily distinguished from those of normal control participants. On Axis I, anxiety was associated with unresolved status, and AAI scales were able to discriminate depression and eating disorder. On Axis II, borderline personality disorder (BPD) was linked to experience of severe trauma and lack of resolution with respect to it. Both preoccupied and unresolved classifications appear to be characteristic of this psychiatric sample. The significant differences between mean AAI scales for the psychiatric and control groups showed that Positive Experience (e.g., loving, nonrejecting parents) and State of Mind (coherence of mind, transcript, metacognition) were lower and that Negative Experience and State of Mind scales were higher for the psychiatric group. The study provided overwhelming support for the association of psychiatric disorder with unresolved difficult early relationships, in line with the predictions of attachment theory (Bowlby, 1980, 1988).

Results of these investigations indicate that the occurrence of autonomous attachment is exceedingly low among clinical groups and individuals with psychopathology. Furthermore, these studies suggest that the Unresolved and Cannot Classify groups are observed with significant frequency in association with psychiatric diagnosis (see Hesse, 1996, for a review).

These pioneering studies provide evidence that attachment organization lacking security and coherence in adulthood may lead to "enduring vulnerabilities to psychopathology" (Allen et al., 1996, p. 254) by impairing the capacity to be part of satisfying social relationships, as well as the ability to understand and evaluate social interactions appropriately. Non-autonomous states of mind specifically may impair ability to attend to social interactions in a flexible and non-defensive way. Similarly, insecure states of mind may lead individuals to have negatively biased expectations of self and others, leading to self-fulfilling and self-perpetuating patterns of atypical interpersonal interactions and relationships. Indeed, patterns of adult attachment may mediate the transmission of psychopathology across generations (Allen et al., 1996).

During the 1980s and 1990s, measures of adult attachment were refined. They included measures of pattern of attachment and measures of styles of attachment. In the same period diagnoses of psychopathology also were made more reliable among raters, beginning with the revised third edition of the Diagnostic and Statistical Manual of Mental Disorders (DSM III-R). A standardized semi-structured diagnostic interview based on the DSM III-R, The Structured Clinical Interview for DSM III-R (SCID), permits a clinical investigator to reach a reliable diagnosis, using a standardized method.

2.2 Attachment, psychopathology and DSM

In the following, we are going to provide a brief excursus about possible connections between Axis I and Axis II DSM-IV disorders and attachment issues.

Our purpose was not to provide an exhaustive review of all studies on psychopathology study, but to explain some of the most representative researches in the last 10 years. This review started from the complete existing literature reported in PsycInfo. We are going to focus on adult samples and on the most classical instruments to assess attachment. However, not all the disorders according to DSM will be reviewed, because some of them were never studied in connection with attachment in the existing literature. For instance Though Disturbances were never extendedly investigated within the framework of attachment. Our brief and not exhaustive review, will follow the following pathway. First we will review studies on attachment patterns, then studied carried out with self-report measures.

2.2.1 Axis I

Attachment and eating disorder. Bowlby (1973) proposed a model in which also eating disorders seemed to be related with specific family attitudes: when the child feels out of control or unlovable could express this kind of grief through externalizing symptoms. Most of the times these children tried to turn the attention away from own distress by uncontrolled eating behaviours. Family environments characterized by overcontrolling parents or perfectionist mother that communicate lack of support, could be considered as risk factors.

Cole-Detke (1998) administered the Adult Attachment Interview (AAI) along with the NEO Five-Factor Inventory, and the COPE to examine the role of attachment organization, personality, field dependence, and coping in the development of depressive and eating disordered tendencies in 66 college women, selected for high or low levels of depressive and/or eating disordered symptoms were. AAI transcripts were rated using both the Attachment Interview Q-Sort and Main and Goldwyn's (1994) scoring method. Results indicated that depression was associated with use of an insecure and preoccupied attachment strategy as well as with a neurotic, introverted, disagreeable, and un conscientious personality profile and the use of negative coping methods rather than positive ones. Moreover, regression models revealed that the effects of attachment organization on depression were mediated through personality and coping. In particular, there were several direct correlations between attachment strategies and personality. Eating disorder, however, was not uniquely associated with any particular attachment, personality, or coping profile other than the use of food or exercise to deal with stressors.

Ward et. Al., (2001) examined the attachment status of patients with severe anorexia nervosa and their mothers, using AAI. Twenty consecutive in-patients with a DSM-IV diagnosis of anorexia nervosa and 12 of their mothers were interviewed using the AAI. A 95% level of insecure attachment in the patients with anorexia nervosa (75% D, 20% E) was found. The majority of mothers also had insecure attachments (58% D, 8% E and 17% CC). In fact, only one patient and two mothers received secure ratings, and of these three, two were unresolved with respect to loss. The distribution in both groups was significantly different from that of published norms (van Ijzendoorn & Bakermans-Kranenburg, 1976). The patient subscale scores were broadly similar to published data on eating disordered patients. The subscale scores in the mothers were closer to the eating disorder groups than to those of published controls. However, there was no significant association found between the attachment classifcations of mother–daughter pairs. The preponderance of dismissive attachment styles was a marked feature of the analysis, both of the patients with anorexia nervosa and their mothers. These eating-disordered patients were similar to the Fonagy et al. (1996) group on these two scales.

Another group of researches assessesed attachment in eating disorders also with self-report measures, addressing both adolescents and adults in different clinical contexts (Orzolek, & Catherine (2001), Hochdorf, Latzer, Canetti, & Bachar (2005) Tasca, Kowal, Balfour, Ritchie, Virley, & Bissada (2006) Tasca, Balfour, Ritchie, & Bissada, (2007), Tasca, Balfour, Ritchie & Bissada, (2007))

We are going to describe two of the most meaningful and well-done studies.

About adults, the first study was carried out by Hochdorf, Latzer, Canetti, & Bachar (2005) and examined how attachment styles were connected to attraction to death in a sample of 34 anorexic and 34 bulimic patients, matched by age, sex, and socioeconomic status to 37 normal controls. Adult Attachment Scale, the Beck Depression Inventory, and the Multi-Attitude Suicidal Tendency Scale were administered. A significant difference between the three attachment styles was found beyond depression. ED patients scored significantly higher on the insecure attachment scale and were less attracted to and more repulsed by life than controls. Insecure attachment style may explain the repulsion by life, while the illness itself may serve as a false "secure base" and may protect from the fear of death.

Tasca, Kowal, Balfour, Ritchie, Virley, and Bissada (2006) tested a model of attachment insecurity in a clinical sample of 268 eating disordered women. Structural relationships among attachment insecurity, BMI, perceived pressure to diet, body dissatisfaction, restrained eating, and negative affect were assessed. The data suggested that attachment insecurity may lead to negative affect. As well, attachment insecurity may lead to body dissatisfaction, which in turn may lead to restrained eating among women with eating disorders.

Another consistent group of studies was focused on teenagers or college student sample (Mccarthy (1998), Bowman, (2000) Suldo, & Sandberg (2000) Kiang & Harter (2006)) Some of these papers assessed attachment dimension with Parental Bonding Instrument, and found specific pattern of attachment related to eating disorders. Among them we chose to review two studies.

Suldo, & Sandberg (2000) examined the relationship between Bartholomew's 4-category model of adult attachment (1990) and eating disorder symptomatology in female college students. 169 undergraduate females (aged 18-72 yrs) completed the Relationship Questionnaire (K. Bartholomew and L. M. Horowitz, 1991) and the Eating Disorder Inventory. Results showed that only preoccupied attachment scores were positively correlated with the eating disorder symptoms of drive for thinness and bulimia.

Kiang & Harter (2006) proposed a model that predicted eating disorder symptomatology. This single model was aimed at integrating sociocultural and attachment processes, determining their relative influence. The model was tested on the basis of 146 female undergraduates self-report data. Path analyses tested the fit of the conceptual model with two hypothesized pathways: (1) attachment avoidance and anxiety (modeled separately) across mother, father, and romantic partner domains would predict psychological correlates of eating disorders, thereby increasing risk for disordered behaviors. (2) higher awareness of sociocultural values about appearance would lead to less perceived appearance satisfaction which would, in turn, lead to eating disordered behaviour. Attachment avoidance exhibited stronger effects than anxiety (explaining 31% and 25% of variance in psychological correlates, respectively).

Attachment and depression. According to Bowlby (1980), depression in adulthood seemed to be correlated with three particular events that could have been occurred in childhood experience: (1) the child could experience a strong sense of hopelessness and desperation after one of the caregivers'death, (2) the child capacity to create a meaningful bond with caregivers seemed to be very important in order to avoid a model of the self as a failure, (3) parents could provide to the child the idea that he or she could be lovable and competent, in other word accepted by them. In particular, one of these attachment elements that seemed to be related with depression is the availability of the parents. The sense of total despair of the child, is connected not only with the real loss of mother or father, but just with unloving and rejecting parents behaviours.

Some studies in this field assessed attachment in relation with depression using different tools and addressing different kind of samples, also very specific as gay communities (Allen, Porter, McFarland, McElhaney & Marsh, 2007, Zakalik & Wei (2006) Scharfe (2007) Troxel, Cyranowski, Hall, Frank & Buysse (2007).

First, we are going to describe the study using the AAI. Allen, Porter, McFarland, McElhaney & Marsh (2007) studied the relation between pattern of attachment measured with the AAI and multiple domains of psychosocial functioning in a community sample of 167 early adolescents. Secure attachment organization was linked to success in establishing autonomy, to the capacity of maintaining a sense of relatedness both with fathers and with peers, even after accounting for predictions from qualities of the mother-teen relationship. Insecurity was associated with patterns of externalizing behaviour and higher and stable patterns of depressive symptoms across adolescence.

The following two studies are example of investigations conducted with well known self-report measures of attachment in women samples.

Scharfe (2007) explored the association between women's attachment representations and episodes of depressed mood during pregnancy and early postpartum months. 235 women completed attachment, the *Relationship Scales Questionnaire (RSQ)*, (Bartholomew & Horowitz, 1991; Griffin and Bartholomew, 1994a, 1994b), and depression questionnaires to assess attachment twice (prenatally and 6 months). The results showed that prenatal attachment scores were associated with both prenatal and several postnatal assessments of depressed mood, and correlations did not differ over time despite a significant decrease in depressed mood from pregnancy to 6 months postpartum. The self-model of attachment was negatively associated with depression over time, and depression was negatively associated with the other-model over time.

Troxel, Cyranowski, Hall, Frank & Buysse (2007) examined the relationship between attachment anxiety, marital status, bed-partner status, and sleep quality in recurrently depressed women. Women were categorized as high or low in attachment anxiety based on *Bartholomew and Horowitz's Relationship Questionnaire* (1991). Polysomnography (PSG) and subjective sleep quality was measured in 107 women with recurrent major depression. Anxiously attached women displayed a reduced percentage of stage 3-4 sleep. Moreover, a significant interaction between attachment anxiety and marital status suggested that anxiously attached women who were previously married (i.e., divorced, separated, or widowed) displayed a particularly low percentage of stage 3-4 sleep. Depressed women who exhibit an anxious attachment style and have experienced a marital rupture showed reduced stage 3-4 sleep, which may signal a concomitant reduction in restorative cognitive and metabolic processes.

Attachment and anxiety disorder. According to Bowlby (1973) specific features of family environment in childhood seemed to be related with anxiety disorders in adulthood, such parental control, overprotection or rejection. Both parents difficulties to let the child go because of excessive concerns and child's worries about being abandoned or rejected by attachment figure, are strictly related to the availability of the caregivers.

Studies in this field assessed attachment in relation with anxiety disorders using different tools and addressing different kind of clinical samples or normative sample with anxiety disorders (Kasoff (2002), Zuellig (2003), Eng (2004), Eng and Heimberg (2006), Lewis (2007).

We would like to stress that there are no studies using AAI. We are going to present some studies on the assessment of the relationship between this kind of disorder and self-report measure, in clinical and in non clinical samples.

Zuellig (2003) examined the hypothesis that clients' IWMs would change after a course of cognitive and cognitive-behavioral therapy. Pre and post-therapy IWMs measured using *scales* were compared in clients who underwent 14 weeks of cognitive therapy, self-controlled desensitization, or a combination of cognitive therapy and self-controlled desensitization for treatment of Generalized Anxiety Disorder. Results showed no significant differences among the three therapy conditions on scales measuring IWMs, and little clinically significant change on those scales. Change was found across therapies on two scales, suggesting that cognitive, cognitive-behavioral, and behavioral therapy aided in reducing client's angry/oscillating feelings toward their mothers, as well as their memories of having enmeshed/role-reversed relationships with their mothers during childhood. Finally, clinically significant change on the angry/oscillating, no memory, and rejected scales was associated with clinically significant change on outcome measures for anxiety.

Lewis (2007) examined relationship among early recollections, adult attachment, and self-reported psychiatric symptoms. *The Experiences in Close Relationships Questionnaire-Revised (ECR-R)* and the *Psychiatric Diagnostic Screening Questionnaire (PDSQ)* were used to operationalize adult attachment and psychiatric symptoms, respectively. 31 clients receiving outpatient psychotherapy at the Driekurs Psychological Services Center in Chicago, Illinois participated in the study. They were culturally, ethnically and socioeconomically diverse. Results revealed a significant relationship between internal locus of control, as measured by an early recollections procedure, and adult attachment, as measured by the ECR-R. A positive correlation was found between the anxiety and avoidant attachment scales and various dimensions on the PDSQ. The anxiety scale on the ECR-R had positive correlations with self reports of symptoms synonymous with Generalized Anxiety Disorder, Agoraphobia, Social Phobia and Major Depression. The avoidance scale on the ECR was positively correlated with self reports of symptoms synonymous with Generalized Anxiety Disorder, Agoraphobia and Panic Disorder.

About non clinical samples, Eng (2004) examined the specific interpersonal correlates of GAD and the centrality of relational distress to the extreme worry that is the hallmark symptom of GAD. Forty-eight undergraduate college students who met self-reported criteria for GAD ("GAD-analogue participants") and 53 students who did not meet these criteria ("control participants") were compared *on measures of interpersonal difficulties, attachment styles, security of attachment to parents and peers, coping styles, and social support*. Friends of the participants also reported on the perceived quality of friendship with and the interpersonal difficulties of the participants. Compared to the control participants, GAD-analogue participants were more likely to report a preoccupied attachment style and lower security of attachment to parents (but not to peers). Security of attachment to either parent or peers did not moderate the relation between GAD symptomatology and dimensions of interpersonal functioning.

Attachment and post traumatic stress disorder. Originally dissociation seemed to be related, in an adaptive way, with attachment trauma because it allows an individual not to be overwhelmed by the trauma itself. This kind of reaction is similar to a trance or freezing experiences that could make the person able to sustain a continuous helpless state. Main and Hesse (1990) suggested that just children who experienced, in threatening situations, a pervasive sense of lack of protection, could occur in dissociative disorders. Moreover, frightening parental behaviours could be considered as a cause of dissociation (e.g. abuse). Finally, also multiple models in which the caregiver shift from frightening to loving behaviours toward the child (e.g. from perpetrator to competent caregiver), can create an unintegrated model of self and others.

A group of studies assessed attachment in post traumatic stress disorder using self report measure in adults (Dieperink & Thuras, 2001; Cohen & Dekel, 2002; Tilus, 2003; Declercq & Palmas, 2006; Korlin, Edman, & Nyback, 2007) and in college students (Rothman, 2004; Kokaliari, 2005).We are going to present to the readers two of these studies.

About adults a study carried out by Tilus (2003) investigated the health-enhancing roles of and adult romantic attachment and spiritual orientation in response to traumatic exposure, and the relative presence or absence of Post Traumatic Stress Disorder (PTSD) symptoms following exposure to traumatic events. A non clinical sample of 44 military couples (88 adults) completed the Experience in Close Relationship questionnaire, the Spirituality Orientation Inventory, the Self-Report Inventory for Disorders of Extreme Stress, the Traumatic Antecedents Questionnaire, the PTSD Checklist, the Traumatic Events

Questionnaire, and a demographic questionnaire that inquired about military history, military rank, religious affiliation, religious attendance, and spiritual practice. Statistical analyses found a significant, negative correlation between spiritual orientation and adult romantic attachment. Adult romantic attachment and spiritual orientation were found to moderate PTSD symptoms after traumatic exposure. Increased adult romantic attachment, specifically secure style, was found to mediate PTSD symptoms after traumatic exposure. These findings suggested that stronger levels of spirituality may mitigate the adverse effects of exposure to trauma and adult romantic attachment secure style. If distressed by traumatic symptoms, couples that have high levels of spirituality and a secure style of attachment may significantly reduce traumatic distress and mitigate the development of PTSD.

Adult attachment style and perception of social support in a population of 544 subjects working for a security company and the Belgian Red Cross, in the occurrence of post traumatic stress disorders (PTSD) (Declercq & Palmans, 2006) that investigated the influence of subjective factors of. Results suggested that adult attachment style differentiate between individuals who are more, and who are less prone, to suffer from a PTSD after having experienced a critical incident.

About college students, Rothman's (2004) examined in 271 college students with different exposure the World Trade Center Disaster (WTCD). They examined : (a) whether an individual's attachment to his/her romantic partner, measured by The Multi-Item Measure of Adult Romantic Attachment (MIMARA), reliably would predict an individual's response to the World Trade Center Disaster (WTCD) (WTCD); (b) if self-reports of how college students exposure (physical, emotional and media-related) to the WTCD was related to the development of symptoms of Post Traumatic Stress Disorder (PTSD), measured by the Screen for Posttraumatic Stress (SPTSS). Multiple regression analyses were employed to assess group differences in a variety of areas that included whether the amount of exposure and degree of attachment affected PTSD symptom severity. Results of a follow-up assessment, at 8 months post WTCD, indicated that physical, emotional, media-related exposure, insecure adult romantic attachments, and being female significantly predicted PTSD symptom severity. In addition, in insecurely attached individuals (in contrast with those more securely attached) the level of emotional exposure one had to the WTCD was more directly associated with the reported development of PTSD symptoms. With regard to PTSD diagnosis, physical exposure, media-related exposure, insecure attachment, females and those less exposed to WTCD were significant predictors. The only variable that predicted PTSD symptoms or diagnosis 8 months later was PTSD symptoms and diagnosis from the initial data collection. One important implication from this study is that college students who are exposed to trauma, even indirectly may still suffer from PTSD symptoms. Furthermore, those students with insecure romantic attachments will likely have more difficulty coping with traumatic events and more likely suffer from PTSD symptoms. Recognizing an individual's pattern of romantic attachment is important for it provides a framework for understanding the important role that close personal and interpersonal play in his or her life relationships and provides a rationale for using interpersonal rather than exclusively symptom-focused interventions to reduce the distress of traumatic events.

Kokaliari (2005) proposed a two-phase study assessing psychosocial factors influencing deliberate self-injury among students attending an all-women's college. In Phase-I participants completed inventories that measured demographics, attachment style, post-traumatic stress disorder (PTSD), self-injurious behaviors, and borderline personality. Phase II tests indicated that race, sexual orientation, borderline pathology, PTSD, attachment style, and secondary caregiver's education levels were significantly correlated with self-injurious behavior. A logistical regression model predicted self-injurious behavior with 67% accuracy. To account for the remaining error, a sub-sample of 10 women with histories of self-injury, but no PTSD or borderline diagnosis, who were securely attached, were interviewed. They indicated that self-injury serves as a form of control over feelings related to productivity and achievement, as a response to high expectations for autonomy and self-reliance, and in reaction to societal demands for performance.

Another consistent group of studies for adults (Caviglia, 2004; Riggs, 2007) were focused on trauma and attachment measured with AAI. We suggest to the reader a brief overview of the two studies.

Caviglia et al., (2004) used the AAI to study the state of mind of 26 adults, all Jewish, who live in Italy and belong to the so-called "second generation" of the Shoa; i.e. they were born after 1945, from Jewish parents who survived the Nazi extermination camps and, therefore, have not directly experienced the Nazi persecutions. The authors hypothesize that the intergenerational transmission of the "shadow" of the Holocaust has weighed heavily on the "second generation" of survivors, through the mechanism of "frightening/frightened" responses given by the parent. The distribution according to the AAI categories showed that the sample was not thoroughly "traumatized". Rather, a relevant percentage of the subjects (46.2%) seems "Secure". This suggested that there are a number of variables that helped many survivors reinstate themselves in the civil and social environment in which they came back, growing up and taking care of their children in a sufficiently adaptive way.

Riggs et al., (2007) examined AAI pattern of attachment, personality dimensions (measured by the Millon Clinical Multiaxial Inventory—III), psychopathology, and romantic styles in a psychiatric sample of 80 inpatients trauma survivors. AAI unresolved trauma was uniquely associated with dissociation and posttraumatic stress disorder, whereas unresolved trauma and unresolved loss jointly contributed to schizotypal and borderline personality disorder scores. Self-reported romantic attachment style was significantly associated with personality dimensions, with fearful adults showing the most maladaptive personality profiles. Findings suggested that self-report dimensions of self and other independently contribute to different forms of psychological dysfunction. Self-report romantic styles measures and AAI attachment classifications were not related, and different results emerged for the two measures. The differences in findings between the two measures were discussed with a view toward the developmental and clinical implications.

2.2.2 Axis II

Narcissistic. The link between attachment and narcissism is that the attachment process is intimately connected with the parent's validation of the child. Later in development, the regulation of self-esteem moves into different domains such as peer relations, romantic relations, and recognition or validation within groups. In other words, from early development the need to be protected and the need to be validated are inextricably related. Consequently, self-esteem progression usually follows the experiences of the secure or insecure developmental pathways build on the attachment relationship during infancy. Attachment models, be they secure, insecure, or disorganized, penetrate all parts of the child's development, including affect regulation, arousal, and sense of self-worth.

A child who develops an internal working model of a secure attachment will, most likely, also develop a healthy sense of self-worth because this child has internalized a mental representation of someone both available and responsive to the child's need for protection and validation. If, the child develops an insecure avoidant model of attachment based on the internalization of a parent's dismissive pattern of relating, the child is at risk of narcissistic pathology due to deficits in the interpersonal interpretive capacities that emerge from this attachment model.

Now we will describe some of the most recent papers that focused on the link between attachment and Narcissistic disorder.

Bennet, 2006 focused on the relevance of attachment theory and research in the conceptualization and treatment of pathological narcissism. The author proposed that the relational context of individual development and the interpersonal interpretative capacities that emerge as part of the attachment system may be salient factors in the etiology and treatment of narcissism. He included is an overview of research on attachment models and their correlation to adult psychopathology and to narcissistic personality disorders. It is suggested that internalization and maintenance of a "secure base" and improvement in self-reflective functioning informs and enriches the clinical treatment of adults with narcissistic features.

Some studies used the questionnaire to investigate this topic (Feintuch, 1999; Selby, 2001; Popper, 2002; Andrews, 2004; Neumann, & Bierhoff, 2004; Smolewska & Dion, 2005). We chose to describe two contributions.

Feintuch's (1999) examined the relationships between attachment styles measured with self-report questionnaires) and narcissism, shame, defences, and the positive and negative affects in 538 undergraduates. Narcissism was measured with the O 'Brien Multiphasic Narcissistic Inventory (OMNI) (O'Brien, 1987) and Narcissistic

Personality Inventory (NPI) (Raskin & Hall, 1979). The study showed close association between security of attachment and shame and affects. Secure attachment revealed positive correlation with positive affects and negative correlation with shame and negative affects. Feful-avoidant and preoccupied attachment were correlated in the opposite direction on these same affects. The two instruments used to evaluate the narcism showed oppositive predicted correlations with attachment on the various dimensions. On OMNI narcissism, secure attachment showed a negative correlation with narcissism while fearful-avoidant and preoccupied attachment showed positive correlations, as predicted, while in the NPI narcissism scale (Raskin, 1979) the correlations were more usually opposite the prediction. The predicted correlations between attachment and choice of defence mechanisms did not achieve significance.

Smolewska & Dion (2005) examined the relationship between attachment anxiety, attachment avoidance, and maladaptive narcissism (using questionnaires) in 171 women. The study also explored the differences between overt and covert forms of narcissistic vulnerability. Canonical correlation analysis (CCA) explored the multivariate relationship between overt and covert narcissism, on one hand, and adult attachment dimensions of anxiety and avoidance, on the other hand. Within the adult attachment set, both anxiety and avoidance were important, but the former more than the latter.

Schizoid/avoidant. From an attachment perspective, extreme levels of avoidant attachment are linked to schizoid disorder, which marked by aloofness and lack interest in others and maintain of interpersonal distance. However it is important to distinguish the schizoid disorder and avoidant personality disorder. Although both disorder involve social detachment the differences is that in the avoidant there a negative vision of self while in schizoid personality there no evidence of negative models of self.

One of the very few studies on the schizoid and avoidant disorder and attachment is Meyer, Pilkonis & Beevers's study (2004). They carried out a study on 176 college students to evaluate the link between personality disorders and attachment. The students completed questionnaires measuring attachment styles and personality disorder features, and each rated 10 emotionally neutral faces on 18 bipolar appraisal dimensions. The results showed that the Schizoid personality is weakly associated with avoidant attachment. about the avoidant structure, the results showed that is linked to anxious and avoidant attachment and to negative face appraisals (e.g., tendencies to rate faces as less friendly and more rejecting).

Antisocial. Bowlby (1973) proposed that when children experienced threatening behaviour from parents or they felt abandoned from attachment figures, they can feel an high degree of anger. This kind of resentment is functional in order to communicate to the parents their feeling about separation. The combination of threatening experience and long-lasting separations, could lead to a disfunctional level of anger. At the beginning this intense hate is directed toward parents, then to different targets: this shifts is functional for the child in order to maintain relationships with parents anyway.

We have found various contributes in the literature focused on the link between antisocial disorder and attachment (Frodi et al., 2001; Turton, 2001;Voss 2001; Levinson, 2004; Marin Avellan et al., 2005).

Frodi et al., (2001) examined the current mental representations of early attachment relationships using the AAI in 24 psychopathic male criminal offenders (aged 20-48 yrs), incarcerated in a forensic psychiatric hospital or a medium-security prison. The results pointed to an extensive over-representation of individuals who were dismissing of attachment and attachment-related experiences (close to three times as many as in the normal population), no secure individuals, and with the remainder being either unclassifiable or unresolved with regard to severe early abuse/trauma.

Levinson (2004) employed the AAI to examine early childhood trauma and attachment patterns, and the Reflective Function (RF) Scale on twenty-two prisoners compared with 22 personality disordered patients without an offending history, and 22 normal controls. The prisoners had experienced more abuse and neglect than the patients, yet were more likely to be coded resolved to their abuse on the AAI. Prisoners were more likely to be dismissive in their attachment patterns, and the prisoners' RF was more impaired than that of the patients. Violent offenders showed the greatest deficits in RF.

A group of research was carried out specifically in the forensic context; among them Turton (2001) examined major procedural and coding challenges non normative sample can pose to interviewers and raters of the Adult Attachment Interview (AAI), with reference to interview transcripts drawn from a population of personality disordered offenders detained in a high-security hospital. The source material comes from 45 AAI transcripts collected from a sample of mentally disordered offenders detained in a high-security hospital. All were diagnosed in separate interviews rated by the research team using the Structured Clinical Interview for DSMIV (First, Gibbon, Spitzer, Williams, & Benjamin, 1997) as having personality disorder. Interviews difficulties have their roots in three separate but overlapping areas: extreme attachment-related experience; interviewees' psychological or psychiatric state; and factors relating to the context in which the interview is conducted. Interviewees in their early lives may have suffered adversity and deprivation of such gravity and complexity that a speaker's attachment history is almost impossible to follow and the assumptions underlying some of the questions do not hold. Also they may have psychiatric symptoms (i.e. delusional thinking, impaired affect) or be receiving treatment (e.g. sedative medication, ECT) that could influence the way they respond. Additional procedural problems may arise when conducting interviews in institutional settings where other agendas may be pressing and the demands of organizational and therapeutic routines intrude.

Marin Avellan et al., 2005 studied AAI in a forensic population of 30 subjects from a high security hospital. They were assessed with the AAI, the SWAP-200, the Structured Clinical Interview for DSM-IV Personality Disorders (SCID-ll), and the Chart of Interpersonal Reactions in Closed Living Environments (CIRCLE). AAI classifications differentiated five of the DSM prototypes of personality disorder diagnosed by the SWAP-200 compared with only one category diagnosed by the SCID-II.

Obsessive Compulsive Disorder. The experiential antecedents of compulsive care-giving is likely in the activation of the child's attachment system evoked anxious and ineffective concern, rather than comforting responsiveness, from the parent. Through repeated experiences, the child has learned that attachment behaviours provoke distress in the parent. Consequently, conflict is experienced whenever the child's attachment system is activated. Paradoxically, then, proximity to the parent is gained at the cost of the child's attachment behaviours; that is, deactivation of the child's attachment system offers, in these circumstances, the best chance to achieve a degree of proximity to the parent. The child's need for care is renounced for the sake of maintaining proximity to the parent. In adulthood such persons' representational model of attachment includes a view of relationships that emphasizes the importance of giving care, and attitudinal biases that function to control or deny their own attachment desires and emotions.

We have found just only research that investigated the link between Obsessive Compulsive Disorder and attachment. Marcel (2000) assessed the attachment styles of obsessive-compulsive personality disorder (OCPD) and Patients with BPD, to the two groups was administred the Reciprocal Attachment Questionnaire. The results showed that patients with OCPD don't exhibit angry withdrawal and compulsive care-seeking attachment patterns and also scored lower on the dimensions of lack of availability of the attachment figure, feared loss of the attachment figure, lack of use of the attachment figure, and separation protest.

Borderline. As mention above, Main and Hesse (1990) suggested that children incapacity to integrate opposite qualities of their caregiver could be correlated with personality disorders onset. In specific, borderline personality disorders is associated with an unusual concern about current and previous relationship difficulties: it means that this kind of individual are not able to experience a unique model of self and others, considering caregivers as incompetent and unavailable.

In literature there are many studies concerning the relationship between adult attachment dimensions and Borderline Personality Disorders (BPD), assessed with different kind of measures. Before showing some example of theses studies we are going to quote a meta-analysis examining the types of attachment found in individuals with this disorder or with dimensional characteristics of BPD.

Agrawal, Gunderson, Holmes, Lyons-Ruth (2004) proposed a meta analysis of 13 empirical studies. The limit of their review is the variety of measures and attachment types these studies have employed. Nevertheless, every study concludes that there is a strong association between BPD and insecure attachment. The types of attachment found to be most characteristic of BPD subjects were unresolved, preoccupied, and fearful. In each of these attachment types, individuals demonstrate a longing for intimacy and at the same time concern about dependency and rejection. The high prevalence and severity of insecure attachments found in these adult samples support the central role of disturbed interpersonal relationships in clinical theories of BPD. This review concludes that these types of insecure attachment may represent phenotypic markers of vulnerability to BPD, suggesting several directions for future research.

In literature we found different kind of studies. Some of them investigated adult attachment pattern using classical tools –AAI- (Barone (2003), Leavy, Klarking & Kernberg (2004), some other self-report measures (Nickell, Waudby,; & Trull (2002)Fossati, Donati, Donini,Novella, Bagnato, Maffei (2001), Meyer, Pilkonis & Beevers (2004) Fossati, Feeney, Carretta, Grazioli, Milesi, Leonardi, Maffei, (2005);)Meyer, Ajchenbrenner, & Bowles (2006) Mauricio, Tein, Lopez, (2007). On the same line some studies consider attachment from a psycho-social point of view (Minzenberg, Poole, Vinogradov, (2006).

Regarding AAI, Barone (2003) examined the early attachment experiences, and their subsequent mental representations, using the AAI, among 80 adults: 40 non clinical and 40 with Borderline Personality Disorder. The specific goals were, besides to identifying the main classification to discriminate potential protective or risk factors of BPD, to identify specific dimension and to study the phenomenon of dysregulation in BPD, using the scale system. The results obtained showed a specific distribution of attachment patterns in the clinical sample: free/autonomous subjects (F) represented only 7%, dismissing classifications (Ds) reached about 20%, entangled/preoccupied (E) 23% and unresolved with traumatic experiences (U) 50%. The two samples differed in their attachment patterns distribution by two (secure vs. insecure status), three (F, Ds and E) and four-way (F, Ds, E and U) categories comparisons. So interviews from the participants with BPD are almost exclusively insecure, with more than half being unresolved regarding past loss or trauma. The results provide support that the Borderline Personality Disorder corresponds to specific types of response to the Adult Attachment Interview. Results support the hypothesis that some developmental relational experiences seem to constitute pivotal risk factors underlying this disorder. In order to identify more specific protective or risk factors of BPD, 25 one-way ANOVAs with clinical status as variable (clinical vs. nonclinical) were conducted on each scale of the coding system of the interview. The results pertaining to the dimensional rating scales demonstrate that some aspects of the quality of attachment mental representations in the borderline pathology may be better explained and clarified by exploring the probable past experiences, and current state of mind, regarding attachment. Specifically, the current sample of respondents with BPD showed a marked tendency toward an angry-involving relationship with the parents against the background of a role-reversing relationship with the mother. Results also demonstrate a failure of meta cognitive monitoring, stressing how this ability can be considered an essential protective factor.

BPD were nearly always associated with non autonomous – mostly preoccupied – states of mind. This finding, associated with difficulties in the area of emotional regulation (as involving anger and impairment in metacognitive monitoring), could indicate specific risk factors for the development of BPD.

Leavy, Klarking & Kernberg (2004), administred the AAI to 90 Borderline before and after treatment (transference-focused psychotherapy, dialectical behavioral therapy and supportive treatment) in order to measure structural change. Moreover they coded all AAIs with respect to reflective functioning (RF). About half of the patients showed a change in their state of mind with respect to attachment after one year of treatment. About 80% of initially unresolved patients showed *resolution* of trauma after one year of treatment, with some patients showing a shift from *unresolved* and *insecure* states of mind to *secure* states of mind and others from *unresolved* and *insecure* states of mind to *cannot classify* or *mixed* states of mind with respect to attachment. The findings on the patterns of change in attachment organization lend support to the idea that the AAI may be a valid and reliable measure of intrapsychic change in borderline patients, although the findings also suggest different trajectories of change. RF significantly increased during the course of treatment, but only in the TFP treated group. In the DBT and supportive treatments, we did not see an increase in RF.

We are now going to review some interesting findings about BPD and attachment distribution, investigated by self-report tools.

Meyer, Pilkonis & Beevers (2004) carried out a study on 176 college students to evaluate the link between personality disorders and attachment. The students completed questionnaires measuring attachment styles and personality disorder features, and each rated 10 emotionally neutral faces on 18 bipolar appraisal dimensions. The results showed that the borderline structure is linked to anxious attachment and to negative face appraisals (e.g., tendencies to rate faces as less friendly and more rejecting).

Fossati, Feeney, Carretta, Grazioli, Milesi, Leonardi, Maffei, (2005) tested four competing models of relationships (adult attachment patterns, impulsivity, and aggressiveness) to understand the associations among Borderline Personality Disorder (BPD) in 466 consecutively admitted outpatients. They used the Structured Clinical Interview for DSM-IV Axis II Personality Disorders (V. 2.0), the Attachment Style Questionnaire, the Barratt Impulsiveness Scale-11, and the Aggression

Questionnaire. In the first model, BPD was associated with the personality traits of impulsivity and aggressiveness, but adult attachment patterns predict neither BPD nor impulsive/aggressive features; in the second, adult attachment patterns were significant predictors of BPD but not of impulsive/aggressive traits, although these traits correlate with BPD; in third adult attachment patterns were significant predictors of impulsive and aggressive traits, which in turn predict BPD; and for the last model adult attachment patterns significantly predicted both BPD and impulsive/aggressive traits. Maximum likelihood structural equation modeling of the covariance matrix showed that model (c) was the best fitting model (chi superscript 2 (21) = 31.67, p > .05, RMSEA = .023, test of close fit p > .85). This result indicates that adult attachment patterns act indirectly as risk factors for BPD because of their relationships with aggressive/impulsive personality traits.

Meyer, Ajchenbrenner, & Bowles (2006) suggested that both avoidant and borderline personality disorder (APD and BPD) are theoretically associated with temperamental vulnerabilities, adverse attachment experiences, and negative (pessimistic or catastrophic) reactions to the threat of perceived rejection; however, more work is needed to differentiate how these processes account for the etiology and maintenance of disorders. A sample of 156 adults completed questionnaires measuring APD and BPD features, temperament (sensory-processing sensitivity), mood, and attachment experiences. Both APD and BPD were associated with temperamental sensitivity, but BPD was uniquely linked with a subscale measuring sensitivity to mental and emotive stimuli, whereas APD was uniquely linked with a subscale measuring the control and avoidance of aversive stimulation. BPD was more strongly linked with negative moods (anxiety, anger, sadness) and insecure attachment to parents, whereas APD was more strongly linked (than BPD) to pessimistic cognitive-affective responses to rejection-related situations.

Concluding our review on psychopathology and attachment we proposed a study (Ward et al., 2006) aimed at addressing the question of whether adult psychopathology may be related to insecure mental representation of attachment, the authors administered AAI and SCID to 60 mothers from a community sample. As existing studies are limited to clinically-referred populations, they supported that this studies may include only more severe cases of psychopathology and thus inflate the association between attachment and psychopathology. Furthermore, in cases of severe psychopathology, memories of attachment experiences could be influenced by retrospective distortion. Secure subjects had significantly less psychopathology than insecure subjects. Correspondence between maternal attachment (F, Ds, E, U) and DSM-III-R diagnoses was investigated. Mood disorders were associated with Preoccupied (E), Unresolved/Preoccupied (U/E) and Cannot Code (CC) classifications. Personality disorders were associated with Dismissing (Ds) classifications. Within the Unresolved (U) category, subjects with secure main attachment classifications (U/F) had significantly less psychopathology than Unresolved/insecure (U/Ds or U/E) subjects. So results suggest that psychopathology was associated with insecure attachment, as classified in the AAI, in this community sample. Secondary analyses suggested that dismissing attachment may be associated with Axis II Personality Disorders, while preoccupied classification may be associated with affective and anxiety disorders. Of note is the evidence that underlying secure attachment within the unresolved classification is associated with reduced probability of psychopathology, suggesting that secure state of mind with respect to attachment may provide a subject with insight and resilience to protect against psychopathology, despite the impact on function associated with both loss and abuse.

2.3 Attachment and psychotherapy outcome

Bowlby (1981) suggested that the way in which adults talk about themselves and their feelings reflect how they have internalized and organized their attachment experiences and how they have regulated their behaviour toward others. This hypothesis allows the therapist to postulate and build a imagine of their clients' earlier life, and the defensive mechanisms they have used to front off negative aspects of attachment relationships (Slade, 1999).

In the therapeutic setting, the therapist becomes a "relatively secure base" (Bowlby, 1981, p. 251) when he can establish a meaningful connection with clients so that they will feel safe enough to begin to explore the past events and experiences that have influenced their lives in the present.

Sable (2008) underlined the importance in attachment theory of the two concepts: stability and security. These constructs accentuate the positive aspects of affectional relationships and how they were linked to the process of adult psychotherapy. Sable supported that the research has shown that positive and supportive attachment experiences are related to feelings of joy, protection, contentment during lifespan. In contrast, the presence of trauma or hurtful experiences, can negatively affect the thoughts and emotions.

In the psychotherapeutic contest, the role of the therapist can be seen as providing a positive emotional experience with others. In this positive encounter the individual have the possibility to remember, reflect, understand and build a new perspective in his personal experience. The presence of comfort and safety in relationship with the therapist allows to the individuals to explore and reanalyze, in a more coherent way, his history and rearrange internal working models.

For example the personality pattern of anxious attachment is used to illustrate that experiencing a relationship of secure attachment with the therapist can enable a client to reconstruct negative representations about the past into more adaptive, optimistic representations of herself, her past, and the future.

Shorey (2006) suggested that as a theory of life span development, psychopathology, and psychotherapy, attachment theory has a great deal to offer people (e.g., researcher, therapists and clients, and lay people) in understanding their own or others' motives, goals, and goal-attainment strategies. For example, by not considering the implications of attachment theory, clinical researchers may fail to detect meaningful results relating to treatment outcomes. This is because failure to identify meaningful subgroups (i.e., attachment styles) within research samples has the potential to obfuscate otherwise significant findings— particularly when those subgroups relate differentially to the constructs or systems under investigation. Thus, the continued ignoring of individual differences in attachment may undermine future advances in psychotherapy outcome research. Researchers may want to look at attachment groups within their samples particularly in studying dynamic systems where in multiple variables reciprocally and iteratively influence each other. The mechanisms for this effect, however, are likely to differ according to attachment styles even if the isolated outcome (in this case levels of depressive symptomology) does not. Identifying differential mechanisms of action then should inform the design of future interventions so that they can be specifically modified to maximize treatment outcomes for each of the attachment style groups. Maximizing treatment outcomes also should be the goal of individual therapists. Therapists, similar to researchers, may apply ill-advised interventions if they fail to consider how their clients are likely to respond to treatments given the clients' specific attachment styles. Accordingly, an assessment of clients' attachment styles should be standard in client intakes or clinical assessment batteries.

In this section our purpose was to provide a brief review of studies on psychopathology (DSM-IV) and psychotherapy outcome. The existing literature is focused on some of most studied disorders although not for all we found interesting results and connection between attachment and psychotherapy.

2.3.1 Axis I

Depression. A first group of studies (McBride, 2006; Steakley, 2006; Hendriksen, 2008) is focused on attachment and treatment. We describe two of these studies, the first that considered the outcome from a interpersonal psychotherapy and cognitive behavioural therapy, the second one the outcome from Short-Term Psychodynamic Supportive Psychotherapy.

McBride (2006) tested anxiety and avoidance dimensions (measured by self-reports) of adult attachment insecurity as moderators of treatment outcome for interpersonal psychotherapy (IPT) and cognitive– behavioral therapy (CBT). Fifty-six participants with major depression were randomly assigned to these treatment conditions. Beck Depression Inventory—II, Six-Item Hamilton Rating Scale for Depression scores, and remission status served as outcome measures. They found that patients higher on attachment avoidance showed significantly greater reduction in depression severity and greater likelihood of symptom remission with CBT as compared with IPT, even after controlling for obsessive– compulsive and avoidant personality disorder symptoms. Results were replicated across treatment completers and intent-to-treat samples. Attachment anxiety did not significantly predict change in severity of depression across treatment for either IPT or CBT when measured by the BDI–II.

These results robustly demonstrate that attachment avoidance is predictive of differential treatment response to IPT versus CBT, when both self-report questionnaire and interview created measures of depression severity are used. Attachment anxiety did not significantly predict symptom remission for either IPT or CBT; however, attachment avoidance again differentially predicted symptom remission, such that individuals scoring higher on attachment avoidance were more likely to remit in response to CBT and less likely to remit in response to IPT. Further, when measures of obsessive– compulsive and avoidance personality disorder symptoms were included in the model, attachment avoidance contributed to the prediction of remission status even after controlling for personality dysfunction previously related to differential outcome for IPT and CBT (Barber & Muenz, 1996). The sine qua non of avoidance involves the active attempt to deactivate attachment behaviours (Main & Goldwyn, 1994) and to regulate attachment security by denying the importance of close relationships (Fraley & Shaver, 2000). Highly avoidant individuals are remote, cool, and distant (Fraley & Shaver, 2000; Slade, 1999). It may be for these reasons that highly avoidant attached individuals do not respond as well to IPT as to CBT. The explicit focus of IPT is on interpersonal relationships. The approach rests on the premise that interpersonal distress is intricately connected with depression and that change in the interpersonal realm is necessary to bring about change in symptom functioning. Goals in IPT, therefore, include helping patients change relationship-based expectations and interpersonal communication and behaviour, resolve interpersonal conflicts, and adjust to interpersonal losses or changes (Stuart & Robertson, 2003). This approach might lack face validity or prove too threatening for individuals who regulate affect by deactivating relationship issues. In contrast, CBT targets the underlying cognitive system in order to alleviate depressive symptoms (Beck, 1983). Cognitive theory emphasizes the causal role of dysfunctional cognitive pro- cesses in the onset and course of depression (Beck, 1983). A central goal in CBT is to bring about change in cognitive organization. This is achieved by helping patients to understand the connection among their thoughts, feelings, and behaviours, to become observers of how thoughts influence mood, and to develop effective strategies to alter the underlying cognitions, which serve to maintain a depressive episode. This approach may appeal to avoidant attached individuals who may emphasize narrowly the importance of cognition as a way to remove themselves from interpersonal concerns. The results of the study support the view that it is important to consider the interaction between patient characteristics and treatment modality when comparing the efficacy of treatments in the research context and when assigning clients to treatments in the clinical context (Addis & Jacobson, 1996; Beutler, 1991; Shoham-Salomon & Hannah, 1991

The most recent study that we found (Hendriksen, 2008) examined the predictive value of early response for final outcome of psychotherapy and combined therapy in major depression. Patients with a diagnosis from mild to moderately depression were treated with either Short-Term Psychodynamic Supportive Psychotherapy (SPSP) (N = 63) only, or combined with an antidepressant (N = 127). Early response was defined as a reduction of more than 25% on the HAM-D-17 after 2 months. Outcome was determined in terms of complete non response and remission rates. Associations between early response and outcome were examined using logistic regression analysis. In SPSP, early non-response was clearly related to final non-response (OR = 3.57). Nevertheless, remission was not predicted by early response, and 26% of the early non-responders ultimately achieved remission. In combined therapy, both final non-response (OR 7.13) and remission (OR 3.66) were associated with early non-response. Although a number of early nonresponsive patients will achieve remission, this study points out that these patients are at risk factor for ultimate treatment failure.

Anxiety. Biscoglio (2005) explored the relationship between *personality, early therapeutic alliance process and overall psychotherapy outcome in 32 patient*-therapist dyads who mosly met most met criteria for anxious or depressive disorders, and were engaged in Brief Relational Therapy (BRT). The author examined the impact of attachment style and introject quality (as assessed by the Relationship Scale Questionnaire (RSQ, Griffin & Bartholomew, 1994) and the INTREX (Benjamin, 1988), respectively) on psychotherapy process and outcome. Therapeutic alliance process was assessed with questions about perceived tension in the relationship from the Brief Project's Post-Session Questionnaire (PSQ); the Working Alliance Inventory, (WAI-12; Tracey & Kokotovic, 1989); and the Session Evaluation Questionnaire (SEQ; Stiles, 1980; Stiles & Snow, 1984). Outcome measures included the Symptom Checklist-90, Revised (SCL-90-R; Derogatis, 1983); the Inventory of Interpersonal Problems, as rated by patients (IIP-64; Alden, Wiggins, & Pincus, 1990), the Target Complaints measure as completed independently by both patients and therapists (TC; Battle, Imber, Hoehn-Saric, Stone, Nash, & Frank, 1966), and the Global Assessment Scale (GAS; Endicott, Spitzer, Fleiss & Cohen, 1976). Significant results included: higher scores on the Affiliation subscale of the INTREX in therapists were related to positive alliance process; fearful attachment scores on the RSQ in patients were related to negative alliance process. Surprisingly, secure attachment in patients and therapists was related to poorer outcome, and fearful and dismissing attachment in patients was related to better outcome. These latter findings can be explained in part by the methodological limitations of the study, including small sample size, and the exclusive use of self-report measures.

Obsessive – compulsive. We chose to describe a study in which the authors (Stekeetee & Von Nopen, 2003) showed the connection between attachment and familiar background that seemed to be important for the outcome. They reviewed the family constellation of patients with obsessive compulsive disorder (OCD), the presence of OCD symptoms among family members, and familial aspects including parental attachment, expressed emotion (EE), and family accommodation. Some evidence supports a negative effect of hostility, emotional over-involvement, and criticism perceived by the patient on behavioural treatment outcome. However, actual criticism observed by the relative during an interview was associated with more benefit from therapy. Family accommodation predicted poorer family functioning and more severe OCD symptoms after behavioural treatment. A review of the limited treatment literature indicates no actual tests of the effects of psycho-educational and supportive treatments although several reports suggest they are useful for families and patients. Including relatives in treatment has proved beneficial in some studies, especially with children, but not in others.

Eating Disorders. Eating disorders seemed to be one of the most studied disorder in connection with attachment studies were not very much investigated in psychotherapy outcome studies.

Tasca et al. (2006) examined 135 patients with binge eating disorder (BED), randomized to a control condition or to one of two 16-session group treatments: group cognitive-behavioral therapy (GCBT) or group psychodynamic interpersonal psychotherapy (GPIP). The two treatments performed equally well, and each resulted in reduced days binged compared with the wait-list control condition. Twelve-month follow-up indicated that improvements were maintained in days binged and in other outcome variables. For women who completed GPIP, higher attachment anxiety was related to improvements in days binged by post treatment. On the other hand, for women who completed GCBT, lower attachment anxiety was associated with improvements in days binged by post treatment. Higher attachment avoidance was related to dropping out of GCBT. Although both GPIP and GCBT reduced binge eating, the results indicated that individual outcomes differ across treatments based on level of attachment anxiety and avoidance.

Substance abuse. The studies that examined the abuse of substance seemed to be focused on the aim of efficacy and in what way the attachment styles could mediate the outcome.

The first study Frank (2001) explored the association between adult attachment styles and the initiation, maintenance and recovery of substance dependence. Attachment was measured by the Trichotomous Attachment Classification (TAC) and the Attachment Style Questionnaire (ASQ), and recovery outcome as measured by the Addiction Severity Index Composite Scores (ASI-CS). Attachment styles of substance dependent patients were explored with particular attention toward their association with several indices of recovery outcome and recovery-related variables at nine months follow-up after completion of an approximately eight week intensive outpatient rehabilitation program. Of special interest, in terms of recovery-related variables, were behavioral levels of engagement in twelve-step programs such as Alcoholics Anonymous and Narcotics Anonymous. Results suggested that substance dependent patients tended to have more insecure styles of attachment and that avoidance may have been a prominent attachment style for patients presenting to substance abuse treatment centers. While adult attachment appeared to be associated with substance dependence the association between adult attachment and recovery from substance dependence was generally not substantiated. However, minor associations between attachment, and recovery suggested further investigation. While there was practically no association found between adult attachment and recovery as measured with the ASI-CS or the self-report of abstinence, there were some important associations found between attachment and other recovery-related variables although these results were mixed. One important finding concerned a significant association between obtaining a sponsor and the self-report of abstinence. There were some findings in this study that might suggest that an insecure style of attachment could be associated with some positive aspects of recovery outcome.

Bolton (2006) examined several facets of attachment-related themes, substance abuse outcomes, and type of treatment. Three broad research questions were investigated: (a) What is the nature of the relationship between attachment and substance use at baseline? (b) What is the effect of type of treatment on attachment-related behaviors? and (c) Does attachment mediate the type of treatment and treatment-outcome relationship? This study involved 96 families who had an adolescent in one of three types of treatment for substance use: (a) cognitive-behavioral therapy, (b) family therapy, and (c) group therapy. Families completed a pre- and post treatment assessment, which included measures of demographic characteristics and substance use (number of drugs used, percent days used drugs, and percent days used marijuana). Additionally, families participated in a 10-minute interaction that was videotaped. These interactions were coded using the Autonomy and Relatedness Coding System (Allen, Hauser, Bell, McElhaney et al., 1994, 2003), which codes for nine specific behaviors representing four specific categories: exhibiting autonomy, undermining autonomy, exhibiting relatedness, and undermining relatedness. Findings showed that exhibiting autonomy, undermining autonomy, exhibiting relatedness, and undermining relatedness were not associated with adolescent substance use or type of treatment. Three alternative explanations as to the lack of the relationships were offered. First, the sample had limited variance in substance use and autonomy and relatedness scores making the detection of relationships difficult. Second, the use of global scores (summed behaviors of a particular category) may not be sensitive enough to detect subtle behavioral differences. Third, the use of a clinical sample results in many contributing factors and thus it is difficult to tease out all of the influences impacting an adolescent seeking and receiving treatment for substance use.

Inpatients. To conclude our review on Axis I we suggest a study with a sample on general inpatients that could be used as an example of psychotherapy outcome mediated by attachment patterns.

Sachse (2002) examined the video recorded interviews of 34 inpatients, using the Adult Attachement-Prototypes Rating and interpersonal problems (IIP; Horowitz). The results showed the existence of a link between the attachment pattern and variables for the indication and prognosis of psychotherapy. The three subgroups, differentiated according to their attachment patterns (avoidant, ambivalent, mixed insecure) differed marginally with respect to their psychodynamic group treatment success. The ambivalent patients showed the most positive outcome (especially with regard to symptoms and self-system-related outcome criteria). There were also, indications for a differential assessment of group related therapeutic factors by the subgroups. The patients with an avoidant attachment pattern considered group-related factors such as cohesion and altruism as least helpful.

2.3.2 Axis II

Borderline. The studies on borderline personality disorder and outcome showed only preliminary findings but some changes in attachment styles.

Diamond's (2003) reported preliminary findings from a longitudinal study on the impact of attachment state of mind and reflective function on therapeutic process and outcome with borderline patients in Transference-Focused Psychotherapy. Preliminary findings showed the presence of changes in attachment classification and reflective function ratings at four month and one year for a subsample of ten patients and therapists.

Leavy, Kenneth et al. (2006) examined changes in attachment organization and reflective function (RF) assessed during one of three year-long psychotherapy treatments for patients with borderline personality disorder (N=90). The BPD patients were randomized to transference-focused psychotherapy (TFP), dialectical behaviour therapy, or a modified psychodynamic supportive psychotherapy. Attachment organization was assessed with the AAI and the RF coding scale. After 12 months of treatment, participants were more secure according to attachment state of mind for TFP only for one of the three treatments. Findings suggest that one year of intensive TFP can increase patients' narrative coherence and RF. All types treatments did not produced changes in resolution of loss or trauma.

PART II

ATTACHMENT IN PERSONALITY
ASSESSMENT INSTRUMENTS

The purpose of this part is to introduce the reader to some tools that assess personality and attachment. Our attention will be focused on AAI, AAP, Rorschach and MMPI. The first two as the best known measures of attachment patter, the two others as the most used instruments in personality assessment. Within the Rorschach, space will be given above all to Exner's Comprehensive Method. The brief description of the MMPI and the Rorschach will be accompanied with a review about the existing literature on connections between these two instruments and attachment.

3 THE ADULT ATTACHMENT INTERVIEW

S. Salcuni, A. Raudino, F. Segato

3.1 AAI description

The Adult Attachment Interview (AAI; George, Kaplan, & Main, 1984/1985/ 1996) was the first attachment theory-based measure developed to assess adult attachment (Bowlby, 1969; 1973; 1977; 1980). The AAI is a about one hour semi-structured clinical-style interview that guides the individual through a series of questions about childhood and current experience with attachment figures. It is entirely audio recorded and then precisely transcript (Main, 1991).

Over the course of the two past decades, the AAI has become the *gold standard* adult attachment assessment. The AAI attachment classification groups are defined as analogous to the four groups identified for infants (Ainsworth, Blehar, Waters, & Wall, 1978; Main & Solomon, 1990): secure, avoidant-dismissing, preoccupied-ambivalent-resistant, and disorganized-unresolved. Classification group is assigned using a meticulous discourse analysis that is applied to the verbatim transcript of an individual's responses to the interview questions. Classification decisions place particular emphasis on mental coherence and distortion against the reported *facts* of childhood history (Main & Goldwyn, 1985/1990/1994/ 1998).

AAI researchers have demonstrated that the interview provides a rich, construct validated picture of adult mental representations of attachment based on evaluations of transcript coherence and other features of attachment state of mind, such as idealization or preoccupation with attachment (e.g., Bakermans-Kranenburg & van IJzendoorn, 1993; Fonagy, Steele, Steele, Leigh, Kennedy, Mattoon, &Target, 1995; Steele & Baradon, 2004). Interviews patterned after the AAI have been developed to assess other aspects of relationships, including parental caregiving (Aber, Slade, Berger, Bresgi, & Kaplan, 1985; Bretherton, Biringen, Ridgeway, Maslin, & Sherman, 1989; George & Solomon, 1989, 1996; Zeanah & Barton, 1989) and adult attachment with current intimate partners (Crowell, 1990). Crittenden (1992, 1994) has developed a somewhat different system the goal of which is also to classify children who do not fit into the traditional Ainsworth system.

Classification using the AAI protocol is defined as able to *surprise the unconscious* because of the order and the structure of the questions during the interview, which provoke an exploration between semantic and episodic memories of the past.

After an initial phase, in which the subject is asked to tell about general family environment and habits of infancy, he/she is invited to think about the relationship with his/her parents. Then, the subject is asked to give 5 adjectives to describe the relationship with the mother when he/she was from 5 to 14 years old, and to prove every definition with real episodes or events of his/her life; then, the same is asked for the relationship with the father. After this first phase, a series of questions about illness, fears, separation from the parents, traumatic or abusive experiences, and losses are investigated. Some questions related to the changing period from infancy to adolescence, and then from adolescence to adulthood is then asked, always putting attention to the changes in the relationship with the attachment figures. At the and of the interview, the subject is asked to imagine having a child and to reflect about their possible relationship at the age of one and twenty years.

3.2 The AAI coding System

The main issue of the AAI is to reach the final attachment classification. In order to reach to, the coder is asked to evaluate two different set of scale: Experience Scales and State of Mind -in respect with attachment- Scales.

Experience Scales are 5 different ordinal scales, from 1 to 9 (Main & Goldwyn, 1998) that measure the inferred parental behaviour in childhood, separately for mother and father. These scales reflect AAI coders' impressions of participants' experiences with caregivers during childhood, including assessments of maternal and paternal love, rejection, neglect, pressure to achieve, and role reversal. Although such information is conceptually orthogonal to the assessment of security versus insecurity in the AAI, several investigators have made use of a subset of these scales to distinguish between secure individuals with putatively negative early relationship experiences with at least one parent (i.e., earned-secures) and secure adults with largely positive experiences with their caregivers (Pearson, 1994). Loving scale evaluates the presence of comfort, care, protection and loving physical contact with parents during childhood; Rejection scale evaluates the presence of clear rejecting or cruel behaviours by the parents at the child asking for comfort, care, and protection; Involving/Role-Reversing scale evaluates the presence of role reversing relationship between the child and the parent, who was asking for comprehension, protection and even physical or psychological care by the child; Neglecting scale evaluates the presence of unaffectionate, neglecting, affective unavailable behaviours by the parent, who was physically but non psychically and emotionally present at the child needs; Pressure to Achieve scale evaluates the presence of parent's desires of achievement and success of the child (e.g. in school activities or sport performance), in spite of the child's needs or desires.

The second set of ratings made by AAI coders reflects the coherence of participants' discourse regarding their childhood attachment experiences (i.e., their state of mind). In Main and Goldwyn's (1998) coding system, 9-point scales are used to rate the participant's tendency to idealize and/or normalize childhood experiences with caregivers in contrast to the lack of evidence brought from the relative relational episodes (*mother idealization* and *father idealization*), the inability to recall events from childhood linked to attachment figures and episodes (*lack of memory,* e.g. "I don't know" or "I don't remember"), the extent to which one or both caregivers are derogated with cool, rigid, foolish, laughable or not worth in time sentences (*derogation*), the expression of unreasonable fears that their child may die (*fear of loss*), current active resentment toward parents that brings the patient into run on sentences, with a confusion in respect with past and present, and between self and others (*mother anger* and *father anger*), and passive or rambling attachment-related discourse (*passivity*).

Metacognitive monitoring is the subject's ability to think and speak in a fresh, humoristic, complete way about attachment figures and experiences. It is typical of Free subjects. The speaker is able to recognize an appearance-reality distinction, the diversity from self and other, from mother and father, from internal representation and real episodes, and even the possible influence attachment figures and experiences could have had on his own development and personality (e.g., Theory of Mind; Flavell, Flavell & Green, 1986). Development of this theory brought to the definition of Self Reflection Functioning Scale for AAI (SRF; Fonagy, Steele & Steele, 1996).

Unresolved scale captures material rooted in experiences of trauma or loss through death (Bowlby, 1980; e.g., death of an attachment figure or family member – especially in childhood; physical, sexual, or emotional abuse; abandonment). Some questions about the experiences of loss or trauma leaving the individual in a momentary or more prolonged state of dysregulation due to the breakdown of organized defensive processes (i.e., integration, deactivation, disconnection).

Coherency of discourse describes a quality of thinking and speaking that is logically connected, consistent, clearly articulated and intelligible (Main et al., 1998, p. 44). Coherence of discourse in the AAI is evaluated based on the degree to which the individual is willing to cooperate with the interviewer and follows four Grice's maxims in speaking (quality, quantity, relation, and manner). Secure subjects provide fresh, clear, articulated and consistent transcript.

Coherence of Mind is a 5 points scale, to evaluate the overall correlation between coherence of transcription and ability to be collaborative, fresh, cooperative and truthful. Factual or logical contradictions, evaluative oscillations and contradictions, idealizations, lack of memory in respect with attachment experiences and dysfluency talking about losses and trauma, lower the overall score of this scale, which is the most correlated with security in attachment pattern (Main & Goldwyn, 1998, p. 109).

Classification in AAI is laid out as follow: there are five major categories, each of them with different sub categories, characterised by specific pattern of behaviours and feelings in respect with attachment early ,memories an attachment figures.

– F- Free, secure autonomous
– Ds- Dismissing
– E- Preoccupied
– U/d – Unresolved with respect
  to loss and trauma
– CC – Cannot Classify

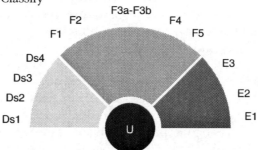

Notice that in AAI one speaker could be scored with more then one classification, such as F/DS or DS3/DS1. Only classifications with a clear oscillations between opposite state of mind in respect with attachment could be classify CC (e.g., CC/DS1/E2). To simplify, patterns of attachment can be imagined as a half circle, beginning with dismissing experiences, passing through free secure experiences and ending with entangled-preoccupied emotions. We decided to put the U category under the half circle, because the U category could be scored in each of the previous cases if evident markers of dysregulation appeared. For example, we could find a U/F or U/DS or U/E.

State of mind scales are used to assist the coder in classifying participants into one of the two major insecure categories (DS or E). Main and Goldwyn (1998) contend that a dismissing state of mind is reflected in any combination of high scores on scales that tap a participant's tendency to idealize parents (DS1, dismissing of attachment), derogate them (DS2, devaluing of attachment), or show failures of memory (DS3, restricted in feelings), and according to the categorical coding system, dismissing adults also occasionally fear the loss of their own child (DS4, cut-off from the source of fear of death of the child). Preoccupation is identified through signs of anger (E2, angry/conflicted) or passivity (E1, passive) or passive and anger together (E3, fearfully preoccupied by traumatic events, combined with or E1 or E2). Security, in contrast, is defined not only by the relative absence of high scores on these indicators but also by clear signs that an adult is able to explore his or her thoughts and feelings about childhood experiences, with fresh speech, humour and forgiveness, without becoming angrily or passively overwhelmed while discussing them (F3a, prototypically secure). By definition, such an ability to freely evaluate one's experiences is reflected in the overall *coherence of mind* and *coherence of transcript* scales. Adults who are able to modify their outlook on their childhood experiences during the interview are given high scores on *metacognitive monitoring*, another indicator of security. Inside the Free category, it is possible to define different kinds of autonomy and security: F1 subjects presents some setting aside of attachment, with harsh childhood experiences; F2 subjects are somewhat dismissing or restricted of attachment; F3 subjects present strong expressed valuing of relationship, accompanied by some manifestation of preoccupations with attachment figures or past trauma events; F5 subjects are definitively secure, but somewhat resentful/conflicting while accepting of continuing involvement with attachment fissures. There is another important category of secure: F3b "earned secure". This secure subjects show a clear actual secure state of mind in contrast to reported or inferred negative experiences in childhood.

Participants that receive a primary unresolved classification (irrespective of whether they are classified as secure, dismissing, or preoccupied) when they score at or above the midpoint on either the *unresolved loss* or *unresolved abuse* scales, which reflect the degree to which individuals' discourse becomes disorganized while discussing loss or abuse experiences, respectively.

Cannot Classify category (CC) is scored every time the transcript indicates a text that cannot be fitted to any "organized" (DS, E, or F) AAI placement. This is evidence most clearly when the text demonstrates a striking or unusual mixture of mental states (Hesse, 1996, 1999).

3.3 Psychometric studies on AAI

Studies of the psychometric characteristics of the AAI are of particular importance, because the AAI is a semi-standardized interview stressing on *natural* discourse, a circumstance that might affect its reliability. Furthermore, the AAI classification system infers the subject's mental representation of attachment from the form of the interview transcript. This inference is based on the coherence of the transcript, although it may be argued alternatively that subjects' general cognitive and memory abilities are being assessed. As a minimal requirement for establishing the universal validity of the AAI, psychometric studies using different languages and combining different tools should yield similar results. Although not many studies were carried out about that and the ones existing in literature are quite spread in their topics.

The psychometric properties of the AAI have received much less attention (Bakermans-Kranenburg & Van IJzendoorn, 1993; Waters, Crowell, Treboux, O'connor, Posada, & Golby, 1993), although the precise meaning of developmental measures can only be established by psychometric research.

3.3.1 Discriminant validity

Van IJzendoorn and Bakermans-Kranenburg (1996) conducted a meta-analysis of 33 AAI studies including more then 2000 AAI attachment classifications, and concluded that worldwide distribution of the three classification internal working models was as follows: 24% was Ds, 58% F, and 18% E. Additionally, about 19% were also assigned to U attachment category. This distribution related to discriminant validity of attachment patterns in adulthood confirmed the distribution of infants' patterns of attachment (Van IJzendoorn & Krooneneberg, 1988; Van IJzendoorn et al., 1999). The AAI classifications appeared independent of the social desirability bias in three studies (Bakermans-Kranenburg & van IJzendoorn, 1993; Sagi et al., 1994; Waters, Crowell, Treboux, O'Connor, Posada, & Golby, 1993). Waters et al. (1993) also found that the discourse style of individuals participating in the AAI is different from their style of discussing a nonattachment-related topic such as the participants' job. The AAI is not measuring logical reasoning abilities or verbal fluency either, because the AAI classifications appeared independent of cognitive and IQ tests in five studies (Bakermans-Kranenburg & van IJzendoorn, 1993; Sagi et al., 1994; Rosenstein & Horowitz, 1993; Steele & Steele, 1994; Ward, Botyanski, Plunket, & Carlson, 1991). Only in the Waters et al. (1993) study was there an association found between the Henmon–Nelson Test of Mental Ability and the AAI. The overall evidence, however, shows that the AAI coding system with its emphasis on coherence of discourse is remarkably little contaminated by IQ differences between the participants.

Related to cognitive differences is the issue of autobiographical memory. Because the AAI heavily relies on the participants' discourse of attachment-related memories from childhood, AAI classifications might be suspected to be associated with autobiographical memory abilities. In the coding system, lack of memory of childhood attachment experiences can be interpreted as a sign of insecurity. In case of the adults with the DS classification, it is supposed that they are not open to negative aspects of their early attachment relationships and, therefore, fall back on lack of memory to avoid reflecting those aspects. Bakermans-Kranenburg and van IJzendoorn (1993) found, however, that the participants (i.e., mothers) within the three AAI classifications did not differ in their ability to remember childhood experiences that are not related to attachment and that those with a DS classification even showed somewhat better memory abilities. This finding was replicated in the Sagi et al. (1994) study with a different sample (students) and different memory measures.

3.3.2 Predictive validity

Some studies on the application of AAI before the birth of a child, have been found to predict the quality of infant–parent attachment relationships (Fonagy, Steele, & Steele, 1991; Radojevic, 1992). The AAI therefore appears to be predictive of parenting behavior toward the children as well. Although adult attachment should be considered neither a necessary nor a sufficient condition for psychological disorders, Bowlby (1973), for example, assumed that environmentally determined disorders might at least partly be related to insecure attachment representations. In 12 studies, some support for the predictive clinical validity of the AAI classifications was found. Van Ijzendoorn, (1995) meta-analysis showed a combined effect size of 1.03 ($r = .46$; $N = 688$) for the relation between security of adult attachment and whether the participants or their children were diagnosed as clinically disturbed.

3.3.3 Interjudges reliability and divergent validity

Most of the studies were focus on cross-cultural data. Psychometric issues (Bakermans-Kranenburg & Van IJzendoorn, 1993) revealed that the reliability of AAI classifications among Dutch mothers was quite high over time and across different interviewers, and that AAI classifications were independent of nonattachment-related domains of memory and cognitive abilities. In a second study, carried out with American mothers (Waters, Crowell, Treboux, O'Connor, Posada, & Golby, 1993), the AAI appeared to be independent of coherence of reasoning about a nonattachment-related issue (i.e., job experience) but was found to be related to a general measure of mental ability.

Some studies on attachment data were carried out in Israel, and showed cross-cultural validity of attachment theory (Van IJzendoorn, 1990). Although the AAI was administered and classified in Hebrew, it yielded results similar to those found when comparable methodologies were used in Dutch (Bakermans-Kranenburg & Van IJzendoorn, 1993).

3.3.4 Test-retest and interjudges reliability

Bakermans-Kranenburg and van IJzendoorn (1993) found that 78% of the AAI classifications remained stable across a 2-month period; Sagi and his colleagues (1994) found that 90% of the classifications were stable across a 3-month period. In two other studies in different countries and with different samples, these results were basically replicated and extended: Steele and Steele (1994) found that 77% of the AAI classifications of 26 English staff and students remained stable across a 1-month period, and Benoit and Parker (1994) showed that 90% of their sample of 84 Canadian mothers received the same AAI classification across a 1.5-year period.

Sagi, Van IJzendoorn, Scharf, Nina, Tirtsa & Ofra, M. (1994) analysed 59 male and female Israeli students twice by 2 different interviewers at 3-month intervals to assess the AAI's test–retest reliability and the effects of the interviewers on the interview itself as well as its subsequent classification. Various memory measures were used to obtain a wide range of information about subjects' memory abilities. Information was also obtained from the students' records about various intelligence-related skills. Results showed high degree of interjudge and test–retest reliabilities, irrespective of interviewers. They found that percentages of agreement between raters for the three attachment categories (autonomous, dismissing, and preoccupied) had a range of k score .82-1.0. Agreements for the self-rated interviews were therefore very similar to what was obtained in cases in which the interviewer and rater were different persons. Test–retest stability is high for all three pairs of raters across the first and the second time of assessment: 87%, 87%, and 95% ([kappa] = .77, .70, and .89, respectively). On a more specific level, a comparison of autonomous versus nonautonomous, dismissing versus nondismissing, and finally preoccupied versus nonpreoccupied indicates a high rate of stability: 90% ([kappa] = .77), 93% ([kappa] = .81), and 97% ([kappa] = .78), respectively.

This finding was supporting the stability of the AAI classifications over time. The classifications on the AAI were not found to be associated with nonattachment-related memory and intelligence abilities. Classifications of the AAI were found to be independent of interviewers. Also, when the interviews were administered twice over a time interval of 3 months, a high rate of stability in classifications was found. Not only was it found that the three AAI classifications were independent of nonattachment-related memory and intelligence measures, but it was also found that in some cognitive and memory tasks the dismissing subjects even performed better than nondismissing subjects. Also, further replications that include additional cultures and languages as well as clinical groups can provide stronger foundations for enhancing the utility of the AAI.

Research studies on relationship between AAI and psychopatology were already reported in Chapter II.

4 THE AAP - ADULT ATTACHMENT PROJECTIVE PICTURE SYSTEM

A. Lis, D. Di Riso, C. Mazzeschi

4.1 AAP description

The Adult Attachment Projective picture system (AAP, *George & West, 2001)* is an adult attachment classification system based on the analysis of a set of projective stimuli. The AAP includes 8 pictures that, with the exception of a warm-up picture, depicts scenes that have been found to activate the attachment system (West & Sheldon-Keller, 1994). Scenes depict a child or adult alone, child-adult and adult-adult dyads. Although the pictures were designed as projective stimuli, the method of administration more closely follows the format of semi-structured interviews (e.g., AAI, child doll play) than the traditional projective format (e.g., TAT). Subjects are invited to make up a story for each picture in which they have to describe what is going on in the picture, what led up to the scene, what characters are thinking or feeling and what might happen next. Picture presentation follows a prefixed order, in which alone picture are alternated with dyadic picture. The purpose of the AAP is to guide the participant to tell stories in response to all eight AAP stimuli. Specific administration rules and probes are described in a very detailed manual. The AAP has to be tape-recorded and transcribed verbatim.

The AAP classification system has integrated features from three representational methods of classifying attachment in adults and children: the AAI, child doll play (Solomon et al., 1995), and adult care giving (George & Solomon, 1996, 1999; Solomon & George, 1996). The AAP was developed to provide researchers and clinicians with a construct validated measure of adult attachment that places the emphasis on mental representation and defensive processing two primary features of attachment theory – e.g., Bowlby, 1969; Cassidy & Kobak, 1988; Main, Kaplan, & Cassidy, 1985; Solomon & George, 1996), yet circumvents the limitations of administration and analysis of interview measures. The AAP emphasizes evaluation of unconscious defensive processes. The AAP was developed to enable researchers to examine new and unique construct-based features of attachment that cannot be examined using the AAI. These include, for example, adult representations of the goal-corrected partnership, the role of agency in attachment, and representational interaction of the attachment, affiliative, and sexual behavioral systems. The AAP is "user friendly" in terms of resources and training; administration, transcription, and the classification process itself are all easy to expedite.

Protocols are classified into four attachment groups: Secure (F), Dismissing (Ds), Preoccupied (E), and Unresolved (U). No criteria has been developed at this time to identify AAI subgroups (i.e., F1, F2, etc.).

George and West (2001) showed that the AAP is a reliable, valid measure of adult attachment. Interjudge reliability was calculated based on 140 cases and convergent agreement between AAP and AAI classifications was determined based on a set of 122 cases (see George & West, 2001, for further details on case selection and sampling). A second large-scale psychometric investigation of the AAP (see George & West, unpublished manuscript) was conducted in 2005. This study examined AAP concordance with the AAI, interjudge reliability, test-retest reliability (retest after three months) and discriminant validity. The study consisted of a sample of 144 participants that included two sub-samples of individuals. One subsample was recruited from Calgary, Alberta (n = 73) and the others were recruited from northern California (n = 71). Participants included females (n = 100) and males (n = 44), ages 18-65 (mean age female = 36.2 yrs; mean age male = 26.4 years). The results of this large scale study provide clear evidence of the reliability and validity of the AAP. Verbal intelligence (WAIS Vocabulary and Similarities subtests) and social desirability (Bindra Inventory of Desirable Responding) were not related to AAP classifications.

Reliability data for AAPs collected in German clinical and normative samples confirmed these results. (Buchheim, Erk, George, Kächele, Ruchsow, Spitzer, Kircher, & Walter, 2006)

All coding is done from the transcribed narrative of the story responses. Coding variables include discourse variables (attachment coherence and personal experience) and content variables (agency, connectedness, and synchrony), and defensive processing markers, including resolution or lack of resolution of any markers of segregated systems in the story. Finally, the protocol is classified according to a decision tree that leads to the classification of the protocol in one of the four classification groups.

4.2 The AAP coding system

All coding variables are strictly connected with Bowlby's attachment theory, giving to the AAP fundamental construct validity. Moreover, they are all operationalized and described in detail in a manual. Reliability has to be reached for the correct use of the AAP.

We will briefly describe the meaning of the content and the discourse variables that are useful in clinical settings. Then examples follow in which they are illustrated.

Agency of the self: The secure base effect in older children and later in adulthood is highly dependent on the ability of the individual to form enduring models of the relationship with the initial caregiver (Internal Working Models, IWM). Over time, a highly differentiated internal representational capacity emerges such that the older child's and later adult's sense of security is maintained not by seeking physical proximity to the attachment figure (except in times of high activation of the attachment system) but by reference to the working model of the attachment figure. The secure base effect in adults is demonstrated in the absence of the attachment figure; that is, maintenance of proximity to the attachment figure becomes almost exclusively an internalized representational process. Secure base is demonstrated by behavior in the presence of the attachment figure when there is no threat. In such situations, the presence and active support of the attachment figure promotes exploration.

There are different forms of connecting with a secure base. Haven of safety has been conceived as a retreat to the attachment figure to reestablish threatened or loss security, and implies a suppression of exploratory behaviors. Haven of safety can be evidenced by an individual's capacity to appeal to relationships to assuage the attachment system. Reparation is an important aspect of haven of safety. From an attachment perspective, reparation is the self's internal resources combined with the desire and capacity to reintegrate a distressed, broken or threatened relationship. In the AAP, the Capacity to act is portrayed when the character is able or confident to make things happen or behaviourally change. Agency of self assesses the degree to which the self is involved in moving psychologically or behaviorally in the direction of empowerment, integration, or understanding. Internalized secure base (ISB), haven of safety (HOS) and capacity to act (CTA) are the three forms of 'agency of self' measured in the AAP. In contrast to being lonely, bored or restless, "internalized secure base" refers to the ability to be content, with solitude as well as to the willingness to engage in self-reflection occasioned by solitude. Internalized secure base is often evidenced by the story character's capacity to be content with solitude in contrast to loneliness, usually implied through descriptions of genuine self-reflection or thoughtfulness. This quality of internalized secure base represents the character's attempt at integration at the level of mind and is often found in responses where the character is portrayed as an adult. The topic of thought is personal, for example, about an experience or person in the present or past with whom the character has a relationship or who has influenced the character in some way. Haven of safety is often found in responses where the character is portrayed as a child; in these scenarios, either the child or the adult may demonstrate this quality. In this instance, the individual either tells a story where a relationship is used for support or exploration, or if the attachment relationship has been threatened; the individual describes one member of the relationship as actively seeking reparation. Capacity to act is evidenced by specific behaviors that demonstrate that the character has taken steps in his or her mind to change the situation.

Connectedness: assesses the desire and ability of the character in the story to be in a relationship defined by any behavioral system (e.g., attachment, caregiving, affiliative, sexual).

Synchrony: This coding variable derived from Bowlby's (1969) concept of the goal-corrected partnership. The goal-corrected partnership captures the child's experience of the caregiver in a "warm, intimate, and continuous relationship with his mother (or permanent mother substitute) in which both find satisfaction and enjoyment" (Bowlby, 1951, p. 13, as quoted by Bretherton, 1992). Later the synchronous elements of attachment were defined more carefully by Ainsworth (Ainsworth et al., 1978): sensitivity, contingency, and responsiveness. Synchrony assesses the degree to which the story characters are portrayed in dyadic scenes engaged in a contingent, reciprocal and mutually engaging relationship. Synchrony is evaluated based on the elements of the caregiving partnership (frequently in adult-child dyadic stories) or elements of mutual enjoyment (frequently in adult-adult dyadic stories).

Defensive Processing: The purpose of the defensive processing dimensions is to identify the quality of defensive exclusion evidenced in the AAP responses. Three aspects of defensive exclusion are delineated: deactivation, cognitive disconnection, and segregated systems (George & Solomon, 1996).

Cognitive disconnection describes a form of defensive exclusion that has been found to be associated with uncertainty, ambivalence, and mental preoccupation with experiences, individuals, or feelings (George & Solomon, 1996). In the assessment, the individual, most commonly, reveals this form of defensive processing by expressing his or her uncertainty directly or by oscillating between descriptions of images of polar opposites (disconnected themes) in telling the story.

Deactivation describes the degree to which the individual uses a form of defensive exclusion to deactivate, diminish, dismiss, or devalue themes in response to the picture stimuli. Deactivation produces representational "distance" between the individual and the attachment-activating event.

Secure individuals, defined theoretically as flexibly integrated and relatively undefended with regard to attachment, have been found to use fewer forms of defensive exclusion when responding to the AAP; the processes that are revealed are usually not confined to any one defensive process.

Segregated Systems describe a mental state in which painful attachment-related memories are isolated and blocked from conscious thought. This material is likely to be rooted in experiences of trauma or loss through death (Bowlby, 1980; e.g., death of an attachment figure or family member – especially in childhood; physical, sexual, or emotional abuse; abandonment). In the assessment some pictures may literally unleash this material, leaving the subject in a momentary state of dysregulation due to the breakdown of organized defensive processes (i.e., integration, deactivation, disconnection – see George & Solomon, 1996; Solomon & George, 1996). It is fundamental to decide if the subject is able to resolve or at least to reorganize his attachment system when segregated systems are unleashed.

4.3 Reading the variables: example of stories in clinical cases

We give an intuitive meaning of these variables showing two groups of four stories derived by the four different classifications groups (F, Ds, E, U). The stories are all based on the Window picture and the Departure picture. The Window depicts a little girl near a window. We can see her from her back and she seems to look outside. In the Departure picture there are a man and a woman with coats and hands in their pockets, standing, and some luggage is between them.

The stories we report do not give a comprehensive picture of the overall protocol. To decide if an individual can be included in one of the four classification groups, the coder needs to compare all seven stories.

F; (Roberto, male, 32 year old medical doctor)

*Uhm, uhm…o.k. a little child. She is sick or she is at the end of her sickness (**Cognitive Disconnection**). The illness is finished, but for the next three days she cannot go out of home. So she is looking outside, because it is already summer. Outside it is sunny. It is afternoon and she is bored (**Cognitive Disconnection**), because she has nothing to do. She is thinking (**Internalized Secure Base**), that in a little time she would be able to go out and that in the first days she will play with other children under the trees in the park outside. Then in few days she will leave and go to the mountains with her grandparents (**Capacity to act**). She is thinking about her feelings (**Internalized Secure***

> *Base) she looks outside and she is <u>bothered, frustrated, irritated</u>* **(Cognitive Disconnection)** *because she would like to go outside and do something, but she <u>is patient</u>* **(Cognitive Disconnection)**. *<u>She watch a little bit of TV</u>* **(Deactivation)**. *She <u>thinks about herself</u>* **(Internalized Secure Base).** *then turns and go to the kitchen where mom is making a cake and <u>they enjòy baking together</u>* **(Internalized Secure Base)**.

The story reveals that Roberto's thinking and speaking was logically connected, consistent, clearly articulated and intelligible. The story is precise, organized and specified. The story included an attachment plot were the internal states of the character were described. The child is thinking about her feelings. Roberto appeared willing to explore his/her internal working model of attachment ("internalized secure base"), which is a central aspect of attachment development. Roberto's sense of security was derived largely from his internal relationship to the attachment figure. Roberto's internalized secure base is evidenced by the story character's capacity to be content with solitude (in contrast to loneliness), as it is usually implied through descriptions of genuine self-reflection or thoughtfulness (the child is thinking, the child is thinking about her feelings) . In the same story Roberto refers also to Haven of Safety. The girl searches and finds mom for mutual enjoyment. According to attachment theory, internalized secure base and haven of safety are promoted in individuals who have developed mental representations of the self as integrated and connected in relationships. Roberto makes a clear and precise description of what the girl will do in the next few days: to play with children in the park and to go to the mountains with her grandparents. In the present moment, she watching TV and baking with mom. The story character was able and confident in making things happen and change after her sickness. Together, all these processes, ranging from internalized processes to specific actions, indicate that Roberto's self was involved in moving psychologically or behaviorally in the direction of empowerment, integration, and understanding according to two forms: internalized secure base and capacity to act. The story also shows connectedness, which is the desire and ability of the character in the story to be in a relationship defined by different behavioral systems: attachment (mother and grandparents) and affiliative (friends).

In the story there are no segregated systems.

Roberto, also, uses cognitive disconnection. The story begins with some uncertainty (the child is sick or at the end of sickness, is bored, later she is frustrated and irritated). Roberto deactivates the attachment system by making the character watch TV. Secure individuals, defined theoretically as flexibly integrated and relatively undefended with regard to attachment, have been found to use fewer forms of defensive exclusion when responding to the AAP; the processes that are revealed are usually not confined to any one defensive process.

For a clinician, it is interesting to follow all the complex variety of processes that Windows has activated in this medical doctor. The child is sick or at the end of the sickness. The first reaction is uncertainty and ambivalence, followed by the activation of ISB. But then Roberto makes his attachment system organized and integrated through specific actions, in which attachment figures are involved grandparents. It is not enough and the individual shows again some uncertainty and ambivalence so at this point, he needs to deactivate his attachment system. Again his secure base appears as ISB and as Haven of Safety. This individual shows how, when in danger, he will be able to use some defences flexibly, but also to have internalized figures of attachment to whom to make reference.

Ds; (Anna, female, 29 year old, working in computers)

Uhm, a little girl is looking outside alone.... Then let see. Before she was doing school task *(Deactivation). She is not very willing to make them. So sometimes she gets up, looks outside. It is nice because there are trees with many foliages. Her home is very small and ugly because there are no windows . She is* uncertain *(Cognitive Disconnection), they said to her that she has to finish* her school tasks *(Deactivation), but she would like to go for a walk. But not a girl friend is coming. So she will continue to make* her school tasks *(Deactivation). What she can think or feeling? She is curious, I think, she is looking outside, she is curious.. she is also a little bit* shy *(Cognitive Disconnection) because she is not completely leant out.. no... but may be it is only because she is living on the eighth floor.*

Anna's story is about a little girl who is involved in school tasks. The story characters are not completely identified. We do not know who said she has to finish the school tasks. No descriptions of genuine self-reflection or thoughtfulness are present. No ability or desire to be connected with attachment or affiliative or sexual systems are present (no girl is coming, there is no mother or parent or friend). She is able to keep organized her attachment system by doing specific actions.

There isn't a segregated system. Although, some mental preoccupation with her experiences appear through cognitive disconnection (the child is uncertain, shy), above all she repeats a consistent use of deactivation under the form of achievement/intellect. Anna develops a story along the duty to perform school tasks. She is not flexibly using her defenses. She rigidly uses deactivation. The development of the story line shows how much she needs these kinds of defenses when her attachment system is activated.

E; (Maria, female, 45 year old, nurse)

So this other picture. First I see a small girl that is looking outside the window. It gives me a sense of solitude, so probably ...//

(Cognitive Disconnection) I do not know ((Cognitive Disconnection) In looking at the picture it comes to me...I associated it, I do not associated it (Cognitive Disconnection at a peaceful (Cognitive Disconnection) moment, I associated it to a moment in which this child is alone... and she simply looking outside the window. So what could lead this child to be like this....May be I do not know it can be (Cognitive Disconnection ... a ehm ... a moment in which she was scolded (Cognitive Disconnection) by her parents. So simply she wants to be alone, or may be she feels sad (Cognitive Disconnection) and so she wants to spent few moments alone ... and... anyway she gives me the sensation surely of happiness (Cognitive Disconnection), and probably the thing will led up at ... a moment in which there would be a clarification. That means that the feeling she is feeling now will finish and surely things will go better (Cognitive Disconnection).

Maria's story is not organized and precise. We only know that the girl was scolded by her parents and that maybe she will stay alone. There is no indication that Maria is really willing to explore her internal working model of attachment ("internalized secure base"), which is a central aspect of attachment development. Although Maria repeatedly talks about being alone there is no evidence of the story character's capacity to be content with solitude (in contrast to loneliness), usually implied through descriptions of genuine self-reflection or thoughtfulness (the child is thinking, the child is thinking about her feeling) . Nor is there indication that she can use the Haven of Safety. Moreover, the girl is unable to make any kind of specific actions that can help to keep organized her attachment system. She able to connect with her parents, but the relation described is only about scolding.

There are no segregated systems. The main defenses used are cognitive disconnection. She described disconnected themes (sadness and happiness), but she also uses entangling (scolded) and glossing over. When using entangling, the individual describes story events that entangle characters or chooses words to describe self or events as emotionally entangled or preoccupied. Glossing over appears when Maria stresses that the child is looking to be serene, happy- making the material less disturbing or negative.

U; (Enrico, 40 year old, inpatient)

This child is alone. She was abandoned (Segregated System) in an orphanage(Segregated System) . She looks outside the window, she will stay in the orphanage(Segregated System) . She will go back to do what she was doing before. What she can think or feeling? Desperate (Segregated System) . Anything else. No.

Enrico makes up a story all about segregated systems. They were unleashed by the picture. Enrico is unable to use any kind of internal secure base or haven to safety or specific action that keeps organized his attachment by making the child act a specific action. The child described is blocked in his traumatic experiences. No cognitive disconnection or deactivation can be activated.

F; Roberto, male, 32 year old, medical doctor)

*So... two fiancés (**Deactivation**) who are leaving in a trip togeth-er. They agreed to go. She has a think she is absorbed in. He under-stands that something is going on in her mind, he stays near her and support and reassure her to make her feel better (**Synchrony**) He is worried (**Cognitive Disconnection**)for her. She fells a sense of despair (**Segregated System**) that she is unable to hide her feelings and to enjoy the trip. They are at the station waiting (**Cognitive Disconnection**) for their train. May be it is a planned trip for some job interviews (**Deactivation**). He is smiling, she is perplex (**Cognitive Disconnection**). They will go on the train (**Capacity to Act**), She will look outside the window. He will be silent, but understanding and thinking about how to support her (**Internalized Secure base**, we can score Agency also in Dyadic pictures if there are some evidences).*

Again, Roberto's story is made up in a very precise and clear way. In this dyadic story, Roberto showed, in a significant way, the story characters portrayed in a synchronic *goal-corrected partnership*. Roberto's story captures how the man in the story is able to understand his fiancés profound distress, and try to support her. He is thinking about what is going on in her mind. This is the highest level of synchrony. In this story there is also a segregated system (despair). The segregated system is resolved by the highest level of synchrony. As for the defences, in this story Roberto also appears a secure individual and defined as flexibly integrated and relatively undefended with regard to attachment. He uses few forms of defensive exclusion (mainly uncertainty and entangling) and he also uses the deactivation markers of romanticism (fiancé) and achievement (job interview). The processes that are revealed are not confined to any one defensive process.

Ds; (Anna, female, 29 year old, working in computers)

*A man and a woman with luggages. So they are at the station. They have to leave and the train is late. No they are coming back because they have their hand in their pockets (**Cognitive Disconnection**). So they are relaxed (**Cognitive Disconnection**). They know each other, because... anyway they are distant (**Deactivation**). They talk, I do not know (**Cognitive Disconnection**)*

I do not know (Deactivation) about what…. As always the train is late they go or they come back. Who knows? I do not know (Cognitive Disconnection) What led up to this? They go or come back (Cognitive Disconnection) from job (Deactivation). They work very very hard like Stakanov (Deactivation). They discuss about their job (Deactivation). They are very competitive (Deactivation).

Anna makes up a story centered on a functional relationship. The man and woman are not involved in mutual enjoyment or in a "goal connected partnership". They are together because of their job. There is no mutual relationship based on an attachment system. Anna uses cognitive disconnection (uncertainty, disconnected opposite themes), but above all she deactivated using achievement/intellect defenses. However, cognitive disconnections are not enough for her when the attachment system is activated. She needs to deactivate.

E; (Maria, female, 45 year old, nurse)

Oh God… another picture. People who are talking or just standing (Cognitive Disconnection)) … eh.. the fact that there are luggages involves detachment, at least this comes to my mind.. I don't know (Cognitive Disconnection)…it recalls me of detachment, also because I see that they are serious, there is no expression, but also from their kind of body, from the way they are drawn… they give me a sense of rigidity and so of detachment. One of the person is detached… what could have led to a detachment, may be one has to go abroad for a business trip or to come and visit parents (Cognitive Disconnection) In the future may be these people would not meet again…it is hard to say..(Cognitive Disconnection) They will go in different directions. There is some sadness, in the sense that the thing is not …// (Cognitive Disconnection) there is some bitterness. This is what comes to my mind, what I feel.

Maria's story is not precise. Two people are talking, they will go in different directions, and they will never meet again. Their meeting is very functional and not guided by a "goal corrected partnership". There is no specific relation between them. Again Maria makes up a story with many words but no specific attachment relation is described. She described disconnected themes showing her profound preoccupation experiences.

U; Enrico, 40 year old inpatient

This woman is leaving by train or with some other kind of transportation (Cognitive Disconnection). and her husband is saying her good bye. What would happen next. She leaves and the man, the husband is a little sad. Anything else. No.

In this story there are no segregated systems. It is important to notice that one unresolved story is enough to score a disorganized protocol. Enrico is already U in the Window story. That means that the Departure stimulus did not unleashed traumatic segregated experience. The story describes a functional relation because the husband just accompanies the wife and tells her goodbye, but no real mutual relationship is described. The only defense activated concerns cognitive disconnection and so experience of preoccupations.

4.4 AAP - Personality, Psychopathology and Psychiatric Status: The State of the Art

The Adult Attachment Projective (AAP) is a relatively new measure of an adults' state of mind regarding attachment. As we have already seen, this test had shown a high convergence with the Adult Attachment Interview (George & West, 2001). There are only a few studies that have examined the relationship among attachment and personality, psychopathology or psychiatric status using the AAP.

The following review shows the studies conducted with this instrument.

4.4.1 AAP and defence mechanisms as a measure of degree of psychopathology

Hoffman (2007) examined the relationship between adult attachment and maturity of defence mechanisms. He administered to 100 undergraduate student the Adult Attachment Projective (AAP) and the Thematic Apperception Test (TAT). Defence mechanisms were scored on the TAT using Cramer's Defence Mechanism Manual (DMM). This score leads to three hierarchy levels of defence: denial, projection, and identification, with denial being the most primitive and identification being the most mature. The AAP four scoring categories were condensed into two groups reflecting secure and insecure attachment. These two groups were then compared to the three levels of defences measured by the DMM scores. Insecure attachment was related to primitive defences of denial and projection. No differences were found between the insecure and secure groups for the mature defence of identification. These results suggested that immature defences could be a better measure of psychological deficits than mature defences. According to Hoffman (2007) the findings of this study argue for the idea that attachment may be a factor in the development of defensive structures. Two explanations for this finding are discussed: (a) primitive defences may become adopted during childhood because of an inability to use an attachment figure for comfort and protection; (b) individuals with insecure attachment may not be able to use identification effectively as a defence, necessitating the greater use of other more immature defences to cope with distress.

4.4.2 AAP, Unresolved Attachment and immigrant status

Van Ecke, Chope, and Emmelkamp (2005) and Van Ecke (2007) compared attachment status of Dutch and Belgian immigrants in California with non immigrant Californians. The authors analyzed attachment at the representational level by comparing coherence in responses of 69 immigrants (29 men and 40 women) and 30 non immigrants (12 men and 18 women) in the AAP. They found that immigrants had significantly higher rates of unresolved attachment than did non immigrants, unrelated to their length of time in the United States, to their marriage status, or to their reasons for immigration.

Analysis of variance indicates that being unresolved with regard to attachment is linked to greater perception of danger in general, and to a lower ability to resolve danger once perceived. Resolution of danger in story responses to AAP images shows that the immigrant group is most troubled by images of departure and isolation, but non immigrants are most disturbed by images of illness.

4.4.3 Attachment and externalizing behaviour problems

Mazzarello (2007) examined associations between attachment representations in a sample of 42 adolescent mothers and their 4-7 year old children. The study investigated : (1) the correspondence between maternal representations linked to insecurity (i.e. low agency of self on the AAP and child attachment classifications designated using the Preschool Attachment Classification System (Cassidy & Marvin with the MacArthur Working Group on Attachment, 1992); (2) potential mechanisms involved in attachment transmission, namely mother-child interactions rated using an observational coding system developed by Moss, Humber, & Roberge (1996) and callous-unemotional traits assessed using the Antisocial Process Screening Device (Frick & Hare, 2001); (3) the roles of both mother and child attachment in the prediction of externalizing behaviour problems (measured using the Child Behaviour Checklist (Achenbach & Edelbrock, 1983); (4) a mediation model in which child attachment acts as a mediator in the relation between mother attachment and externalizing behaviour problems; and finally (5) a moderation model investigating interactions between child and mother attachment in the prediction of externalizing behaviour problems. Results showed a significant correspondence between maternal representations of attachment and child attachment.

4.4.4. AAP and Dysthymia

West and George (2002) evaluated the relationship between preoccupied attachment and dysthymic disorder in women. Attachment patterns were assessed using the AAP. The sample consisted of 420 women, 129 women were identified with depressive symptoms as assessed by the Centre for Epidemiological Studies

Depression scale (CES-D). Twenty-four of these 129 dysthymic women were assessed according to the Structured Clinical Interview for DSM-III-R-(non-patient edition) (SCID-NP). The results indicate that preoccupied attachment is associated with the diagnosis of dysthymia in women: 58% of the 24 women with a diagnosis of dysthymia were classified as preoccupied. Dysthymia was not associated with unresolved attachment. This result differs from the findings of Fonagy and colleagues, who reported that 72% of depressed adult inpatients were unresolved. These findings suggest that loss is not as clearly linked to depression as Bowlby had assumed. According to the authors, depression represents a basic reaction to a sense of frustration experienced by preoccupied individuals in their efforts to achieve an internally coherent representation of the world and of attachment. The authors discussed the association between preoccupied attachment and depression, with attention to the possibly complicating factor of unresolved mourning.

4.4.5 Research for evaluation of the insecure attachment in a foster mother

Odipo (2002) examined associations between a foster mothers' state of mind in regards to attachment (as measured by the AAP) and 37 foster mothers' descriptions of their foster children (as measured by the Parent Development Interview, PDI). Sixteen foster mothers were classified as secure-autonomous while twenty-one were classified as insecure in regards to attachment. Approximately sixty percent of the insecure foster mothers were classified as unresolved with regards to attachment. The distributions of attachment classifications suggested that foster mothers were unresolved in regards to attachment. Findings suggest foster mothers' attachment status is related to their representations of their foster children. Results indicated that the two groups (secure and insecure foster mothers) differed significantly on 7 of the 13 PDI subscales scores; namely pleasure, business of caregiving, achievement, comfort/safe haven, perspective taking, enmeshment, pleasure and pain.

4.4.6 AAP and FMRI studies

Buchheim, George, Kächele, Erk, Walter (2006) administered the AAP in a FMRI environment. The FMRI measures neural activity correlated with regional increase in blood flow. The signal is based on "BOLD" effect (BOLD= blood oxygenation level dependent) and the FMRI reveals the signal of oxygenated and deoxygenated haemoglobin. The subjects are placed inside a scanner and have to give answers to AAP pictures. The researchers showed that the neural underpinnings of these unique intimate emotional states are linked to functionally specialized areas in the brain. This paper supported that the AAP is a fruitful measure to use in an FMRI environment to examine brain activation patterns in adults while they are speaking overtly about attachment stories in a standardized setting. In another study, Stanley

(2006) investigated the association between individual differences in emotional reactivity of the prefrontal cortex as measured by EEG, and attachment in 124 college students classified for attachment organization by the AAP. Participants viewed video clips of separation and reunion scenes designed to activate and terminate the attachment system with increasing intensity. Skin conductance data was also synchronized to the separation and reunion scenes. Supporting attachment theory's continued emphasis on reunion, there was a significant main effect for attachment organization during the reunion condition.

5 ATTACHMENT AND RORSCHACH ASSESSMENT

S. Salcuni, L. Laghezza, G. Rondanini

5.1 The Rorschach test

The Rorschach Inkblot Test (Rorschach, 1921) is a well known method to evaluate personality structure. The test consists of 10 ambiguous stimulus cards (inkblot cards). Many methods have been devised to administer, score and evaluate the Rorschach test after the premature death of its author. Generally, for all of them, at the presentation of each card the subject is asked *what can they be* and a specific inquiry is conducted at the end of the administration. The inquiry is an integral part of the administration.

Some of the existing methods approach the Rorschach from a psychometric point of view (e.g. Exner's Comprehensive System (CS; Exner, 1991)), while others use a clinical idiographic approach (Chabert, 1983; Lerner, 1991; for comments see Weiner, 2001). In most methods, idiographic and nomothetic approaches are integrated. These methods start with the scoring of quantitative data which are compared with norms and a qualitative idiographic analysis is later added. The variety of methods used for the Rorschach both highlight the richness and complexity of the information the instrument can give, and make the Rorschach a very specific technique. From an idiographic point of view, historically the test has often been criticized because of a lack of psychometric features. The richness and complexity of the possible uses of the Rorschach test is also demonstrated by the numerous scales, based on Rorschach responses. The scales include: the Ego Impairment Index (EII; Perry & Viglione, 1991); the Aggressive Contents Scale (Gacono & Meloy, 1994); the Mutuality of Autonomy Scale (MOA; Urist, 1977); the Rorschach Oral Dependency Scale (ROD; Bornstein & Masling, 2005); and the thought Disorder Index (TDI; Johnson & Holzman, 1979).

Although psychologists often debate the question of validity and usefulness of the Rorschach Inkblot Test (Rorschach, 1921), the Rorschach is in wide clinical use to investigate personality structure (Brown & McGuire, 1976; Lubin, Larsen, Matarazzo, & Seever, 1985; Piotrowski & Keller, 1989; Piotrowski et al., 1985 Ritzler & Alter, 1986; Ritzler & Del Gaudio, 1976; Sweeney, Clarkin, & Fitzgibbon, 1987). The Rorschach helps psychologists to describe the complex interaction among psychological, biological, environmental, and behavioral domains (Viglione & Perry, 1991). Useful applications of this assessment instrument include identifying and ruling out potential or unrecognized problems, non obvious overt and covert behaviors, respondent characteristics and individual patterns relevant to diagnosis (Viglione, 1999).

5.2 Exner's Comprehensive System

The debate about the Rorschach test has been and is still very alive. Despite a wealth of creative thinking and extensive research efforts, the unsystematic nature of these early endeavors prevented the Rorschach assessment from establishing much claim of scientific status. Since the early 1970s, however, with the advent of the CS (Exner, 1991, 1993; Exner & Weiner, 1995), Rorschach assessment evolved into a carefully standardized procedure. Over the years, the CS has become the most widely used approach to Rorschach Assessment. As the only carefully standardization approach to collecting and codifying Rorschach data, the CS is the primary Rorschach Method that should be considered in evaluating the scientific worthiness of the instrument.

The observations on Rorschach standardization have three important implications for the basic nature and utility of the Rorschach Inkblot Method (Weiner, 2001). First, Rorschach data, specifically with CS, are not theory bound and can be interpreted within the framework of diverse ways of conceptualizing personality processes: provided that one believes in the existence of personality states and traits and the implications of Rorschach responses can be couched in whatever theoretical language one prefers. Second, the Rorschach stimuli and instruments are essentially cultural free, and the instrument can be administered in a standard manner independent of a respondent's age, gender, ethnicity, nationality, or other demographic characteristics. Finally, Rorschach data lend themselves to both nomothetic interpretation based on comparison with available normative data and to idiographic interpretation that allows for individualized case conceptualization. The previously published article by Stricker and Gold (1999) and by Viglione (1999) elaborate each of these advantages of Rorschach Assessment.

The most recent contribution to the debate is given by the series of articles in the Journal of Personality Assessment coordinated by Meyer (e.g. Meyer, 2001; Meyer & Archer, 2001), which demonstrated the psychometrics validity of the Comprehensive System devised by Exner (1991, 1993). This system rests on three methodological pillars: standardized administration, objective and reliable coding, and a normative database (Weiner, 1998). It enables the integration of the objective aspects of the test with its projective and dynamic aspects in scientifically controlled ways.

In particular, the great majority of Rorschach CS variables and configurations have shown impressive psychometric characteristics (Perry & Viglione, 1991; Perry, McDougall, & Viglione, 1995; Exner, 1995; Sloan, Arsenault, Hilsenroth, Handler, & Harvill, 1996; Sloan, Arsenault, Hilsenroth, Havill & Handler, 1995). In the CS the Rorschach test is essentially a behavioral problem-solving task (Viglione, 1999), and the CS scores are simply a summary of problem-solving behavior collected under standardized conditions. The task complexity and personal relevance of the answers probably contribute to the possibility of generalization of the Rorschach variables, as supported by empirical findings .

5.2.1 A brief description of the CS Clusters

The CS proposes an interpretation based on clusters. The order by which the cluster is addressed is not always the same. Twelve key variables have been identified to define the best order of cluster review. The presence of a key variable predicts which combination of two or three clusters of data will yield the data sources that will contribute the most substantial information about the core psychological features of the person. Considerable importance is given to these features in forming the description of an individual. They are dominant elements of personality structure and have a major impact on the psychological organization. The variables exert a significant influence on the way in which the other features are organized.

Controls and Stress Tolerance

Controls are defined as the capacity to form decisions and implement deliberate behaviours that are designed to contend with the demands of the situation. They refer to the person's ability to remain organized and directed in response to a specific situation. The controls may vary: they may diminish or strengthened depending on the circumstances of a situation. Some people have less capacity for control and they are prone to becoming overwhelmed temporally or chronically with a loss of control over feelings and thinking. The capacity of control is contingent on the person's ability to draw on available sources to form and implement deliberate actions that are designed to contend with demand situations.

There are three important conceptual issues to understand control capabilities: resources, stimulus demand and stress tolerance. The concept of *resources* refers to the collection of cognitive capabilities that have been developed, including the manner by which feelings are identified and utilized. Resources do have a direct relationship to the ability of the individual to control his behaviours. The more resources available, the more likely the person is able to form and direct behaviours regardless of whether or not those behaviours are productive or adaptive. The *demands* experienced by a person are an important issue in understanding capacities to control because if the level of demands exceed the level of resources available to contend with the demands, some sort of psychological disarray is bound to occur. The result is a reduction or loss of control. Demands on the individual can originate both externally or internally, but the impact is always internal and takes the form of mental activity. The third concept is the *stress tolerance* that relates directly to the capacity of control: as resources increase, also the ability to tolerate the stress increases. Conversely as resources are more limited so too is a person's ability to tolerate stress.

Situational Related Stress

Situational stresses can evolve from any of a variety of personal trauma: failures, emotional loss, conflicts about decisions. They create a considerable discomfort and they have an impact on some aspects of the psyche.

Affect

This cluster determines the role of the emotion in the psychological organization and functioning of the person and the way in which people process emotional experience. The affect cluster identifies whether people have adequate capacities to experience and express emotion sufficiently, pleasurably, and in moderation, or whether, instead, they are prone to process affect in a constricted, dysphoric, or intense manner that leads to adjustment difficulties.

Self Perception

This cluster provides information about two specific aspects: self –perception and self-involvement. The cluster investigates how people view themselves, particularly with respect to their level of self-esteem, the extent of their self-awareness, and the nature of their self-image. The self-involvement analyzes the level of interest of the person on them self and their capacities to confront the external world. There are two types of people that are over concerned with themselves: people who have a high consideration of themselves and people who perceive themselves with a low value. These people are highly focused on themselves with a very low involvement and interest in the external world. The Self Perception cluster tries to identify whether people feel satisfied and comfortable with themselves or if they have negative self-attitudes; whether they are excessively preoccupied with or pay little attention to themselves; and whether they have a clear and stable sense of their identity or if they have an uncertain and unrealistic imagine of the kind of person they are.

Interpersonal Perception

This cluster of provides information about how people perceive other people and relate to others, particularly with respect to their attitudes toward other people and the degree of interaction they have with them. This cluster tries to understand if people are able to sustain an adaptive level of interpersonal interest, involvement, and comfort, or are instead inclined to be disinterested and disengaged in social situations. This cluster also measures if people are able to produce intimacy and security in their interpersonal interactions, or tend instead to regard interpersonal closeness with a preference to keep their distance from others. Finally, it tries to understand if they perceive other people and social situations accurately or are they prone to misunderstand the reasons of others and the implications of interpersonal events.

The cognitive triad includes three clusters which provide information about the following cognitive skills: processing, mediation, ideation.

Mediation

This cluster provides information about the manner in which people perceive their environment, particularly with respect to whether they perceive people and events the way most other people do. This cluster analyzes reality testing: the individual's ability to produce a response that is adapted to the stimulus shape and the way in which the person interprets reality. Being able to perceive one's experience realistically and with a minimum of conventionality constitutes a personality strength that typically contributes to good adjustment. Conversely, difficulties in seeing oneself and one's world in a realistic light is a personality limitation that often causes adjustment problems.

Ideation

This cluster provides information about the way people think about their experiences and the impressions they form about events in their lives. Ideation represents the core of psychological activity from which decisions and behaviours take shape. This cluster analyzes the way in which the input is changed into concepts or symbols. The ideation focuses on thinking's features and its quality and coherency. People adapt best when they are able to think about their experiences and impressions in a logical, coherent, flexible, and constructive manner. Conversely, being inclined to illogical, incoherent, inflexible, overly fanciful, or excessively pre-occupying ways of thinking constitutes a personality liability that interferes with psychological adjustment.

Processing

This cluster provides information about the manner in which people focus their attention on events in their lives and how they organize the perceptions of the stimulus. This cluster evaluates the effort, the quality, efficiency and coherency to process the information. The processing strategies are influenced by different variables: motivation, defences, attitudes, ideas, and need to reach a aim. A good adaptation is promoted by openness to experience and efficient organization of the impressions one forms, whereas viewing the world in disorganized way makes a person susceptible to various types of adjustment difficulty.

5.3 Rorschach and attachment

The Rorschach test and the attachment theory have occupied center stage in recent years. The aim of this chapter is to present a brief review of studies and theoretical essays that have addressed the relationship between attachment theory, patterns and styles of attachment and personality structure as investigated by the Rorschach variables.

The existing literature on Rorschach and attachment shows two broad sets of studies. A first group of studies examined the relations between Rorschach variables and other separate instruments aimed at evaluating patterns and styles of attachment according to attachment theorists. Among them we can distinguish studies that used questionnaires (attachment styles, socio-cognitive approach) and studies which used the AAI (attachment patterns from a developmental narrative approach) and, recently, the AAP (attachment patterns from a defenses mechanisms approach). In a second group of studies, attachment was identified using only Rorschach variables. Even if we embrace Bowlby's classical definition of attachment, such as identified by George and West (2001), in literature attachment was sometime connected with Bowlby's theoretical model, and sometimes it was defined simply and reductively as interpersonal relatedness or an interpersonal relation construct.

At the end of the chapter some conclusion are presented, which are aimed at highlighting limitations and strengths of the different tools and methodologies analyzed.

5.3.1 Rorschach and Adult Attachment Interview (AAI)

Very few studies have sought to explore the association between attachment patterns measured by the Adult Attachment Interview (AAI) and Rorschach data.

Rothstein (1997) investigated the association between the constructs of mental representation of interpersonal relationships posited by object relations theory and attachment theory. The author administered to a non clinical sample of 39 middle-class primiparous women, in their third trimester of pregnancy, the Rorschach and the Adult Attachment Interview. Rorschach tests were scored with two object relations measures: Urist's (1977) Mutuality of Autonomy Scale, and Blatt et al.'s (1976) Developmental Analysis of the Concept of the Object Scale. No significant differences were found in quality or developmental level of object representations among subjects grouped by security versus insecurity of attachment. A post hoc independent t-test of subjects grouped by minimizing and maximizing affective styles, rather than attachment category, indicated that affective minimizers had a greater number of Urist scale malevolent scores than affective maximizers.

Jones (2000) compared adult internal working models of attachment as assessed by the Adult Attachment Interview to the two Rorschach object relations scales already used by Rothstein (1997) on a sample of 37 mothers of diverse backgrounds. The structural level of accurately perceived object relations was developmentally more mature for securely attached mothers than insecurely attached mothers. However, the developmental level of the thematic content of object relations did not differentiate securely and insecurely attached mothers.

5.3.2 Rorschach and Adult Attachment Projective Picture System (AAP)

Jacques (2002) investigated the relationship between disorganized attachment (U) and disordered thinking and affect dysregulation using the CS in adults. The AAP and the Rorschach were administered to a sample of 25 adult community volunteers who self-reported a history of childhood trauma. Major findings were as follows: 52% of the sample was classified as U (n = 13). One-way analysis of variance demonstrated significant relationships between the U group and Rorschach affect variables *C* (pure color) and *DEPI* (Depression Index). An analysis of variance also demonstrated a significant relationship between U and *PTI* (Perceptual-Thinking Index). Disorganized attachment and its multiple mental representations may be a more useful way to conceptualize thought disorder, confusion, incoherency and affective instability. The participants were extensively quoted.

5.4 Measures of construct of attachment in the Rorschach compared with other measures of construct of attachment (questionnaires and others)

Few studies have examined attachment constructs on conduct disorders, psychopathy, antisocial personality disorder and delinquency using a multi-assessment approach; comparing attachment construct in the Rorschach and attachment styles measures devised by questionnaires or other measures of attachment styles.

Disruptive behaviors refers to those behaviors specified as Conduct Disorder and Oppositional Defiant Disorder in the DSM-IV (APA, 1994). A robust literature indicates that these behaviors can be differentiated into two groups, aggressive and non-aggressive/delinquent, each with its own developmental trajectory. The aim of Pinto's (1999) contribution was to examine whether or not children manifesting different behavioral disturbances, manifest different attachment styles or differences in object representations, which have been found to mediate behavior. The frequency of certain Rorschach determinants, considered to reflect attachment needs, dysphoria and attachment was examined on the Rorschach protocols of 50 adolescent boys, ages 13 through 15, identified as in need of service for disruptive behaviors, significant enough to cause dysfunction either in school or the community. The Mutuality of Autonomy Scale (MOA; Urist, 1977) was also used. This scale measures object representations along seven dimensions, reflecting different developmental levels. The youths' self-report of their attachment to each parent and to their peers was also examined, using the Inventory of Parent and Peer Attachment (Armsden & Greenberg, 1987). The subjects were subdivided in two groups: aggressive (overt group) and non/aggressive (covert group) No difference was found between the groups in their use of Rorschach determinants, nor in their ratings of attachment of parents and peers. On the MOA, the covert group showed a significantly higher frequency of Most Adaptive Responses (MAR) than the overt group, indicating a greater capacity for collaborative and reciprocal relationships. The groups did not differ in the frequency of their Least Adaptive Responses (LAR), suggesting that malevolent and destructive interactions are equally expected by each group. Further research in this area is required. Pinto's (1999) exploratory analysis of the frequency of distorted or unusual perceptions (X-, Xu) found that this population of adolescents manifesting disruptive behaviors produced a significantly greater number of these responses when compared to the non-clinical sample reported by Exner (1993).

CS Rorschach variables and questionnaires were used to explore the relationship between quality of paternal attachment and the development of violent behavior. Measures of attachment included the Parental Bonding Instrument (PBI; Parker, Tupling, & Brown, 1979) and the Ranking of Attachment Scale (RAS; Delucas, 1997), a measure developed for this study. The following personality variables were explored: egocentricity, disturbed interpersonal perceptions and relatedness, and aggressive perceptions. The personality variables were explored by CS scores and other Rorschach scores: Texture and Aggressive Responses, Human Experience Variable (Perry & Viglione, 1991) scores and Gender Scores (Morgan & Viglione, 1992). Three groups from a military brig were compared: 33 violent offenders group including subjects convicted of or with a documented history of violent behavior towards another person; 32 non-violent offenders group, whose crimes were non-violent and who had no documented history of violent behaviors; and a control group of 32 prosocial aggressive subjects comprised of military corrections staff personnel assigned to the brig. Although the results of these analyses were non-significant, 10 out of 12 analyses showed only a *trend* towards significance in the hypothesized direction. The lack of differences may have been influenced by the homogeneity of military subjects (Delucas, 1997).

Some studies used a multidimensional approach to compare attachment styles and attachment construct in the Rorschach for other psychopathologies. They examined normal and pathological children, adolescents and adults.

Muras (1996) categorized 60 adolescents receiving psychiatric treatment by using a self report on attachment (Bartholomew, & Horowitz, 1991) into one of three attachment groups: secure, avoidant, and anxious-ambivalent. The measure was given to both patient and therapist. As a way to integrate attachment and object-relations theories, the Rorschach Mutuality of Autonomy Scale (MOA; Urist, 1987) was administered to assess level of object relations. According to therapists' ratings of attachment, these adolescents were categorized predominantly into the two insecure attachment groups. The frequencies of categorization into both the avoidant and anxious-ambivalent groups differed significantly from normative data. No relationships were found between attachment status and level of object-relations. As predicted, the anxious-ambivalent group experienced more anxiety (Y) than the avoidant group, but that was the only variable that discriminated between the two insecure groups.

Farrar (1996) compared 29 adult female outpatients who had experienced father/daughter incest in childhood with a group of 31 female outpatients who had experienced no incest in childhood. Each participant completed the Rorschach and a set of self-report measures, including demographic and sexual history questionnaires, a revision of the McMaster Family Assessment Device (FAD; Epstein, Baldwin, & Bishop, 1982), and the Bell Object Relations and the Reality Testing Inventory (BORRTI; Bell, 1991). The Rorschach was scored using the Developmental Analysis of the Concept of the Object Scale (Blatt, Brennis, and Schimek, 1976a). Incest survivors experienced significantly more difficulty than the controls with issues of trust in intimate relationships, as measured by the Alienation subscale of the BORRTI. Their level of current distress was higher (as measured by the BSI) and they described their family's functioning (FAD) as more pathological. Level of object relations, as operationalized by the Alienation subscale on the BORRTI, was predictive of subjects' report of family pathology. And level of object relations, as measured by Alienation and Insecure Attachment on the BORRTI, was predictive of level of overall current distress. Results indicating investment in fantasies rather than realistic relationships (OR-score on the DACOS) approached significance.

Solano, Toriello, Barnaba, Ara and Taylor (2000) explored the similarities and differences between 20 mentally ill patients and 20 psychosomatically ill patients on measures of alexithymia, perceived closeness to parents, and mental representations of interrelationships. All subjects were given the Toronto Alexithymia, (Bagby & Parcker, 1997), the Family Attitude Questionnaire (Targum, Dibble, Davenport & Gershon 1981), and the Rorschach Interaction Scale (Graves, Mead, & Pearson, 1986). Both the psychotic and psychosomatic subjects showed a high degree of alexithymia. They also showed a lack of general closeness to parents and a predominance of maladaptive Rorschach interaction patterns suggestive of internal working models associated with poor affect regulation, and insecure attachment styles. While the majority of the psychosomatic patients showed an Avoidant interaction pattern, the majority of psychotic patients were Ambivalent (55%) and Flexible (25%).

Novick (1997) compared object relations of 38 mothers and their children (grade 3 through 6) from an inner-city neighborhood and examined the mothers' empathic ability and quality of their attachment to their own parents. Children attended public elementary school, half were boys, half girls. Object relations were measured by the Mutuality of Autonomy Scale (MOA; Urist, 1977), applied to child and mother Rorschach imagery; maternal empathy by the Interpersonal Reactivity Index (Davis, 1980); and maternal attachment by the Adult Attachment Scale (Collins & Read, 1990). Data showed a correlation between only one of the three mother and child scores. The proposed relationships of both maternal attachment status and maternal empathy to level of maternal object relations were not supported by the data. The proposed relationship between maternal empathy and attachment was supported by several moderate correlations. Single correlations indicated relationships between those aspects of the mother's functioning and the object representations of her child.

Rorschach orality, number of Rorschach Human responses (*HMR*) and self-reported attachment style were examined on a college sample (n = 198) (Duberstein & Talbot, 1993). High orals were more often classified as more insecure than low orals. However, heterogeneity was found within the low-oral group: subjects who produced no oral responses (78%) were more likely to be classified as insecure than subjects who produced one oral response (35%). Neither orality nor attachment security was meaningfully related to the number of HMRs provided, but the quality of *HMRs* provided by insecure subjects more frequently evidenced themes of struggle.

75 college students subdivided in three groups of 25 participants, each representative of one of three adult attachment styles (secure, preoccupied, and

avoidant) were compared on CS Texture response, Morbid content response, and Burns and Viglione's (1996) Human Experience Variable (Rhonda, 2001). Securely attached participants displayed significantly more interpersonal characteristics indicative of healthy adjustment than avoidant attached participants. Conversely, participants classified as preoccupied failed to be significantly different from either secure or avoidant participants.

The results of the administration of the Rorschach, the Relationship Questionnaire (Bartholomew & Horowitz, 1991) and the Relationship Scales Questionnaire (Griffin & Bartholomew, 1994a, 1994b), both measures of adult attachment style, to a total of 79 married or dating men (n = 40) and women (n = 39) provided support that moderate levels of texture (T = 1) indicated a secure attachment style, high levels of T (T > 1) indicated a preoccupied attachment style, and low levels of T (T = 0) indicated either a fearful, dismissing, or general avoidant attachment style (Cassella, 1999). Accounting for gender differences, separate analyses were conducted with the result that high T women were no more preoccupied than other women while high T men did score higher than all other men. T = 0 participants did not score higher on either fearful or dismissing attachment than those who gave more texture responses, however, they scored higher on a general measure of avoidant attachment. Finally, the general avoidant measure correctly classified more of the T = 0 participants than did a measure of psychopathology.

Frank, Tuber, Slade and Garrod (1994) studied the relationship between 25 first-time pregnant women's fantasy representations on the Rorschach test and later, attachment status of their 1-yr-olds. The Manual for Assessing Primary Process Manifestations in Rorschach Responses (Holt, 1968) was used to score Rorschach protocols and the Strange Situation was examined to assess infant attachment behaviors. Findings supported that primary process integration during pregnancy is significantly and positively related to infant security of attachment and suggested a relation between empathic maternal behaviors and dimensions of mothers' unconscious mental representations measurable prior to the infant's birth.

Priel (2001) performed an empirical study of the relations between assessments of adult attachment styles and object representations in the context of first-time 120 pregnant mothers' emotional ties to their unborn babies. Mothers' representations of their own mothers, were found to fully mediate the association between internal working models and antenatal ties to their babies.

Reid (2001) determined if adult attachment style was predictive of various interpersonal characteristics as measured by the Rorschach inkblot method. Specifically, Exner's (1993) Texture response, Morbid content response, and Burns and Viglione's (1996) Human Experience Variable were utilized as indicators of interpersonal health and adjustment. Participants were 75 college students, 25 participants were each representative of one of three adult attachment styles: secure, preoccupied, and avoidant. It was hypothesized that participants' Rorschach profiles would be theoretically consistent with their adult attachment classification. It was found that securely attached participants were significantly more likely to display interpersonal characteristics indicative of healthy adjustment than were participants classified as avoidantly attached. Conversely, participants classified as preoccupied-ly attached failed to be significantly different from either securely or avoidantly attached participants. Implications of results are discussed and directions for future research are suggested. Particularly, it is suggested that research within this area of study should utilize multi-modal methods of assessment when determining adult attachment classification, and that research aimed at validating Exner's (1993) Comprehensive System for the Rorschach continue to be vigorously pursued.

The psychometric properties and predictive validity of the Dependency Index (DI; Hilsenroth & Bornstein, 2002) and the Rorschach Oral Dependency Scale (ROD; Masling, Rabie, & Blondheim, 1967) were examined by Fowler, Brunnschweiler, Swales and Brock (2005) to determine if these implicit measures of dependency predict observable attachment-seeking behavior in 66 female inpatients diagnosed with borderline personality disorder. The DI was predictive of nursing staff observation of positive attachment/treatment compliance ($r = .28$, $p = .02$) but not excessive isolation. By contrast, the ROD predicted positive attachment/treat-ment compliance ($r = .38$, $p = .002$) and excessive isolation ($r = -.35$, $p = .004$). Texture responses predicted excessive isolation ($r = -.25$, $p = .05$). Discriminant validity was supported when neither dependency measure predicted hostile inter-actions or self destructive behaviors. Hierarchical regression analyses revealed that the ROD demonstrated incremental validity over the DI and select CS variables asso-ciated with dependency.

Berant, Mikulincer, Shaver and Segal (2005) examined associations between self-reported attachment anxiety and avoidance and responses to the CS. Seventy-two, non patient Israeli adults participated in a 2-session study. In the first session, they completed a self-report scale tapping the dimensions of attachment anxiety and attachment avoidance. In the second session, they completed the CS. Self-reports of attachment anxiety were associated with Rorschach scores thought to indicate difficulties in regulating and controlling emotions and self-perceptions of being relatively helpless and unworthy. Self-reports of attachment avoidance were associated with Rorschach scores thought to reflect lack of acknowledgment of need states and maintenance of a grandiose self.

5.5 Measures of construct of attachment in the Rorschach variables set

Attachment theory postulates that based upon experiences in early childhood, par-ticularly relationships with early caregivers, individuals develop internal representa-tions of themselves and others which organize subsequent interpersonal behavior. Those individuals who experience parenting which does not adequately meet their emotional or physical needs of protection and care, or who experience early child-hood trauma develop internal representations of others as hurtful and unavailable and are likely to react with hostility and aggression toward others. This is probably the reason why Rorschach variables as measures of attachment were often studied in conduct disorder, psychopathic and delinquent subjects. Most of these studies used CS variables, others used scales applied to the Rorschach protocol.

Three CS Rorschach variables, texture, diffuse shading, and pure human content were used to investigate the constructs of anxiety (diffuse shading) and attachment (texture and pure human content) in inpatients conduct-disorder adolescents compared with dysthymic adolescents. 48 inpatient conduct-disordered and 30 inpatient dysthymic adolescents (all aged 13-16 yrs) participated in the study. Conduct-disordered subjects came from homes in which the mother figure was significantly less present. Mild, moderate, and severe conduct-disordered subjects were also compared on the 3 selected Rorschach variables, and family characteristics for the two groups were investigated. There was a lower frequency of texture (lower anxiety) and pure human content responses (lesser attachment) responses in conduct-disorder adolescents and a greater frequency of diffuse shading responses in dysthymic adolescents (Weber, 1991; Weber, Meloy, Gacono, 1992).

Moderate and severe psychopaths were compared on CS variables related to attachment and anxiety. 42 male offenders (aged 18-43 yrs) who met criteria for antisocial personality disorder were assessed with the Hare Psychopathy Checklist (Hare, 1998; Hare, Harpur, Hakstian, Forth, Hart, & Newman, 1990). According to this checklist the subjects were divided in two groups: severe psychopaths (scoring >= 30), and moderate psychopaths (scoring<30). Three Rorschach variables related to attachment, anxiety, and coping were compared between the two groups. Moderate psychopaths produced texture and diffuse shading responses at a significantly greater frequency than Severe Psychopaths. These results add construct validity to the lack of attachment in psychopaths and the role of anxiety in differentiating secondary from primary psychopathy (Gacono, & Meloy, 1991).

CS Rorschach variables and Rorschach object relations and defensive operations supported the absence of attachment in psychopathic, antisocial personality disorder subjects selected from a population of prison inmates (Gacono, & Meloy, 1992). The data were analyzed in 60 antisocial personality disorders subjects compared with 43 psychopath subjects. All the subjects were selected from a population of prison inmates. The Rorschach was able to differentiate antisocial groups based on level of psychopathy. Data supports the absence of anxiety and attachment and the presence of pathological narcissism and borderline personality organization in psychopathic antisocial personality disorder subjects (Gacono, & Meloy, 1992).

Meloy (1992) applied attachment theory in the tradition of Bowlby and Ainsworth, and object relations theory in the tradition of Klein, Jacobson, Mahler, and Kernberg, to case studies of bizarre and unusual homicides. Psychological patterns include both psychoanalytic constructs and the specific psychological test data from the case studies that support such constructs. CS variables of the Rorschach test were utilized as psychological test data, among others. The idiographic portraits of these case studies supported murder as a form of pathological attachment. Such individuals show a fixated or regressed pre-oedipal personality structure and are organized at a borderline or psychotic level, and most often utilize defenses of projection, projective identification, and omnipotent control (Meloy, 1992).

Three Mental Disorders-III (DSM-III) Cluster B personality disorders: narcissistic personality disorder, borderline personality disorder outpatients, and incarcerated antisocial personality disorder patients, divided into psychopathic and non-psychopathic groups were compared on CS Rorschach variables. The variables investigated internal psychological operations and in particular attachment and object relations. The sample included: 18 narcissistic personality disorder (NPD) outpatients, 18 borderline personality disorder (BPD) outpatients, and 43 incarcerated antisocial personality disorder (APD) patients, divided into psychopathic (P-APD) and non psychopathic (NP-APD) groups. incarcerated Psychopathic antisocial personality disordered subjects and narcissistic personality disorder outpatients were highly narcissistic, but the latter indicated more anxiety and attachment capacity and less borderline object relations and damaged identity. Borderline personality disorder outpatients were more anxious than psychopathic incarcerated antisocial personality disorder patients and evidenced greater potential for attachment. incarcerated Non psychopathic antisocial personality disorder patients were less narcissistic than narcissistic personality disorder outpatients and incarcerated psychopathic antisocial personality disorder patients, produced less evidence of attachment capacity than narcissistic personality disorder outpatients and borderline personality disorder outpatients but more than psychopathic incarcerated antisocial personality disorder patients, and were similar to borderline personality disorder outpatients in proneness to anxiety (Gacono, Meloy, & Berg, 1992).

Eighteen incarcerated sexual homicide perpetrators were compared to 23 non sexually offending but violent male psychopaths on select CS Rorschach variables to investigate attachment and personality and object relations. Sexual homicide perpetrators were similar to psychopaths in their attachment abnormality, deep structural anger, pathological narcissism, moderate and pervasive formal thought disorder, and borderline reality testing. They were distinguished, however, by a more frequent affection hunger, a tendency to engage in more dysphoric rumination, and abnormal elevations of non volitional ideation due to unmet instinctual need states. They also showed a greater interest in others as whole, real, and meaningful objects (Gacono & Kenney, 1994).

Attachment and anxiety, aggression, pathological narcissism and level of personality organization, and the antisocial psychopathic reference groups' ages and genders were investigated in antisocial subjects. Rorschach test results from archival data gathered on 380 antisocial children (mean age 9 yrs), adolescents (mean age 15 yrs), and adults of both genders (mean ages were 30 and 29 yrs for males and females respectively) were examined on these variables. The results answered affirmatively to some general questions. First, the Rorschach test discriminated between psychopathic and non-psychopathic antisocial samples, and among DSM Cluster B personality disorder. Second, the test empirically generated quantitative data from which certain psycho-structural and psychodynamic properties of antisocial individuals could be inferred (Meloy & Gacono, 1998).

CS variables were selected based on a psychodynamic and cognitive-behavioral model of pedophilia to study attachment and other personality features in incarcerated pedophile men. 60 incarcerated men who met Mental Disorders-IV (DSM-IV) criteria for pedophilia were compared to 60 incarcerated men with no history of sex offenses. Pedophile's Rorschach contained significantly more responses and revealed signs of anxiety and helplessness, painful introspection, distorted views of others, and primitive dependency needs than did those of the comparison group. Pedophiles possess many core personality features associated with narcissistic personality disorders, but were less well-defended against feelings of vulnerability and painful introspection than other incarcerated men. Like other incarcerated men, the pedophiles exhibited disturbances in self-worth, tendencies to abuse fantasy to avoid emotionally tinged stimuli, and chronic negativism and hostility. The pedophile and non-pedophile men showed signs of impaired attachment and failed narcissism (Bridges, Wilson & Gacono, 1998).

CS Rorschach variables were also selected to compare 39 non violent pedophiles, 32 non sexually offending psychopaths, and 38 sexual homicide perpetrators on attachment and other personality features to add to the understanding of sexual deviation and violence among these three groups. The three groups were similar in pathological narcissism, formal thought disorder, and borderline level reality testing. Non sexually offending psychopaths are distinguished by their lack of interest in and attachment to others and their seemingly conflict-free internal world. Both sexually deviant groups evidenced interest in others and appear to experience a very dysphoric internal world. Pedophiles show significantly more characterological anger and cognitive rigidness, less acting out style, and a introversive inability to gratify their needs. The sexual homicide perpetrators are distinguished by high levels of obsessive thought and an inability to disengage from environmental stimuli (Gacono, Meloy, & Bridges, 2000).

The Rorschach Test and Roemer Symbol Test were compared through examination of select variables on a sample of individuals distinguished in levels of psychopathology. The participants of the study were 44 male inmates, 18 years and older, convicted of drug offense crimes. Participants were classified as moderate and severe psychopaths according to the Hare Psychopathy Checklist-Revised (PCL-R). Five CS Rorschach and Roemer variables related to attachment, anxiety, coping, and narcissism were analyzed. The absence of texture responses among the overall sample, adds construct validity to the lack of attachment in individuals who are psychopaths, and the role of anxiety and grandiosity in differentiating moderate from severe psychopathy. The overall sample produced a significant frequency of vista responses on the Roemer test compared to the Rorschach test. Significant correlations between most of the select variables on the Rorschach and Roemer stimuli were found and lend support for interchangeable use of theses instruments on psychopaths. Moderate psychopaths produced shading and personal responses on the Roemer test compared to the Rorschach test at a significantly greater frequency than the participants classified as severe psychopaths. No firm distinctions were found between the Roemer and the Rorschach tests in their ability to detect significant differences among individuals classified as severe psychopaths (Egozi & Virginia, 1999).

Reid (2001) studied if adult attachment style was predictive of various interpersonal characteristics as measured by specifically CS variables: Texture response, Morbid content response, and Burns and Viglione's (1996) Human Experience . They were utilized as indicators of interpersonal health and adjustment. Participants were 75 college students, 25 participants were each representative of one of three adult attachment styles: secure, preoccupied, and avoidant. It was found that securely attached participants were significantly more likely to display interpersonal characteristics indicative of healthy adjustment than were participants classified as avoidantly attached. Conversely, participants classified as preoccupiedly attached failed to be significantly different from either securely or avoidantly attached participants. Implications of results are discussed and directions for future research are suggested. Particularly, it is suggested that research within this area of study should utilize multi-modal methods of assessment when determining adult attachment classification, and that research aimed at validating Exner's (1993) Comprehensive System for the Rorschach continue to be vigorously pursued.

Ingle (2002) studied the etiological and phenomenological characteristics of three types of pedophile using Rorschach structural variables. The author examined the Rorschach protocols of three pedophiles differentiated using a new typology of pedophilia. Each case manifested, in their Rorschach protocols, different internal working models of attachment. The 'intimate' pedophile manifests features of anxious/ambivalent attachment; the 'aggressive' manifests features of disorganized attachment; and the 'criminal/opportunist' manifests a detached interpersonal style. The intimate pedophile produced object relations content implying fear of engulfment, symbiotic merger, separation/division conflict, and womb imagery. The aggressive pedophile's object relations content implied violent merger, malignant internal processes, boundary disturbance, and primitive birth and womb imagery. The criminal/opportunist pedophile produced content implying narcissistic mirroring and boundary disturbance.

All the research studies we have reviewed highlighted how attachment based on selected CS Rorschach variables distinguished deviant groups among themselves or in comparison with control groups. Other studies on the same topic did not support completely this hypothesis.

CS Rorschach indexes of attachment were partly unable to differentiate: female inmates with low, medium, and high psychopathy; female inmates from the normative female sample; and female inmates from their male counterparts (Murphy & Donna, 1996). Subjects were female inmates confined for a range of 26 violent and nonviolent offenses. CS Rorschach variables indexing seven domains of psychological operations were also assessed in 47 female inmates and compared to the normative female sample. Female inmates displayed a paucity of affective resources, vulnerability to depression, poor coping capacity, a lessened likelihood to perceive interpersonal relationships as positive, a lack of introspection despite self-absorption, a tendency to oversimplify issues, and unconventional or distorted perceptions. Instead, offenders resembled the normative sample in anxiety, constraint of negative affect, and information processing. 64 female inmates with low, medium, and high psychopathy, measured by the Psychopathy Checklist (PCL-R), were also compared on Rorschach indices of narcissism, attachment, anxiety, hysteria, and introspection. All of these indices were unable to differentiate the three groups of female offenders. Finally psychopathic and non psychopathic females were compared to their male counterparts on Rorschach indices of narcissism, attachment, anxiety, hysteria, introspection, cognitive ideation, and cognitive mediation. The first four domains of psychological operations did not distinguish between males and females. A sex difference was noted in the other two domains, with the males uniformly displaying higher cognitive distortion and lesser perceptual accuracy (Murphy & Donna, 1996).

CS measures of attachment, reality testing and personality functions and the Human Experience Variable (Burns & Viglione, 1996), as measure of object relations, were compared in 40 Rorschach protocols of matched-pairs of male delinquent and nondelinquent subjects. This was done in order to predict which youth were most at risk to develop conduct disorder, antisocial personality disorder, and psychopathy. The authors explored the hypothesis that poor early attachment and object relationships were pivotal in the development of later antisocial behavior. The subjects were derived from the Glueck and Glueck (1950) longitudinal study, which attempted to discover the causes of juvenile crime. The Rorschach, with the Human Experience Variable scale (HEV), did not identify subjects who developed psychopathy. Although when the follow-up data behaviors of later antisocial behavior (delinquent and non delinquent) of these youth were explored, the Rorschach was effective in distinguishing delinquent from non delinquent protocols by examining Rorschach variables and HEV scores on the basis of follow-up data of antisocial behavior in these youths. Significant between-groups differences were found for W, Afr, and $F+\%$. No significant between groups differences were found for H, $M-$, $3r+(2)/R$, Lambda, $X+\%$, $X-$, Isolate Index, primitive responses, and the Human Experience Variable scale (Loftis, 1997).

83 inmates diagnosed with Antisocial Personality Disorder and 88 inmates with other diagnoses were compared for five CS Rorschach scores white space,

texture, pure human content, diffuse shading, and vista responses. These CS Rorschach constellations of scores were often associated by several researchers with anger, interpersonal detachment, shallow emotions, and impaired interpersonal relatedness, which are characteristic of these individuals. The frequencies of the five CS scores were compared in the two groups of inmates. Results were analyzed for the entire sample, for a sample excluding individuals with IQ scores below 80, and for a sample excluding suspected malingerers. Although the data supported the association between the dependent variables and incarcerated individuals, a series of nonparametric statistical procedures revealed no significant differences between the groups for these 5 scores for any of the samples. Although the study supported a constellation of Rorschach scores typical of incarcerated individuals, it failed to provide empirical support for their validity as specific measures of antisocial character traits (Howard, 1999).

Fewer studies investigated attachment by use of Rorschach variables on other psychopathologies.

A series of studies (Mccarroll, 1998) compared disruption in caregiving and attachment measured by use of CS interpersonal indexes (texture, pure human content, cooperative movement, aggression, food, and the isolation index) in 95 adolescents inpatients in psychiatric treatment. In addition, subjects Rorschach data were compared to normative adolescent Rorschach data within several domains. Significant differences were found between all compared subjects Rorschach data and normative data with the exception of the Isolation Index. Disruption groups were compared for Rorschach interpersonal variables and differences between groups were expected. The comparisons concerned: a) subjects with no disruption prior to age five and subjects with disruptions at or after age five; b) subjects with disruption in caregiving and subjects with no disruption; c) subjects who had within family disruption to those who had at least one out of family placement; d) groups with different numbers of disruptions to each other. Comparison of all kinds of disruption in caregiving to interpersonal Rorschach variables revealed no significant differences. However, trends were found in several disruption studies. Subjects who had experienced no disruption in caregiving reported more Pure Human Content, showing more interest in people than those with disruption. The variable Food was observed more frequently by subjects with disruption outside the family, suggesting more neediness and dependency within this group. Finally, the relationship between caregiving disruption and depression was examined. Disruption in caregiving was found to not be related to depression.

Rorschach scores have seldom been used to examine attachment in normal samples.

The manifestations of dependent and self-critical personality styles, following Sidney Blatt's perspective (Blatt, & Ford, 1994; Blatt, & Lerner, 1991; Blatt, & Lerner, 1983a, 1983b), using Rorschach variables were investigated in 21 students with a dependent and self-critical personality style and in a control group of 20 students.

Discriminant analysis revealed that 4 Rorschach variables best differentiate the two styles, 4 variables reflect the way the self-critical style expresses itself in Rorschach and 4 variables reflect the way dependent style expresses itself (Campos, 2002).

Howard (2005) examined the correlation of defences in mother-son pairs. Defensive behaviours were studied utilizing the Rorschach. The study found that the defences of regression, repression, avoidance, a personal defense stance and the quality of inner resources were positively correlated between mothers and sons. The results indicated that, for this sample, mothers and sons' defensive behaviours were correlated across several variables. These results suggest the Rorschach may be a useful instrument in studying the sequelae of the attachment relationship.

5.6 Conclusion

The state of the art of the relationship between personality assessment by the Rorschach and attachment theories and measures of attachment is currently in a complex state. The reviewed literature evidenced two categories of studies. A first category showed an attempt to identify in the Rorschach or in scales applied to the Rorschach specific scores that can measure the construct of attachment. Specifically two types of scores were identified: (a) Exner's Comprehensive System scores included in the clusters of self-perception and interpersonal perception; (b) scales that measure the level of object relations (specifically Urist's MOA and Blatt's Object Relation Scale). These scores demonstrate discriminant validity comparing certain categories of pathological subjects, above all deviant subjects (antisocial, psychopathic, delinquent subjects). But studies on other categories of subjects or pathologies are lacking and almost absent.

A second category of studies showed an attempt to correlate instruments devised within the attachment theory, specifically AAI, AAP and some types of questionnaires with Rorschach scores hypothesized associated with the construct of attachment. The Rorschach scores are often the same identified in the first category of studies we indicated. The studies on nomothetic associations between questionnaires and Rorschach involved a wider range of categories of subjects besides antisocial people. Unfortunately, the results showed significant associations only in few studies. Regarding the AAI, associations were explored only in two studies. Just one study explored an association with AAI. These studies did not used Rorschach scores, but only scales of levels of object relations. The results again did not show significant relations between different tools. Apparently in these studies more limitations then strengths were evidenced.

Concerning the samples, the interest was focused on specific types of subjects; above all were the ones in which disturbances in attachment were hypothesized.

6 ATTACHMENT AND THE MMPI

A. Raudino, D. Chessa, C. Marogna

6.1 The MMPI

The Minnesota Multiphasic Personality Inventory (MMPI, Hathaway and McKinley, 1943) is an empirically based self report measure of psychiatric symptomatology, that provides an objective assessing of personality and intrapersonal functioning. The instrument was developed in the late 1930s by Hathaway and McKinley, at the University of Minnesota. The original MMPI was published in 1943 and has been in use without any revisions for over 50 years (Butcher 1990). A standardized revised version of the MMPI, the MMPI-2, was released in 1989 for adults of 18 years old and over (Butcher et al., 1989). A subsequent revision of some test elements of the MMPI-2 was published in 2001 (Butcher et al., 2001). The MMPI-2 includes 567 items or questions, in true/false format, and usually takes between 1 and 2 hours to complete. The MMPI-2 (1989) includes a sample of 2600 persons, with a different racial composition (white 81%, black 12%, Hispanic 3%, American Indian 3%, Asian-American 1%). There is a less used short form of the test that includes the MMPI-2 first 370 items, used where circumstances do not allow the full version to be completed (e.g., illness or time pressure). The MMPI-2 is a revision which was developed to answer the many problems raised with the original MMPI. When compared with the original MMPI, the MMPI-2 is the preferred test at the present time, although many computer test interpretations will include both profiles. A new revised version of the test, the MMPI-2 Revised Form, was released in 2007. This form needs further research (Karp & Karp. 2007).

Hathaway and McKinley (1943) utilized an empirical keying approach in the construction of the MMPI. This atheoretical point of view was maintained also in the second version, the MMPI-2 (Butcher et al., 1989). This approach requires items to be determined empirically, in order to differentiate between groups of subjects. The keying approach represented an innovation at the time of the MMPI's construction. It was an atheoretical approach in contrast to the contemporary psychodynamic testing. The instrument validation respected empirical criteria. Some authors considered this kind of validation a strength for the use of the questionnaire while others (Sanavio & Sica, 1999) evaluated it as a deficiency of construct validity that could negatively influence the scale's inner consistency. Clinical interpretation of the instrument is based on five groups of scales: validity scales, clinical scales, content scales, and supplementary. Historically, the clinical scales have been used as the core interpretation for the first version and also for the second one. The MMPI-2 (1989) modified old scales, added new scales, and elaborated on the new scales; for instance the MMPI–2 Restructured Clinical (RC) Scales (Tellegen et al., 2003). The RC Scales were constructed using contemporary models of personality and psychopathology.

The MMPI-2 validity scales include three basic types of measures. First, scales are designed to detect overtly random or non-responding subjects (CNS "cannot say" identify the number of omitted item, VRIN "variable response inconsistency" is an indicator of tendency to respond inconsistently, TRIN "true response inconsistency" is the tendency to respond true or false indiscriminately. Second, scales are designed to detect when clients are intentionally or unintentionally over reporting or exaggerating the prevalence or severity of psychological symptoms (*F* detect deviant or atypical ways of responding to test items, *Fb* the respondent stopped paying attention to the test items). Thirdly, scales are designed to detect when clients are intentionally or unintentionally underreporting or downplaying psychological symptoms: *L* (Lie) the subject presents him/herself in a favorable light, *K* denies or exaggerates psychopathology. The validity scales are extremely important in the interpretation of the entire test since they indicate the degree to which the clinical profile is a valid picture of the person being evaluated.

The basic 10 clinical scales capture complex and critical dimensions of human psychopathology. As a result of the empirical keying process, many of the clinical scales measure several highly correlated symptom clusters, such as anxiety disorders and obsessive compulsive disorder. They are labeled: *Hs* (Hypochondriasis): concern over bodily functioning; *D* (Depression): poor morale, lack of hope in the future, and a general dissatisfaction with one's own life situation; *Hy* (Hysteria): conversion-type symptoms as a means of resolving conflict; *Pd* (Psychopathic Deviate): psychopathic personality, asocial or amoral type; *Mf* (Masculinity/Femininity): possibility of sexual concerns and problems;

Pa (Paranoia): feelings of persecution, grandiose self-concepts, suspiciousness; *Pt* (Psychastenia): inability to resist specific actions or thoughts regardless of their maladaptive nature; *Sc* (Schizophrenia): including bizarre thought processes and peculiar perceptions, social alienation; *Ma* (Hypomania): hypomanic symptoms; and *Si* (Social Introversion): insecure and uncomfortable in social situations. These scales are designed to measure common types of psychopathology.

The Content scales included 15 scales. *ANX* (Anxiety): the scale investigates generalized anxiety problems; *FRS* (Fears): recognizes specific fears and phobias; *OBS* (Obsessiveness): regards the presence of obsessive thoughts and compulsive behaviour; *DEP* (Depression): evaluates the symptomatic depression; *HEA* (Health Concerns): indicates presence of somatic disorders; *BIZ* (Bizarre Mentalization): investigates serious thinking and psychotic ideation; *ANG* (Anger): investigates loss of control in the anger acting out; *CYN* (Cynism): detects the presence of negative attitudes to others people or clinical belief; *ASP* (Antisocial Practices): identifies people that have behavioural problems; *TPA* (Type A): identifies competitive and aggressive; *LSE* (Low Self-Esteem): high scores in this scale indicate that the subjects have a bad opinion and undervalue themselves; *SOD* (Social Discomfort): problems in social relationship; *FAM* (Family Problems): identifies the familiar discomfort; *WRK* (Work Interference): values lack of adaptation in working environment; *TRT* (Negative Treatment Indicators): indicates incapacity to accept help and to find copying strategy.

6.2 MMPI and attachment

As we have already stressd in other chapters of this book, that over the years, there has been considerable interplay between attachment theory, and the broad field of mental health research and practice (e.g., Belsky & Nezworski, 1988; Bowlby, 1977,1988). Some studies indicated that insecure attachment status was linked with outcomes suggestive of emerging psychopathology (Lewis et. Al, 1984; Erickson, Sroufe, & Egeland, 1985; Sroufe, 1983). However, in the literature there are only few studies that investigate the possible relationships between the degree of psychopathology, measured with the MMPI (or MMPI-2) and instruments aimed at evaluating styles or patterns of attachment. The most often cited are studies that used questionnaires (attachment styles socio-cognitive approach) while there were very few studies which used the AAI (attachment patterns and developmental approach). However, two studies tried to also measure attachment using items or scales derived from the MMPI items.

6.2.1 Studies on AAI and MMPI

Pianta, Egeland and Adam (1996) examined differences in self-reported psychiatric symptomatology on the MMPI-2 in relation to adult attachment status on the Adult

Attachment Interview (AAI) in first-time mothers from a high-risk poverty sample of 110 women recruited in public clinics during the second trimester of pregnancy. Mothers were randomly assigned to a treatment and control group. Participants reported fairly high levels of symptomatology regardless of attachment status. But the authors found that the preoccupied group endorsed considerably more symptoms of psychopathology on the MMPI-2 than the Dismissing or Secure groups, and the Dismissing group endorsed the lowest levels of anxiety type symptoms. Pianta et al., suggested that the Dismissing individuals might have been under-reporting their symptoms due to their tendency to suppress emotion and provide self descriptions consistent with a view of the self as strong and independent. A significant difference among the attachment classification groups was also found on the Hysteria scale, with individuals classified as dismissing scoring lower than individuals classified as Secure. Again a significant difference was found for the Masculinity-Femininity scale, with individuals classified as dismissing scoring significantly higher than individuals classified as either autonomous or unresolved. Preoccupied individuals, on the other hand, might have been exaggerating symptoms in attempts to portray themselves as vulnerable and to solicit help. The Preoccupied group, consistent with their high Response Infrequency score, endorsed considerably more symptoms of psychopathology than the Dismissing and Autonomous groups. The mean scores of the preoccupied group exceeded 65 on the Response Infrequency, Psychopathic Deviation, Paranoia, and Schizophrenia scales. They presented themselves as in distress, helpless, angry, and mentally confused, consistent with Main's description of preoccupation with attachment (Main & Goldwyn, 1985, 1994). The Secure group's scores ranged between the scores of the other 2 groups on most scales. These different symptom patterns are consistent with adult attachment status as an index of self-representation and as a set of strategies for processing emotions and thoughts related to distress and to attachment relationships. Although the findings of this study are essentially descriptive, these investigations clearly indicate that attachment insecurity is extremely prevalent among individuals diagnosed with mental illness.

Browning (2003) examined the ability to *fake-good* on the AAI using the MMPI-2. The AAI and MMPI-2 was administered to 21 participants under both *control* (non-faked) and *experimental* (instructed to fake-good) conditions. The scores received on the *L* and *K* validity scales of the MMPI-2 under the control versus the experimental conditions were compared to determine if the instructions that were intended to induce faking good in the experimental condition were successful. Significant differences were found between the experimental and control group on the MMPI-2 *L* and *K* scales, suggesting that the instructions did induce faking good in the experimental condition. It was hypothesized that the experimental condition instructional set impacted (1) idealization positively, (2) coherence of mind negatively, and (3) overall attachment classification becoming more dismissing. To verify this hypothesis the scores received on the AAI idealization and coherence of mind scales during the control versus experimental condition were compared. Significant differences were found between the experimental and control group on the AAI idealization scale and on the AAI coherence of mind scale. These results suggest that the individuals' idealization scores were significantly lower in the control versus experimental conditions while the individuals' overall coherence of mind scores was significantly higher in the control versus experimental conditions. Of the 12 subjects, who were found to be dismissing under the experimental condition, 4 had previously not been classified as dismissing when the standard AAI instructions were given. Even though the results were not indicative of a difference in attachment classification under the control versus experimental conditions, a trend was apparent. It appears that one attempting to fake good may appear more dismissing on the AAI than he/she really is. The authors stress the limitations of their study. They are aware how it could be important to replicate the study using a larger sample size and to determine if trying to make oneself look positive will impact overall attachment status.

6.2.2 Studies using questionnaires to measure attachment styles and MMPI

Studies that correlated personality traits measured with the MMPI (MMPI-2) included a range of populations and a range of topics. The population ranged from normal people (elderly people, college students, couples) to psychopathology (psychiatric patients, deviant population).

Early studies tried to make some connection between the original MMPI and attachment. However, they showed some basic limitations. Although they referred to a relation between attachment and the MMPI, attachment was not the principal aim of the study. Attachment was in fact measured using tools not specifically devised to measure attachment. We mention them to give a flavour of the beginning interest in this topic.

Harel and Deimling (1984) measured attachment using data from 1834 subjects aged more than 62 years old. Attachment was derived from one of the four factors (Attachment, Social Interaction, Social Support, and Adequacy of Social Resources) with a factor analysis of the social resource measures included in the OARS, and the Multidimensional Functional Assessment Questionnaire. The results showed only a limited degree of association between Attachment and MMPI.

Robinson and Janos (1986) examined attachment and personality traits of 24 markedly accelerated high school students and compared them with 24 regular-aged university students, 23 National Merit Scholars, and 27 students who had qualified for acceleration but elected to participate in high school. Measures included an inventory of parent and peer attachment, the MMPI, the California Psychological Inventory, and the Tennessee Self-Concept Scale. Accelerated high school students differed minimally from the college-aged groups, and not at all from high-ability, same age students. Both groups of normal-aged college Ss were more socially assertive. Accelerated Ss were less conforming and conventional than the others. Results provide no basis for concern about the psychological and social adjustment of accelerated students. This result identify a finding contrary to the expectation that skipping high school is deleterious to adjustment.

Regarding attachment resent studies have been conducted using the MMPI-2.

Cooke (1997) examined the links between the construct of object relations theory quality of intimate relationships and psychopathology within a non patient sample and examined specific patterns of interrelations. A Relationship Experience Scale was constructed and a factor analysis was conducted in order to provide information about participants' reported quality of relationship experiences. Scores on these factors were then correlated with the Bell Object Relations Inventory, the Continuity and Integration of Self Scale, and the MMPI-2. Subjects classified with Insecure Attachment, identified by excessive worries about being accepted and fears about abandonment, explained the greatest amount of variance in subjects' quality of relationship experiences across a number of domains. The pattern of interrelationships differed for the MMPI-2 variables; individuals with a more fragmented sense of self and women with exaggerated fears of abandonment tended to report much more psychological distress.

Jacobson (2004) investigated the association between the way people behave in romantic relationships, or *romantic attachment style*, and psychopathology. This study explored how the Experiences in Close Relationships (ECR), a self-report measure of romantic attachment style, were correlated with the degree of psychopathology, assessed with the MMPI-2. Two other measures of psychopathology, the State-Trait Anxiety Inventory (STAI) and the Beck Depression Inventory (BDI), were also included to explore the relationships between romantic attachment style and anxiety and depression. Data were collected from both a clinical (n = 188) and non clinical (n = 186) sample. Insecure attachment was more related to psychopathology across measures. MMPI-2 clinical scales differentially related to the two dimensions of romantic attachment; anxiety and avoidance. Furthermore, the relationship between attachment and psychopathology variables was stronger overall in the non clinical sample than in the clinical one.

Taylor (1998) investigated the relationship between attachment and psychopathology in incarcerated adult female psychopaths. Participants in the study were randomly selected incarcerated females with at least one child less than five years old. The test battery consisted of three primary measures: the Attachment Style Questionnaire (ASQ), the MMPI-2, the Psychopathy Checklist; Screening Version (PCL: SV), and one behavioural observation the verification of the custody status of the biological child of the participant. The assessment of attachment was multi-method; the ASQ assessed secure attachment, and the behavioural observation of child custody assessed relinquishment status. A positive association was found for psychopathy and Scale 4 of MMPI-2 (Psychopathic Deviate); negative associations were not found for psychopathy and 5, a subscale of Scale 4, the A scale (Anxicty), and Scale 2 (Depression). The findings suggested that a high level of psychopathy on the MMPI-2 is associated with poor caregiving capacity.

Diehl (2003) explored attachment relationships among adult inmates. The study's main premise was to examine adult reactions to being separated from loved ones. Subjects consisted of 167 male inmates who tested within the first month of their imprisonment, to assess acute emotional and behavioural reactions to being separated from loved ones. The Relationship Questionnaire (Bartholomew & Horowitz, 1991) was administered utilizing a four-category model of adult attachment and assessing individual attachment patterns. It was predicted that *secure* and *dismissing* inmates would adjust better both behaviourally and emotionally to separation from loved ones than either *fearful* or *preoccupied* inmates. Emotional adjustment was measured via scores on specific scales of the MMPI-2, the Brief Symptom Inventory, a mental status interview, and behavioural adjustment was measured by reviewing the number and severity of inmates' disciplinary records. Overall, the analyses lent partial support to the hypotheses. There was some consistency across the objective measures of emotional adjustment in that Secure and Dismissing inmates had BSI and MMPI-2 scores indicative of better adjustment to separation from loved ones than Fearful and Preoccupied inmates, particularly on the depression and anxiety scales. Additionally, the attachment groups, did not differ from each other on the behavioural indicators of adjustment.

Gardner (1996) studied adult attachment style in adult male substance abusers and focused on four areas affected by attachment style: the effect of attachment style on areas of life adjustment, the relationship between attachment style and psychopathology, the relationship between attachment style and psychopathology treatment outcomes, and the occurrence of various attachment styles in this diverse chemically dependent population. Measures included scores on the three dimensions of the Adult Attachment Scale (closeness, dependency, anxiety), MMPI-2 clinical and personality disorder scale scores, staff ratings of treatment adjustment and predicted post-treatment adjustment, and a rating of prior life adjustment. The results suggest that attachment style does help explain differences in life adjustment above and beyond that explained by a composite MMPI-2 scale score (Scale A-Anxiety and Scale 7-Psychasthenia). The results further suggest that those with an insecure attachment style report fewer problems and psychological symptoms. Lastly, higher rates of avoidant attachment styles (46%) and lower rates of preoccupied attachment styles (11%) were found in this chemically dependent sample than are found in non-clinical samples.

6.2.3 Studies where attachment is measured using MMPI items or scales

Two studies used some items of the original MMPI to detect attachment.

Tarnaplo (1958) administered the MMPI to 25 leaders and 25 non-leaders in a California utility company. No significant differences were found on any of the regular pathology scales of the MMPI. However, 40 items did differentiate between the 2 groups, and the non-leaders showed higher attachment to the mother figure.

Bloomquist & Dossa (1988) examined a Family Attachment scale devised together with two other family scales (Family Discord and Family Problems) from the MMPI. All 3 scales (Family Discord, Family Problems, and Family Attachment) have at least some data supporting their reliability and concurrent validity as global measures of perceived family dysfunction. Available research suggests that the Family Problems scale is the best MMPI family scale. This scale was developed using intuitive and empirical methods, has the most extensive normative data and research supporting its psychometric integrity, and is recommended by the authors for clinical use.

6.3 Conclusion

Although not too many studies were interested with the possible relationship between MMPI and attachment, the brief review we have reported showed an increased interest in the topic. Of interest were the two studies devoted to attachment status (AAI). The results of these two studies seem to open very interesting new directions for researchers but also for clinicians.

PART III

CLINICAL
APPLICATIONS

The purpose of the chapters in Part Three is to feature the AAP, the Rorschach and the MMPI as valid and productive assessment measures that can be used in clinical practice, and that together provide a more integrated picture of personality than using them separately.

There are a few clinical papers that have been published on the interplay between attachment patterns and a clinical approach to patients in clinical settings.

Buchheim & Kaekele (2001) presented a single-case study of a female patient diagnosed with a narcissistic personality disorder and a Borderline personality organization. Their study focused on the interplay between attachment measured using the AAI and a psychoanalytic perspective. The psychoanalyst described his impressions of the initial interview with the patient and essential steps during the treatment. The patient was classified as "insecure preoccupied" with an "unresolved state of mind" concerning loss and abuse. The study discussed converging and diverging aspects of clinical and attachment interpretation. Through this case study, the authors showed how using the AAI broadened the therapist's perspective, especially in respect to the patient's unresolved state of mind concerning traumatic experiences of loss.

Dahlbender (2004) questioned how much attachment theory and psychoanalysis would benefit from each other with regard to their clinical interview techniques. Three groups of questions concerning representation of early relationship, early separation, and early loss were taken from the Adult Attachment Interview (AAI) and were integrated into the interview of the Operationalized Psychodynamic Diagnostics (OPD). One female patient suffering from bulimia, cannabis use, and borderline personality disorder was interviewed with both the AAI and the modified OPD interview. The OPD interview benefited from the integration of the evaluation of early representations of attachment, particularly for the assessment of psychodynamic conflicts and psychic structure.

Buchheim (2005) discussed the benefits of knowledge about a precise methodology for capturing attachment experiences in connection with the evaluation of past-in-the-present in first psychoanalytic interviews. According to the author, the AAI provides the clinician with interesting scenic information for purposes of psychodynamic formulation. With due consideration of defence processes, the specifically linguistic approach to attachment narratives can be profitably employed in the observation of biographical memories, both at the outset and in the course of the psychoanalytic process. The vital interaction between these two perspectives was illustrated with reference to the case of a depressive female patient with chronic migraine and unprocessed experience of loss on the basis of a narcissistic/hysterical personality structure.

The following chapters are devoted to the interplay between attachment pattern measures and other assessment measures in clinical cases. The purpose of these chapters is to include three different levels of questions:

1) How and how much is attachment dimension connected or interwoven with other personality dimensions? How and how much has a clinician to rely on attachment to complete the picture of the patient's personality functioning?
2) To stress the importance of a multi-method assessment for personality, contrasting this with a multi-test approach.
3) To demonstrate for clinicians how the intersection of the AAI, AAP, Rorschach, and MMPI - as two or three methods in a multi-method approach - can work together to provide important information, as described using a single case example.

The organization of the cases will be the following:

    I. The case.
       a) Background.
       b) The assessment battery
   II. Integration of the assessment.
  III. Clinical Implications: What the therapist takes away from the case.

The only exception to this organization is the chapter on adoption. In this chapter, before going to the description of clinical couples, case examples later in this book, a review of the literature on the topic is presented.

7 PERSONALITY ASSESSMENT: THE CASE OF EMILY

Mazzeschi, D. Chessa, S. Salcuni

7.1 Background and the assessment battery

Emily is a 17-year-old girl. Two years ago, when she was fifteen, she was diagnosed with anorexia nervosa using the DSM-IV criteria. She is a restrictive type, with periods of elimination behaviours (bulimic crisis, diuretic abuse), depressive and anxious symptoms, obsessive behaviours and high interpersonal sensibility. At that time she was hospitalized for the first time for six months. In 2007 she was again very underweight (31,7 Kg.) and she was again admitted to a clinic for eating disorders. A multi-method psychological assessment was this time required to have more comprehensive information of her functioning and to decide a psychological treatment plan.

Emily is the first of two children of an intact family. Her mother is 45 years old and her father is 50 years old. The mother seems to be very worried although all the family tends to minimize and deny Emily's disease. At least until they cannot avoid recognizing Emily's physical condition.

When she came in for a psychological assessment, Emily was asked to complete some questionnaires. What emerged from the assessment was that she obviously hates her body, she cannot look at her image in the mirror and she doesn't like her flanks and her belly. During the assessment she seemed a little bit stressed.

She looked like a very shy and reserved teenager, younger than her real age. She showed some difficulties in expressing her feelings, her problems and her internal world with the other people and seemed to have the same difficulties with the clinicians. She reported that sometimes she prefers to be silent even when she is surrounded by other people.

The disturbance is completely egosyntonic: she doesn't have awareness of the real severity of her condition. She said that she accepted admittance to the clinic because her parents were worried, but she didn't have a problem. She attends a linguistic high school with no success and appears to put all her energies into the control of her body. Her affectivity is completely flat, the social contacts with peers are poor or nonexistent and she has never had sexual and/or romantic relationships.

The clinical interview showed: 1) a very low subjective awareness of her severe condition; 2) a very low capacity to recognize that she needs help; 3) a picture of a person very fragile and poor from a psychological view point. According to these first data the clinician decided to administer the CS to confirm the existence of weaknesses and strengths in the different clusters of the CS. Moreover, the CS was administered to analyze if some variables such as interpersonal relationships would give some information about Emily's capacity to be involved in a therapeutic working alliance. The AAP was chosen to investigate attachment pattern for two reasons: 1) to investigate the capacity to rely in IWM; 2) to investigate the presence of defences and segregated systems.

7.2 Emily's AAP stories and interpretation

Window:

> *I see a <u>void home </u>(Segregated System) a girl who is looking outside <u>hoping</u> (Cognitive Disconnection) to find some company. What do you think led up to that scene? <u>I do not know </u>(Cognitive Disconnection)... may be <u>she is thinking</u> ("Internalize Secure Base") about the <u>void home</u>, (Segregated System) What are they thinking or feeling ? The child feels alone, there is no one ... and she is looking for someone .. a face.. a figure from outside, something that will give a sense of life ... What do you think will happen next?.. she sees the life outside, maybe deciding to go*

In responding to the Window picture, Emily makes up a story all about Segregated Systems. Already they were unleashed by the first picture. The girl is in an empty container, where there is no connection with attachment figures or with people from other behavioral systems such as friendship or romantic. Emily does not have any secure bases or haven of safety that she can rely on. Nor she is able to organize specific action maintain organization of her attachment, she vaguely decides to go, but she does not know exactly where. However, she tries to maintain a bit of organization "thinking" about the empty room. It is not a good solution, but enough to prevent being completely disorganized when the attachment system is activated, in this case, through emptiness and isolation. Some cognitive disconnection fractures the story.

Bench

It looks like a <u>prison </u>(Segregated System) someone who cries sitting down alone on a bench.. What are they thinking or feeling ? <u>feeling lost</u> (Segregated System) What do you think led up to that scene? She has done something that she not supposed to do, and so she was <u>locked in </u>(Segregated System)... she was <u>punished</u> (Deactivation).. <u>she is sorry for what she did </u>(weak attempt of "Internalizied Secure Base")... What do you think will happen next?. Once <u>she expiated all the guilty things</u> (Deactivation) she has done she will get out from this <u>prison </u>(Segragated System).. Anything else? I see myself here a little bit.

Again the picture unlashes segregated systems of Emptiness\Isolation and Danger/Failed Protection. Again, there is no internal secure base or specific actions that maintain attachment system organized present. The character of the story is not identified, Emily says only "she" is sorry, surely it is not enough to speak about true reparation in terms of attachment. However, it is enough not to become disorganized in her attachment system. Emily uses some deactivation to deactivate her attachment system.

In the Bench story there is a personal experience at the end of the story, that could not be classified as a rupture in the story, but that may give us some information about how she is feeling. The girl is lost, in jail, punished, locked in but it is not clear for what specific reason she was punished. There is no secure base or haven of safety that she can rely on. Again no behavioral system such affiliative or romantic could help. We know from her history that she was in the clinic because she was physically very underweight. We think that this story helps us to know how she feels staying in the Eating Disorders clinic: not like a place where she can be helped and taken care of, but as a prison where she is obliged to stay because she did something wrong, but she does not know what.

Cemetery

A man at the cemetery. He is crying on his father tombstone... a great pain for who ..who died. What do you think led up to that scene? The pain for a big illness, but at the end .. freedom, because .. a <u>incur-</u>

able sickness (Segregated System) and so at the end the death.. What do you think will happen next?.the freedom from the pain.. What are they thinking or feeling ? Loneliness because anyway that person is no more there. Anything else. No

Emily talks about an incurable sickness, again a segregated system, but this time she is really completely unable to find any kind of reorganization. The story is not concrete, there is an inconsistent story plot with lack of specific action or behavior. The fragile and very poor organization she has been able to maintain until now, is now failing her.

Corner

A child who pulls out something, who does not look at something.. like he is trying to reject someone maybe an adult. (Deactivation) He lays down his head and turns his gaze because he does not want to look, to listen ....What was happening before? Maybe someone has done to him something he was not supposed to do or he told him something he was not supposed to tell him (Cognitive Disconnection) and so it is like he is trying to pull out... does not being feeling hurt. And later what could be happen? That may be he will decide to go out from the corner and look for someone who could support him... What can he feel or thinking ? He is trying to defend, to protect himself (Capacity to act)

Emily makes up a very vague story where a child is trying to pull out and to protect himself, no one knows about: something, someone? The only consistent thing is that in this case the child tried to protect himself. This is a good solution as a capacity to act. He is looking for someone who could support him, but this is not an attachment or affiliative or romantic figure. Emily again deactivates attachment using Rejection

Departure

luggages, holidays... have a break.. What would be happened before? The hurry of everyday of lead them to decide to have a holyday together. And the what would be happen? Looking for peace... to spend a while of peace, to come back to everyday life, may be more calm. (Cognitive Disconnection)

A very vague story, where no character is defined. "They" have a very functional relationship but we really do not know who and how many they are. Cognitive disconnection using glossing over permeates the story. Emily makes "them" to be calm, tranquil not making a disturbance or the material negative.

Bed

A child with her mom. The child asks mum to be hugged ... she is ready to hug... And what happened before? May be the child had <u>a nightmare</u> (Segregated System) and <u>mum hearing him crying went to comfort him</u> (Synchrony)... And what happened ? After the hug mum calms down the child, who go back to bed peacefully.

What feeling and thinking? Love. Anything else? No.

This is the only story in which the characters are identified and there is a clear attachment figure who comforts the child after a nightmare.

Ambulance

Mother with a sick child.. he was hurted, they are waiting for <u>medical doctors and paramedics</u> (Deactivation) and for the ambulance that will bring him to be taken care of his illness. Felling and thinking, let me see.. Mother is <u>anxious</u> (Cognitive Disconnection) about her child's health... the child is not aware of how much he is sick, of what .. of his pain... Anything else? No

Only two of the characters are identified. Mother is anxious. Paramedics and medical doctors will take care of the child. There is not synchrony of comfort or even reassurance from the mother. The child is not aware of the severity of his illness.

Emily has an Unresolved attachment pattern and is very interesting how many times the pictures unleashed segregated systems. Two times she was able to maintain a very poor and fragile organization, but, finally, she was unable to maintain it. Only in one story she was able to activate an attachment figure that comforts the child. We hypothesize that Emily would be a very difficult patient to deal with in a psychotherapeutic process. First, she can seldom represent an attachment figure that can give her a secure base or a haven of safety - her attachment internal world is often empty, a prison, a nightmare. Maybe she can not understand that she is very sick and she needs to be taken care of (see Ambulance). Maybe she feels the inpatient clinic, is a place to be locked away in instead of a place where she can be helped. All this make her a very fragile and, maybe, difficult patient. It often happens that anorexic patients are totally unaware of the severity of their disturbance.

7.3 The CS

The CS interpretation is reported cluster by cluster, highlighting strength and weakness for each personality dimension. This procedure helps to combine Rorschach information with those derived from the others tools and with biographical information.

Emily gave a valid protocol that provides reliable information and supports a valid interpretation.

The key variable from which we start the interpretation are CDI > 3

This index gave us basic initial information that we should pay attention to, during the whole Rorschach analysis: Emily seemed to have some coping deficits and interpersonal difficulties.

This is the interpretative strategy:

Controls à Interpersonal Perception à Self Perception à Affect à Processing à Mediation à Ideation

Controls

Liabilities: She tended to greatly avoid the complexity of her experience: it means that she was not able to pay attention to different aspects of reality at one time (very High Lambda style). She had very small amounts of psychological resources to face internal and external demands (*EA*). She experienced both situational and chronic stress (*D* and *AdjD*), and last of all connected difficulties in a free expression of her emotions (*C'*). She had no cognitive awareness of her basic needs (*FM*): Emily showed an ambitent style of functioning (*EB*): she did not have a specific and clear way of facing both internal and external demands in dealing with her experiences. She goes back and forth between emotional and ideational resources. Strenghts: no strenghts

Interpersonal Perception

Liabilties: Emily showed some coping difficulties in interpersonal relationships (*CDI*): she did not consider interpersonal relationships as a fundamental and meaningful part of her experience (*COP* and *AG*). During her interpersonal exchanges, she had a tendency to preserve her personal space showing clear difficulties in close and intimate relationships (*T*). She showed a poor relation representation which means she was not able to create consistent and realistic ideas about others (*H*), resulting in her being poorly adapted in interpersonal relationships (*GHR* and *PHR*)

Strenghts: Emily did not seem to be isolated (Isolation Index) and she did not assume a passive or dependent role (*a:p* and *Fd*)

Self-Perception:

Liabilities: Emily's identity did not seem to be based on realistic identification (*H*). She didn't focus on herself (Ego Index) and also she did not seem to have a good introspective capacity (*FD*). This then means that she doesn't usually pay attention to either her positive features (*Fr+rF*) or negative aspects (*V* and *MOR*).

Affect

Liabilities: Emily's emotional world seemed to be very poor. She did not seem be able to process affective material (*FC:CF+C*) and she had a great difficulty in her feelings expression (*SumC':WSumC*). As a consequence she did not become easily engaged in affectively charged situations (*Afr*). Strenghts: no strenghts

Processing

Liabilities: She processes reality in a very economic way with a low integration of effort (*W:D:Dd*). As a consequence, most of the time Emily did not show an efficient processing quality especially in complex situations (*DQ+* and *DQv*). She showed a strong achievement orientation, not balancing resources at her disposal with her goals (*W:M*). Strenghts: She did not show attentive problems (*PSV*).

Mediation

Labilities: Emily's reality testing is basically compromised (*XA%* and *WDA%*) both in everyday experience and in specific situations. She seemed to read reality in a very personal and atypical way: she seemed to read reality in a more subjective and individualistic way even in simple and well-defined situations, not paying attention to social expectations (*X-%* and *P*). She seemed to be very poor in mediating processes and this pattern is pervasive. Strenghts: no strenghts

Ideation

Strenghts: Emily showed a quite good and consistent ideational domain. First, she seemed to be flexible in her ideational production (*a:p*) and her thoughts seemed to be clear, logic and precise (*Sum6*, *WSum6*, *Lvl-2*). In her ideational functioning, Emily did not use any defences, such as intellectualization, to neutralize emotional content (Intellectual index) or to escape in a fantasy world in order to avoid fearful aspects of reality (*Ma:Mp*). Labilities: Sometimes, in specific stressful conditions, she seemed to have some ideational difficulties.

7.4 Conclusion

Emily's CS confirmed a picture of a very fragile girl that had been already derived by the clinical interview. Also, the CS gave more information about how all the dimensions measured by the CS were compromised.

All together the AAP and the CS give little hope of psychological survival and change for this young patient.

8 A CASE IN COLLABORATIVE ASSESSMENT

A. Lis, C. Mazzeschi, D. Di Riso

8.1 Collaborative/Therapeutic Assessment

Therapeutic Assessment (TA) is a form of collaborative assessment described and introduced in personality assessment by Constance Fischer and Stephen Finn (Finn, 1996, 1996, 1997, 1998; Finn & Martin, 1997; Finn & Tonsager, 1997, 2002). Therapeutic assessment relies on collaboration between the psychologist/psychotherapist and patient, as they work together to reach a creative synthesis using psychological instruments, and test data obtained by the psychologist. The Collaborative approach is an individualized psychological assessment in which the assessor and the client with an active contribution work together to develop productive understandings, which become "therapeutic" in themselves.

The Collaborative Assessment includes two fundamental aspects: 1) patient's activation and collaboration with the assessment process in respect to the working alliance and explanation of the results; 2) the choice of a specific test set which is adequate for the specific client. Swann (1997) supported that "..being understood by a therapist may reduce feelings of alienation for it tells patient that someone thought enough of them to learn who they are. For these and related reasons, when provided in a supportive context, self-verifying feedback may have beneficial effects, even when it is negative". APA guidelines on Ethics and Psychological

Assessment require that all clients should be given testing feedback in a language they understand and that the clients benefit therapeutically from feedback (Ackerman et al, 2000; Finn & Tonsager, 1992).

Collaboration is a mean of individualizing the assessment process, resulting in suggestions, and written accounts. In contrast to the traditional assessment approaches, in the collaborative assessment (CA) the client is an active participant in the process (Fischer e Finn, 1987; Finn & Tomager, 1992, Finn 2003). Life events are regarded as primary data and test scores, categories, and related research are used as bridges into the particular life of a client and as tools for an exploration of their meaning for the patient's life. Feedback is one of the basic components of the TA. Recently, there has been increased interest in how to guide the clinicians in the process, of giving feedback to clients about personality assessment results. The feedback session becomes particular useful for the client, because it allows the generation of good strategies to cope with stress, higher motivation and higher efficacy in the intervention. During the feedback session the therapist uses non technical language, taking into account the client's level of intelligence, education, vocabulary, and psychological sophistication. This kind of feedback provides the client with a new perspective and options in problem solving. The TA becomes a highly individualized, constructive and therapeutic approach very useful in many different setting and contexts. Some clinical studies have stressed the therapeutic effect of TA (Allen, 2002; Byers, 2002; Engelman and Frankel, 2002; Finn, 2003).

8.2 The conceptualization of CA at Clinical Service for Psychological Assistance at Padua University

The aim of this chapter is to illustrate a case of collaborative assessment as it was conceptualized and carried out in the Clinical Service for Psychological Assistance (SAP-SC) following the model we have devised at the SPA-SC, following Finn's guidelines (Lis, 2007).

Only young adults who satisfy the criterion of a low to moderate integration of personality structure can be accepted for a therapeutic assessment. Three instruments are used to make this decision:

Operationalized Psychodynamic Diagnosis (OPD; Task Force, 2001): is a diagnostic interview developed to propose operationalized clinical diagnostic guidelines; it is audio recorded and transcribed to be scored. It defines five diagnostic axis: Axis I, Experience of illness and Prerequisites of Treatment; Axis II, Relational Issues; Axis III, Conflict; Axis IV, Structure; and Axis V, Syndrome diagnostics according to ICD-10.

Symptom Checklist-90-Revised (SCL-90-R, Derogatis 1994): it is a 90-item, brief, multi-dimensional checklist used to screen for a broad range of psychological problems and symptoms of psychopathology; it is a highly structured self report that is typically administered in a fast, simple and non-interactive fashion.

9 primary symptom dimensions are measured, as well as symptom intensity: Somatisation; Obsessive Compulsive; Interpersonal Sensitivity; Depression; Anxiety; Hostility; Phobic Anxiety; Paranoid Ideation; Psychoticism; PLUS Global Severity Index; Positive Symptom Distress Index and Positive Symptom Total.

Global Assessment of Functioning Scale (GAF; APA, 1997): it is a 100-point quick assessment scale that measures a client's overall level of psychological, social, and occupational functioning on a hypothetical continuum, from 100 (good mental health) to 0 (presence of deep psychological disturbance).

After the first meeting with the patient a special team working on TA, meet and discuss:

(a) the severity of the case in view of deciding or not for a TA;
(b) the Axis I of the OPD, above all concerning prerequisite for treatment, to decide if the case will be able to sustain TA;
(c) to decide the psychological instruments that could specifically be used with this patient. All patients in TA would be administered a:

I. *The Minnesota Multiphasic Personality Inventory (MMPI-2;Butcher et al., 1989)*: it provides valid descriptions of people's problems, symptoms, and features.
II. *Rorschach Test (Rorschach, 1921)* administered and scored according to Exner's (Exner, 1974, 1986, 1993) guidelines.

After the tests administration, the psychologist prepares an individualized letter that represents a written feedback for the patient. The letter is very personal. The letter tries to put together a patient's picture that organizes all the material using not only clear and simple language, but uses metaphors and poetic references. Collaborative assessment techniques are powerful because they focus on helping clients "rewriting" the stories they tell themselves about themselves (which psychologists usually call identity). For some people those stories have become problematic or incomplete in important ways. Compared to other forms of therapeutic intervention, psychological assessment has the advantage of quickly gathering detailed specific information about clients' self-schemas and interpersonal schemas. Furthermore, when collaborative assessment techniques are applied, clients are enlisted as active participants.

The material used to write a letter can be derived from all the material at disposal: from the more aware to the less aware level. A team helps the psychologist complete the letter.

The feedback includes: (a) three sessions in which the letter is shared and discussed in a "holding" environment between psychologist and patient; (b) two instruments for the evaluation of the TA process:

Assessment Questionnaire-2 (AQ-2; Finn, Schroeder, & Tonsager, 1995): it is a 48-item inventory measuring the efficacy of the assessment procedure. It is aimed to determine clients' felt satisfaction. We use another AQ-2 version for the therapist to assess also his/her degree of satisfaction about the intervention.

Open Ended Questionnaire: it's a questionnaire concerning client's impressions and satisfaction of the assessment, and to explore: how the client if felt listened to and understood; how much the client felt himself emotionally involved during the sessions; if the client felt to have gained new reading ways about his problem and about the patient itself.

8.3 The case: Samantha

8.3.1 Background and intake clinical interview

NOTE: THIS FOLLOWING PARAGRAPH NEEDS TO BE IN PAST SIMPLE WHEN TALKING ABOUT CLIENT'S DESCRIPTION OF SELF IN THE PAST AT ASSESSMENT:

Samantha is a 20 year old philosophy student. She self-referred because she felt that something was going wrong in her, because she never felt at ease with other people. She has some friends, but every time she goes out with them she always think that something is missing in her relationship with them. Moreover; she complains that she has some difficulty in expressing her own emotions and feelings. This feeling is something that has always accompanied her social life, but now, she thinks that it is time to spend some time to reflect on herself. She never had a boyfriend. She is now interested in a boy who is attending the same theoretical philosophy course she is attending. But the interest looks like only at a level of adolescent *fantasy*.

Samantha has some eating difficulties; it means that when she is much stressed she is unable to eat. Samantha has a significant fear of death and illnesses. When she was 15 years old, an aunt, to whom Samantha was very affectionate and with whom she had a deep bond, died. This aunt took care of her during her childhood and adolescence because her mother was busy working. After the aunt's death, she felt blocked. During that period she lost weight.

Before the University, Samantha lived in a small village, with her family: father, mother and a sister five years younger than she. She complains about a very conflicted relationship with her mother a dentist. The mother is described as a tyrant. However at the same time Samantha says that they seem to be bonded with a reciprocal dependency. The father is defined as a marginal figure, absent in the family dynamics. He is described as a dreamer, not very concrete, but she feels affectively close to him. She describes her sister, as being always easy going, at ease with everyone, spontaneous, and completely different from her.

She came to Padua two years ago to begin the University. She decided to come together with a female cousin of the same age. They share a flat. They appear to have a close relationship. Samantha depends on her cousin when she has to decide something, whether important or not.

The most striking thing about Samantha's interview was in regards to her language. Her language is intellectualized, rational, interspaced with philosophical terms. She seemed unable to process affective meaning, above all when she was talking about death and death experiences. She talks about death and about her fears of death and illness in a very cold, controlled, and non- affective way.

From a general point of view, the structural pattern is on the moderately integrated level which means that in non-conflict situations Samantha is able to maintain a good bond with herself and others. On the other hand, when she has to face complex and highly emotional situations she needs support.

8.3.2 The questionnaires

GAF: The therapist gave a score of 51 because of: a slight flat emotions; (b) moderate difficulties in social functioning: she had few friends.

SCL-90: the highest significant scores were on depression, obsessive-compulsive and Interpersonal Sensitivity. Samantha seemed to have some intrusive thoughts, she felt sad and unmotivated and she felt uneasy in interpersonal relationships.

Team meeting: Since Samantha had the experience of the aunt's loss, the team decided to administer the Rorschach, the MPPI, the AAI and the AAP. Why two attachment pattern measures? The team thought that, beside the attachment classification, those two instruments could give different information about the attachment dynamic in the overall functioning of the patient. The first one helped the clinician get some biographical information related to her relationships with her parents and the second one allowed an investigation, in an indirect way, into the possible trauma she experienced related to her aunt's death.

8.3.3 Test results

MMPI-2

Samantha had a valid profile on the MMPI-2. This indicated her wish to attend to the required task in an active way.

Considering the total of all the scale's scores of Samantha, she has an average level of psychopathology.

Validity Scales	T	
L	65	Moderate 60-69
F	61	Moderate 56-70
K	49	Modal 41-55
Fback	55	Moderate<90

L Scale - Samantha showed sometimes the deliberate and rather unsophisticated attempt to present herself in a favourable light and stereotypic manner; showing a defensive attitude which presents her in a conformist and ethically rigid way.

F Scale – She didn't have deviant or atypical ways of responding to test items. The *F* Scale is a good indicator of degree of psychopathology, with higher scores suggesting greater psychopathology. She didn't have a high score on The *F* Scale, so we can assert that Samantha's degree of psychopathology is mild. She did have some difficulties on maintaining attention, maybe she wishes to be involved in a social, or political life. She has some risk of acting out, and sometimes she is inattentive and critical of herself.

K Scale - The *K* Scale is an effective index of attempts by subjects to deny psychopathology and to present themselves in a favourable light or, conversely, to exaggerate psychopathology and to try to appear in a very unfavourable light.

Some people refer to this scale as the "defensiveness" indicator, as high scores on the *K* Scale are thought to be associated with a defensive approach to the test, while low scores are thought to be indicative of an unusually frank and self-critical approach.

On *K* scale, Samantha has a medium score, which means that she is able to balance defensive strategies with a stance of openness. Her resources seem enough to allow her to handle psychotherapy.

Back F (Fb) Scale – Samantha has on the *Fb* scale, a low score, which means that she didn't answer first test items that occurred later in the booklet and she didn't have a random pattern of responding.

For clinical scales the range of non normative scores are $> T = 65$
Clinical Scales

Clinical Scales	T
1. Hypocondriasis	45
2. Depression	72
3. Hysteria	67
4. Psycopathic deviat	53
5. Mf-f/m	60
6. Paranoia	48
7. Psycastenia	55
8. Schizophrenia	52
9. Hypomania	45
0. Social Introversion	71

Scale 1: Hypochondrias (Hs) – Samantha doesn't have a neurotic concern over bodily functioning. She doesn't have many hypochondriac concerns about her health or body; she is pragmatic and shows a good introspective ability.

Scale 2: Depression (D) - Samantha's scores on the Depression scale were elevated, (T=72): She seems to be lonely, sad, and shy: Samantha perceives herself in a inadequate way, is critical to herself, doesn't have energy enough, could have some problems in attention and sleeping. She feels a high level of subjective depression (subscale T = 77), is nervous, never happy and doesn't have the ability to cope with problems well. Samantha lacks confidence and could feel discomfort in social relationships. From a psycho - behaviour point of view, Samantha is depressed and more slow (subscale T = 79). In social circumstances she feels blocked, and wants to avoid other people.

Samantha could have a somatic disease (T = 70), and she lacks energy and a capacity to manage the problems of everyday life. She has internal stress and a memory deficit. She doesn't gain enjoyment from life (subscale of mental not efficiency T = 66) and could arrive at the conclusion that the life isn't worth living. Samantha is apathetic and sometimes feels that she could lose control of her thinking. This scale was originally developed to assess symptomatic depression. The primary characteristics of symptomatic depression are poor morale, lack of hope in the future, and a general dissatisfaction with one's own life situation. Samantha has high scores but they not significantly elevated on this scale. This suggests she doesn't have a strong clinical depression, but a general attitude or life-style characterized by poor morale, lack of involvement and depressive symptoms instead of a nosografic classification.

Scale 3: Hysteria (Hy) – Samantha has also high scores on the Hysteria scale (T = 67): she demonstrates hysterical reactions when faced with stressful situations. She uses the defensive mechanisms of denial and dissociation, she has troubles and symptoms on specific functions, is naïve, histrionic and seductive. She feels weak and sick, worn out, is unhappy and melancholic (she has a score on subscale of weariness and malaise of T = 83). Samantha could have various somatic symptoms (headache, dizziness) (subscale T = 65). She is not hostile to other people. In situations of conflict, she uses the defensive mechanisms of repression of affection and conversion. Also, Samantha inhibits her aggression (subscale T = 70), and she rejects negativity and hostile impulses. She is susceptible to others' reaction to her.

Scale 4: Psychopathic Deviate (Pd) – She has a modal score in this scale (T = 53), so she is not a psychopathic personality, asocial or amoral type. She is tenacious, responsive, sensible and reliable. Samantha may be seen as conventional, conforming, and submissive.

Samantha has a high score on a sub scale of Psychopathic Deviation (T = 68): in life she feels a lack of love, support and understanding from her family. The family is perceived as over controlling and critical. She might want to leave her home.

Scale 5: Masculinity-Femininity (Mf) - Scale 5 was originally developed by Hathaway and McKinley to identify homosexuality in males. The test authors identified only a very small number of items that differentiated homosexual from heterosexual males. Scores that are markedly higher than expected for males, based on the persons' intelligence, education, and social class suggest the possibility of sexual concerns and problems. High scores are very uncommon among females. When they are encountered, they generally indicate rejection of the traditional female role. Samantha has a T score of 60 which is near a high level, so this means that she wants to be logical, and not emotional, or competitive.

Scale 6: Paranoia (Pa) – She has a low score (T = 48). Samantha is rational, doesn't have paranoid symptoms such as ideas of reference, feelings of persecution, grandiose self-concepts, suspiciousness, excessive sensitivity, and rigid opinions and attitudes.

Scale 7: Psycho-asthenia (Pt) – (T = 55), Samantha doesn't show psycho-asthenic symptoms, characterized by excessive doubts, compulsions, obsessions and unreasonable fears. This diagnostic label is not commonly used today. Among currently popular diagnostic categories, the obsessive-compulsive disorder probably is closest to the original psycho-asthenia label. In addition to obsessive-compulsive features, this scale taps abnormal fears, self-criticism, difficulties in concentration, and guilt feelings. The anxiety assessed by this scale is of a long-term nature or trait anxiety, although the scale is somewhat responsive to situational stress as well. Our subject doesn't have these symptoms, and she seems to be well organized.

Scale 8: Schizophrenia (Sc) – Samantha scored 52 on this scale, which is far from a schizophrenia diagnosis. However, she has some high scores on the schizophrenia subscale above the normal range (T=76) for emotional alienation, (T = 65) for loss of Ego control. Samantha seems to be emotionally alienated; she feels hopelessness, apathetic and also frightened. She could have the desire to die. She has the loss of Ego Control, feels despair and preoccupied. Her life is not gratifying, and she could comfort herself with fantasy and daydreaming when facing stress. She feels hopeless and might want to die. She has a good sense of reality but she feels social alienation, poor familial relationships, difficulties in concentration and impulse control, lack of deep interests, disturbing questions of self-worth and self-identity, and sexual difficulties. Misinterpretations of reality, delusions, and hallucinations may, also, be present. Ambivalent or constricted emotional responsiveness is common. Behaviour may be withdrawn, aggressive, or bizarre. Scale 8 is probably the single most difficult scale to interpret in isolation because of the variety of factors that can result in an elevated score.

Scale 9: Hypomania (Ma) –The lowest score for Samantha (T = 45) is on the Hypomania scale. Samantha has a low level of energy and activity, she seems to hole up, she is careless, apathetic, and could show a chronic level of weariness. She feels depressed and also anxious but she is balanced and does not have an elevated mood. She doesn't feel nervous or suddenly depressed.

Scale 0: Social Introversion (Si) - Samantha also has a high score on Social Introversion (T=71). She feels embarrassed, withdrawn, stiff, and overawed. Samantha) is socially introverted, feels uncomfortable and insecure in social situations. She doesn't feel comfortable in relationships and has difficulty communicating. She tends to avoid parties, and she is ill at ease with males. Other people describe Samantha as cold and distant. She is probably reliable.

Content scales (high scores > T = 65)

Content scales	Score T
Anxiety	66
Fears	52
Obs	61
Dep	59
Hea	54
Biz	45

Content scales

A first group of six content-scales includes internal symptoms and a subject's peculiar perceptions:

1. *ANX* (Anxiety): (23 items) Samantha has positive scores only in the Anxiety scale (T = 64). She has general symptoms of anxiety that indicate internal stress and somatic symptoms - rapid heart beat and shortness of breath, tachycardia, sleeplessness, and excessive worries -, sleep symptoms, excessive concerns and poor concentration. She feels that the life is tiring and she has difficulty making decisions. She could be afraid becoming crazy. She is aware of her problems and doesn't have difficulty admitting them.
2. *FRS* (Fears): (23 items) (T = 52) She doesn't have specific fears and phobias about condition, animals or objects.

3. OBS (Obsessiveness): (16 items) (T = 61) She has a moderate score on this scale. Samantha could have a mild level of obsessive thoughts and mull over attitudes with compulsive behaviour. She could has some difficulties in making decisions and feels some stress with change.
4. DEP (Depression): (33 items) (T = 59) the level of score in this scale is not higher than in the Depression clinical scale but there is probably a mild level of symptomatic depression which includes depressed mood, and little involvement in their life. Samantha feels a sense of emptiness and could have crying spells.
5. HEA (Health Concerns): (36 items) (T = 54) Samantha doesn't have many somatic concerns such as neurological, vascular, or general pain.
6. BIZ (Bizarre Mentation): (23 items) (T = 45) This scale investigates psychotic thinking, which could indicate hallucinations or paranoiac ideation. Samantha doesn't have a psychotic structure.

Aggressive tendencies	Score T
Ang	40
Cyn	47
Asp	44
Tpa	47
Lse	57

A second group of four scales include aggressive tendencies: subject's social behaviour, and the ability to control behaviours and emotions.

On these scales Samantha had low scores: this could be interpreted as reflecting her inhibition of aggressiveness.

7 ANG (Anger): (16 items) (T = 40) She doesn't have problems in the control of her anger or in acting out. Samantha isn't impulsive, impatient, and doesn't loose control to become aggressive.
8 CYN (Cynism): (23 items) (T = 47) Samantha doesn't have negative attitudes to wards other people or psychological thinking.
9 ASP (Antisocial Behaviours): (22 items) (T = 44) She doesn't have behaviour problems at school, or breaking the law with activities like stealing.
10 TPA (Type A): (19 items) (T = 47) Samantha's personality is not hostile, competitive and aggressive.
11 LSE (Low Self-Esteem) (24 items) (T = 57) Her score on this scale is not high enough to be interpreted but there could a tendency to have a bad opinion of and to undervalue herself.

General Problems	Score T
Social discomfort	75
Familiar problems	55
Difficulties at Works	67
Difficulties in Treatment	63

Four content scales measure general problems:

1. *SOD* (Social Discomfort): (24 items) (T = 75) On the general problems scales Samantha has a high score on social discomfort with other people. She feels inadequate, embarrassed. She prefers to stay alone. This scale measures problems in social relationships and discomfort in a group.
2. *FAM* (Family Problems): (25 items) (T = 55) She doesn't identify lot of problems with her family and she doesn't have feelings of hate for her family.
3. *WRK* (Work Interference): (33 items) (T = 67) She could have some problems at work: poor performance, tension, difficulty making decisions. Samantha has personal doubts and could feel any support from her family. She could have problems adapting to a work environment.
4. *TRT* (Negative Treatment Indicators): (26 items) (T = 63) This score in near an acceptable range for interpretation. Samantha has a capacity to accept help and to find coping strategies in an adaptive way. This is a positive indicator that she is willing and able to begin a psychological process.

Supplementary Scales	Score T
Anxiety	64
Repression	70
Ego strength	37
Alcoholism Mac-R	38

On supplementary scales Samantha shows the following scores:

1. **Anxiety:** (T = 64) near the range. She feels anxiety, some distress especially in social situations.
2. **Repression:** (T = 70) this high score means that she tries to avoid disagreements and unpleasant circumstances.

3. **Ego strength:** (T = 37) she is inhibited, expresses physical symptoms and has a feeling powerlessness. She has difficulty coping with problematic circumstances.
4. **Alcoholism:** (T = 38) she doesn't show an alcohol abuse behaviour.

On the Addictional Scales:

Addictional Scales	Score T
Overcontrolled-Hostility	47
Dominance	46
Social Responsability	53
University unadapt	68
Gender role	38
Gf	51
PTDS	59
Married symptoms	68
Potential drug abuse	51
Admitting dependance	54

1. **Over controlled hostility:** (T = 47). She doesn't react with aggressiveness to resolve problems.
2. **Dominance** (T = 46)**:** No interpretation of this score either in leadership attitude or in a lack of confidence in herself.
3. **Social Responsivity**: (T = 53). No interpretation for score either in readiness to accept her behaviour or in lack of honesty.
4. **University non adaptation:** (T = 68) Samantha could have some difficulties in the university. She feels pessimistic, and anxious.
5. **Gender Role**: (T = 38) and *Gf* (T = 51) No interpretation on the gender role scale; she doesn't show stereotypical gender attitudes.
6. **PTDS:** (T = 59) she does not have intrusive and persistent thoughts or lack of control.
7. **Married symptoms:** (T = 68) The high score on this scale could indicate the possibility of Samantha developing difficulties in the marriage relationship.
8. **Potential Drug Abuse:** (T = 51) Samantha is not a potential drug abuser.
9. **Admitting Dependence**: (T = 54) She doesn't show any dependence from alcohol or substance abuse.

RORSCHACH

The CS interpretation is reported cluster by cluster, highlighting strengths and weaknesses for each personality dimension. This procedure helped to combine Rorschach information with those from other tools, in order to structure the feedback session according to the patient's words and the tool's detailed material.

Samantha produced a valid protocol which provided reliable information and supported a) valid interpretation.

The key variables from which we started the interpretation are the following: (a) *AdjD* is minus; (b) Reflection > 0; (c) *Afr* <.46. These indexes gave us basic important initial information. During the complete Rorschach analysis Samantha seemed to have: liabilities with chronic stress management (*AdjD*), some narcissistic features (Reflection), and some difficulties in being engaged in emotional situations (*Afr*).

Samantha interpretative search strategy is:

Controls → Self-Perception → Interpersonal → Perception → Affect → Processing → Mediation → Ideation

Controls

Liabilities: Samantha showed an ambitent style of functioning (*EB*). She did not have a specific and clear way in facing both internal and external demands in dealing with her experiences. She goes back and forth between emotional and ideational resources. Moreover, she had few psychological resources (*EA*) which did not allow her to manage stress, both situational (*D*) and chronic (*AdjD*). Samantha had to manage a great amount of demands (*es* and *Adjes*), both ideational and affective. The specific sources of stress in her life appear to involve ongoing concerns and issues (*FM*, *V* and *T*) rather than merely situational or transient problems and issues (*m* and *Y*). Specifically she had a high awareness that some of her needs were not satisfied (*FM*), she felt some aspects of self-blame (*V*) and she believed that her source of feeling loneliness and grief related to emotional depriving experiences (*T*).

Strength: No strength.

Self-Perception:

Liabilities: Samantha showed a severe conflict of self-image: she seemed to overvalue her personal worth, becoming concerned with just her own needs at the expense of those of others (Reflection). She often failed to obtain reaffirmation, through praise and success, of her high self-value so she experiences feeling of blame (*V*). Such a combination raised the possibility that her narcissistic features did not constitute a pervasive personality characteristic but was instead accompanied by some substantial worries and doubts about herself. Also, Samantha seemed to be concerned about her body functioning (*An+Xy*) which could allow the support of an image of herself as a fragile or vulnerable person. Samantha lacked in introspective process (*FD*).

Strengths: Samantha did not represent herself with too many negative and morbid features. Her self-image was not characterised by pessimistic ideations (*MOR*) and, although she did not achieve a stable and defined sense of identity (Reflection vs *V*), her identity seemed to be based on realistic identifications (*H* : *(H)+Hd+(Hd)*).

Interpersonal Perception

Strengths: Samantha gave evidence of adaptive capacities to be engaged in interpersonal relationships (Isolation Index) and to anticipate them as positive and cooperative (*COP* vs *AG*). This indicates that means she is interested in other people and she seemed to be able to represent others in a realistic way (Human content). Most of the time this features allowed Samantha to interact with other people in a good and consistent way (*GHR:PHR*).

Liabilities: She appeared to be experiencing a great amount of need for closeness and deep contact (*T*). This aspect could often lead Samantha to feel lonely, emotionally deprived and at risk for reaching out for close relationships indiscriminately. Moreover, she tended to be dependent in interpersonal relationships, in order to satisfy her need of closeness (Food).

Affect

Liabilities: Samantha has some difficulties in processing emotionally stimulation. First, she did not seem to able to recognize and analyze affective reality features (*FC:CF+C* very low) and second, Samantha did not become easily engaged in affectively charged situations (*Afr*). This characteristic does not necessarily prevent Samantha from being interested in interactions, but when strong feelings would come up in the relationships, she would often tend to break them off. Moreover, Samantha showed a consistent oppositional tendency toward the world in general. This may be associated with underlying feelings of anger and resentment (*S*). This attitude could lead Samantha to a chronic state of irritation and to difficulties with impulse control. Moreover, she showed a low psychological complexity which means she usually functions in a simplistic and psychologically poor way (*Blends:R*). This would imply that she tends to show maladaptive behaviours in complex situations, involving emotional displays.

Strengths: No strength.

Processing:

Liabilities: Samantha shows an under incorporative processing pattern which means that she usually pays too little attention to information in her reality analyses (*Zd*). She could be at risk for making conclusions in a simplistic way and, consequently, make decisions based on a poor reality processing. Although she shows a strong achievement orientation, she is not able to balance resources at her disposal with her goals (*W:M*). Moreover, in dealing with processing experience, she makes a huge effort to put together and integrate different parts of the stimulus (*Zd*; *W:D:Dd*). These aspects could sometimes lead her to attend to her experience less precisely (*DQ-%*).

Strengths: Most of the time Samantha shows a good and efficient processing quality (*DQ+%*).

Mediation:

Strengths: Samantha's reality testing is good and consistent (*WDA%, XA%, X-% and S-%*). However, she seems to have an idiosyncratic way to perceive people and events (*Xu%*)

Liabilities: Samantha makes a huge effort to keep her reality testing working in a good and accurate way (*XA% and WDA%*) and she does not seem to be conventional (*P*). Samantha seems to understand reality in a subjective and more individualistic way, even in simple and well-defined situations.

Ideation

Strengths: Samantha shows a good and consistent ideational functioning. First, she seems to be flexible in her ideational production (*a:p*) and her thoughts seem to be clear, logic and precise (*Sum6, WSum6, Lvl-2*). In her ideational functioning, Samantha does not use any kind of defence, such as intellectualization, in order to neutralize emotional content (Intellectual index) or escaping into a fantasy world in order to avoid fearful reality aspects (*Ma:Mp*).

Liabilities: no liabilities

AAI: DS2/F2

Samantha's AAI was scored as *dismissing* with derogation of parents and attachment (DS2, devaluing of attachment), but there was some evidence of meta-cognitive monitoring (F2 = somewhat dismissing or restricted in attachment).

On the Experience scales, Samantha presented low levels of Loving experiences, both from mother and father. She saw comfort, care, protection and loving physical contact with her parents during childhood as having been substantially functional to satisfy concrete needs. The Rejection scale evaluated a quite high intensity regarding her mother's behaviours of refusal when she was asking for comfort, care, and protection. On the contrary her experiences of her father's behaviour underlined a quite high neglecting attitude, since frequently he was physically but not psychically and emotionally present for Samantha's needs. For both mother and father we scored quite a high level of Pressure to Achieve, which showed the parent's desires of achievement and success for the child (e.g. in school activities or sport performance), in spite of Samantha's needs or desires. No Involving/Role-Reversing aspects were found.

On the State of Mind scales, Samantha showed a strong tendency to idealize her mother, and to normalize and minimize childhood experiences her father. The inability to recall events from childhood (*lack of memory*) was quite present. The major finding was Derogation of caregivers and, above all, of attachment in general. Some expressions of unreasonable fears that an imaginative child may die (*fear of loss*) were found. No current active resentment toward parents (*mother anger* and *father anger*) was found. Some features of passive and rambling attachment-related discourse (*passivity*) were found, and she was a bit too talkative to be a Dismissing. A little evidence of meta-cognitive monitoring was found and she appeared to be somewhat aware of the nature of experiences with her parents and about the effects of those experiences in her present state of mind and on her personality (*Coherence of Mind*). Although, she remained definitively Dismissing, because she was emphasising her strength and her independency from parents, by endorsing their cold attitude to manage her needs. She was restricted in her emotional expressions, preferring to rationalize and failing in recall episodes of her childhood, in a very defensive way, instead of elaborating and thinking about painful live events.

Experience Scales				State of Mind			
	Mother	Father		Mother	Father		
Loving	3.0	3.5	Idealization	3.5	1.5	Lack of Memory	5.0
Neglect	1.0	5.0	Derogation	5.0	5.0	Preoccupied Anger	1.0
Rejection	5.0	1.0				Passivity	2.5
Pressure to achieve	4.0	4.0				Fear of Loss	4.0
Role Reversing	1.0	1.0				Metacognitive	2.0
						Coherency Transcript	3.5
						Coherency Mind	3.5

AAP:U

Samantha's AAP was classified as U. There were two stories - Bench and Ambulance- that unleashed segregated systems about which she was unable to maintain organized in her attachment system. As we know, the AAP does not maintain the double classification about U that is, a instead part of the AAI. But we think it is important in better understanding Samantha's personality functioning to highlight that she could be a U/Ds. In other words, her main way to deal with the activation of the attachment system is to deactivate it, to shut it out.

We will summarize Samantha's AAP and then we will report completely two stories: one in which the segregated systems were unresolved and one where she is able to maintain organized her attachment system, to be connected with an affiliative figure and where she used deactivation as a major defense.

In the whole protocol, Samantha develops clear and logical stories. The characters in the stories are all clearly identified. However, she never describes the internal states of the characters. No secure base or haven of safety are described in any of the alone stories. So her sense of security is never derived from her internal relationship to the attachment figure. But in Window, in Cemetery, and in Corner she was able to organize her attachment making specific actions e.g. a child asks her father in Window, a man is praying In Cemetery, a child is pushing away in Corner. She never found mother for mutual enjoyment. No real and mutual synchrony is described in the dyadic stories e.g. in Departure, husband and wife work together, in Bed, father reads a book to his child. It is interesting that although sometimes she is able to be connected with a parental figure (Window- the father, this figure acts in the affiliative system more than in the attachment system they have fun together. The mother never appears as major figure of attachment.

Now we are going to explain the representative stories of Samantha's functioning. The first one is organized and shows a Ds typical way of functioning; the second one is prototypical of a disorganized pattern.

Window:
...A girl in her.. room... she is looking outside... and ... she is looking outside .. and she is <u>waiting</u> (Cognitive Disconnection) that mummy will come back from the supermarket to make her make her <u>school tasks</u> (Deactivation) ... So she is looking out and she is <u>waiting, waiting</u> Cognitive disconnection) that she is arriving by car ... .And mummy comes and they make the <u>school tasks</u> (Deactivation) ... The child tells mum that because it is a beautiful day she would like to go out with her. Mummy says no because <u>she is tired</u> (Cognitive disconnection). ..So mummy... mummy is asking father, daddy.. asks daddy to take the girl out. She asks to go to the playground, to the carousels and they go and get fun. *What are they feeling and thinking?* The <u>girl is anxious</u> (cognitive disconnection) because she would have preferred to go with mum instead than with

dad.. at the beginning she was sad about that ... Finally she is able to get fun with her father, but at the beginning she did not accept her mother's answer because she wanted to go with mummy, she feels underneath a little bit disappointed.

Discussion:

The story is clear and coherent. A girl is waiting for mummy, but mummy is not represented as a secure base or as a haven of safety. Mother is just a person which helps to deactivate attachment through achievement. The girl complains because the mother asks the father to have fun with her, because she wants mummy. Using cognitive disconnection, deactivation and capacity to act, Samantha is able to organize her attachment system and to make use of the father as affiliative system.

Bench:

I see a mother... in jail.. in prison (Segregated System).. She is crying.. .. She killed her partner (Segregated System).., the father of her two children.. She is crying because this two children are now orphans. She got a life sentence (Segregated System)... He died (Segregated System).. and she think about suicide (Segregated System).. And.. because her guilty feelings are too much strong (Deactivation) to be tolerates and so she prefers to put an end to her life. *What would happen next?* With the passing of time her children will never go and visit her.. they will never be able to forgive her for the severe homicide (Segregated System).. she has committed. For the crime (Segregated System).. she has marked herself with, to have eliminated tragically (Segregated System).. the life of a person so important for her two children.

Discussion:

In Bench, Samantha gives us a very different picture. The picture unleashed a very threatening and dangerous representation of a mother who killed the father of her two children, which will never will be forgiven. In this case, Samantha is unable to organize her attachment system. The woman, until the end of the story, is unable to represent any kind of containment for her segregated system.

Some reflections about AAP and AAI

It is very important to highlight the differences between Samantha's AAI and AAP pattern. AAI showed a Dismissing classification and AAP an Unresolved one. According to Samantha's experiences we tried to explain these discrepancy. First, we decided to administer an attachment measure according to Samantha history: she described a maladaptive relationship with her mother and she defined herself as *blocked* after her aunt's death. The AAI dismissing scoring was related to her an emotional relationship with her parents and with the impossibility to express emotions freely. The U material is present about her aunt (Unresolved loss = 4,0) but it was still integrated because AAI is based on verbal elaboration. Samantha is able to organize her loss experience through a defensive and cold approach. She seemed to organize her U material through intellectual words. On the other hand, the AAP could investigate her dysregulation in an indirect way, overcoming the defensive processing: in that way the U material is able to come up, also because Samantha seemed to talk about characters as their own experiences, not hers.

8.3.4 Conclusion: passages from the feedback letter

The letter began by recalling the reason for the referral. The psychologist stressed how Samantha has experienced, in the here and now of the session, a new relationship with her therapist, accepting this new experience although she knows that for her it is difficult to face a new relationship. Moreover, she was active and really motivated to complete the many assessment instruments which involved her in very complex situations. The therapist suggested that it was not an easy task, because she knew that that would lead to a new awareness and knowledge about her. The first metaphor was taken from the AAP picture - bench. Like the woman in Bench who is in a prison, she feels sometimes locked in. But differently from the woman, Samantha is in jail because it is her feelings and emotions that are locked in jail. Perhaps she feels so threatened to let them free, that she had to lock a door of a part of her "home". She has locked up her feelings and emotions with a very heavy door of rational and intellectual words. However, all the material that the therapist and she have collected together takes her in a different direction. Besides the locked door, there are many voices that want to be heard and to which she has given the opportunity to be heard through the different assessment instruments that she has accepted to participate in. Now the door can slowly be opened and allowed to let the light come in. Now they can together look as to why it is so complicated for Samantha to look at what is in herself and other people.

According to the MMPI, there are several questions, of such a very long questionnaire of which she was very patient and active in responding, that gave a confirmation, but in a more detailed way of what she briefly expressed in the clinical interview. Directly from the letter according to MMPI scales: *"You fee lonely, sad, shy; you perceive yourself as inadequate, you are critical of yourself, you lack confidence and you feel discomfort in social relationships. In social circumstances you feel blocked, and want to avoid other people. The different items helped you to describe better all these different negative feelings that you get about yourself.*

Samantha feels a high level of subjective depression, is nervous, never happy and doesn't seem to have the ability to cope with problems, lacks confidence and could feel discomfort in social relationship. From a psycho-motor-behavioural point of view Samantha is lethargic. She could have somatic symptoms; she lacks energy and a capacity to manage the problems of everyday life. She has internal stress and memory deficits. She doesn't gain enjoyment from life and could arrive at the conclusion that the life isn't worth living. She is apathetic and sometimes feels that she could lose control of her thinking. Directly from the written report: *"You feel embarrassed, withdrawn, stiff, overawed, socially introverted, and uncomfortable and insecure in social situations. You do not feel comfortable in relationships and you have difficulty in communication. You tend to avoid parties and fun times. You are not at ease with the other sex, the others describe Samantha as cold and distant."*

However, other instruments showed that basically she is very interested in human relationships and that she is able to form a good representation of them. So her feeling is not completely supported by her basic interest in human relationships. The AAI allowed her to analyze her first life experiences with mom and dad and the clinician decided to highlight some aspects of these experiences. Directly from the letter: *"You described low levels of loving experiences both from your mother and father because the comfort, care, protection and loving physical contact with your parents during childhood were substantially functional just to satisfy your needs".* According to AAI classification, we scored for the both mother and father a quite high level of Pressure to Achieve, which showed the parent's desires of achievement and success of the child (e.g. in school activities or sport performance), in spite of Samantha's needs or desires. In the written report: *"You felt yourself as the child in the Window who was waiting for mummy just to do together school tasks. This is maybe the reason why on the one hand you feel value as a dutiful student, a dutiful friend, a dutiful daughter, yet on the other hand, you feel vulnerable and unsatisfied about yourself and maybe you blame yourself. Your aunt was the only person you felt taken care of."*

The letter also stressed the presence of locked aggressive feelings boiling in Samantha that she hasn't paid attention to yet.

These are only passages from the letter, but we think that the meaning of the type of communication that went on between Samantha and her therapist can be understood.

The letter gave Samantha the opportunity to look at herself in a different and more integrated way. The MMPI gave the opportunity to describe her symptoms and difficulties like in a magnifying glass. The Rorschach contributed to giving worth to her strengths in the cognitive triads, but it also gave some information about her and other useful perceptions. The AAI and AAP, give her the opportunity to see how during her childhood, she experienced attachment, and how anger was excluded but could released.

Samantha was depicted as a huge iceberg in which some fresh emotions were locked in. In the feedback session she was able to express anger and rage toward her cousin and toward the therapist. The assessment phase helped her to defrost these unvoiced emotions, and in the feedback session, Samantha's words were less controlled, her tone of voice was lighter and the rigid posture of Samantha in the chair relaxed.

9 THERAPEUTIC CHANGES: THE CASE OF MATILDE

A. Lis, L. Laghezza, A. Raudino

9.1 Background

Matilde is a 20-year-old student. She referred herself to a Clinical Service in order to solve some worries about her University choice. She attends the second year of Medical School, but she is not sure that this is the right Faculty for her. She wears casual clothes and does not use any kind of make up. She is not in fashion at all. She moved away from her native small town in order to study. Now she shares a flat with other students near the Medical School.

She feels confused and quite insecure. This insecurity causes her severe crying crises, pervasive anxiety, and some physical symptoms, such as psychomotor agitation and tachycardia. She had taken light tranquilizers in the last three months. She is fluent, clear and precise in the cognitive evaluation of her disease, but quite inflexible when her reactions, thoughts and reality interpretative patterns are analyzed.

At the beginning of the first session, she seems to be quite distrustful, but she is aware that she needs someone to trust in order to learn new keys and to understand new perspectives to her uneasiness. She recognizes that she needs help to face the state of uneasiness that she is feeling.

Matilde is a smart reflective and trim girl, characterized by a clear and accurate way of speech and thinking.

She does not talk about any other satisfying relationships and she does not have a lot of friends.

In her native small town she lived with her parents and a little sister. She still lives with them when she goes back from the University for her vacations. She is very proud of her family. Matilde has a good relationship with her mother. They usually talk a lot and she tells her about her problems. Sometimes Matilde feels guilty because she makes her mother too much concerned and involved about Matilde anxiety and uneasiness. Matilde describes her father as rigid and very involved in practical duties. Matilde has a 10-years-old little sister. They are very attached. Matilde describes Sarah as really different from her. The little girl is very funny, ironic and she has a great amount of energy. They play together a lot and Matilde becomes unconcerned about her worries when Sarah is close to her. She says that she is very lucky to have such a family.

However, although the descriptions about her family are rich, most of the times they are neutral and dull. She often tells about things they do together, without any reference to shared emotions or feelings.

Matilde says that she had several friends during her high school years: she talks of being very attached to her school-mates. They considered her as their main confident and friend indeed. But they seemed to share just school occurrences. Now that she moved to University, she kept in touch frequently with them. They do not know anything about this uneasy period she is going thought. From the beginning of the University, her life is totally busy with university and academic matters. She seems not to have time and desire to be engaged in social relationships.

She never had a boyfriend. She is very embarrassed to talk about sexual topics. She says that this topic is not important at the moment and it is not a big deal for her.

9.2 The assessment phase

Different tools were used in the assessment phase. Matilde had three semi-structured interviews and a feedback session with her future therapist. Regarding the assessment battery, Matilde filled up the Symptom Check List – 90 (SCL-90; Derogatis, 1983) to obtain a symptom profile and the clinician filled up the Global Assessment Functioning (GAF; APA, 1994) to analyze her general level of functioning. A different clinician administered the Rorschach CS to analyze personality structure and the AAP to catch the attachment pattern. This clinician carried out a feedback session to give Matilde some explanations on the relevant issues that came up during the evaluation.

9.2.1 The assessment results and therapy planning

GAF: The therapist gave a score of 51 on the GAF: moderate symptoms: occasional panic attacks and moderate difficulties in the social functioning (lack of actual friends).

SCL-90: the highest significant scores were on depression and anxiety.

The AAP showed a secure pattern of attachment. This means in Bowlby's terms that Matilde is characterized, at the representational level, by a flexible and well organized thought about attachment situations and relationships (Bowlby, 1992). According to Bowlby's theory, securely attached individuals are confident that they can rely on attachment figures to achieve care, safety and protection, and, when alone they have access to internalized attachment relationships (George and Solomon, 1996, 1999).

The AAP allowed clarifying the specific dynamics of this pattern, and how it could be related with Matilde's personality functioning. The stories were precise, well organized and articulated, and often describe very clearly attachment topics. In the Alone stories Matilde appeared to be comfortable with solitude and willing to explore her internal working model of attachment (*internalized secure base*). Quoting from her *Cemetery* story: "*a gentleman who had a bad day or felt undervalued for an episode that happened during the day and there he goes and visits his father... he feels reassured because he found a place to think about his life by himself and then he will go back at home and will read what happened from a different point of view*". In this attachment plot, the character internal states are well and clearly described and show how Matilde's sense of security was largely derived from her internal relationship to the attachment figure. Matilde's internalized secure base was also evidenced in the *Bench* story where an adolescent "*is thinking about how to make a decision about her relationship with her school mates. They do not appreciate her and she will make a decision of not being dependent of them*". This story shows the character use of internal resources to cope with the distress. In this story Matilde is able to integrate her internal working model with her affiliative system. Other attachment themes were concerned with attachment figures. In the *Bed* story "*a child had a nightmare, screamed. He is frightened, Mother immediately gets up, soothes him and he will go back to sleep reassured. May be the bad dream was really about being alone without mammy and now ... the first thing he needs is his mommy*". In this story Matilde showed how frightened she can be by being left without mother. But she was able to represent a mother that contingently soothed her child allowing him to deactivate the attachment system (*"the child goes back to sleep"*). As the typical secure individual, Matilde seemed to clearly express her desire to be connected to others, depicting balanced and reciprocal interactions. In this story, as in other dyadic stories, Matilde showed how mother and child are portrayed to a high degree in a contingent, reciprocal and mutually engaging relationship (synchrony, "goal- corrected partnership). The goal-corrected partnership captures Matilde's child's experience of the caregiver in a "warm, intimate, and continuous relationship with his mother (or permanent mother substitute) in which both find satisfaction and enjoyment" (Bowlby, 1951, p. 13, as quoted by Bretherton, 1992).

In *Window* the parents are out for the day. The child feels alone and at the same time excited. "she will find friends, she will go out of home and will have fun with them". In this story Matilde, in the absence of her parents is able to find a connection with friends. In other words, when the attachment system is activated (the absence of parents) she is able to activate other kinds of systems: in this case the affiliative system (friends). Matilde, through her stories, showed the desire and ability to be in a relationship defined by different behavioral systems (e.g., attachment, caregiving, affiliative). According to attachment theory, internalized secure base and haven of safety are promoted in individuals who have developed mental representations of the self as integrated and connected in relationships. This is the picture that Matilde showed in the AAP.

Some useful information for the clinician can derive from the defense processing dimension of the AAP. The purpose of the defensive processing dimension is to identify the quality of defensive exclusion evidenced as consequence of the attachment system activation, in the AAP responses. In Matilde's protocol there are two *segregated systems:* one in the alone picture ("a gentleman talks to his dead father") and one in the dyadic pictures ("a child has a nightmare"). The first segregated system is resolved using a metacognitive approach: the man is able to think about what happened in a new way. The second is resolved by her mother's synchrony: the mother's response to his child's need occurs without delay. According to attachment theory, segregated systems describe a mental state in which painful attachment-related memories are isolated and blocked from conscious thought. This material is likely to be rooted in experiences of trauma or loss through death (Bowlby, 1980; e.g., death of an attachment figure or family member – especially in childhood; physical, sexual, or emotional abuse; abandonment). Some pictures may literally had unleashed in Matilde this material, leaving her in a momentary state of dysregulation due to the breakdown of organized defensive processes (i.e., integration, deactivation, disconnection – see George & Solomon, 1996; Solomon & George, 1996). But she was able to deal with and resolve them. What the clinician has to keep in mind is that this transitory state of disregulation due to the breakdown of organized defensive process could have happened just now when Matilde came to the university and could be one of the unconscious reasons for her referral. May be her fear was that this fear of being alone could be renewed in this period of transition toward adulthood. It could also occur that these attachment-related memories could be unleashes during the treatment, thus allowing them to be integrated.

As theoretically expected, Matilde was flexibly integrated and relatively undefended with regard to attachment. She was found to use fewer forms of defensive exclusion when responding to the AAP; the processes that are revealed were not confined to any one defensive process. The stories show very few cognitive disconnections, meaning that Matilde attachment representation are not fractured by anxieties and uncertainties but they seem to be consistent. There were some deactivation markers. That is, sometime Matilde clearly deactivate the attachment system making the character sleep (deactivation), substituting mutual enjoyment with working and planning a job (Departure). But she appears to use them in a flexible and useful way without interfering with an integrated representation of attachment. For the clinician this would mean that in her current life, when her attachment system is activated (danger, abandonment, death, prison) she will be able to cope with the situation in a flexible way. But she will also be more fragile and prone to some states of dysregulation. In therapy she will be able to see her therapist as a person who can represent a secure base from where to start to explore her internal word.

CS Rorschach

Matilde's CS showed a very complex picture regarding strengths and liabilities.

The Rorschach profile was summarized according to 27 CS variables proposed by Exner and Weiner (1991) and named Index of Adjustment Difficulty. In their paper, the authors identified several personality characteristics associated with achieving treatment goals of different forms of treatment. According to classical dynamic psychotherapy, these goals include the ability to manage stress adequately, bring a consistent coping style to bear on problem situations, attend openly to their experiences, engage in constructive self-examination and feel comfortable in interpersonal relationships. Weiner and Exner (1991) suggested that these Rorschach variables relate to specific personality features and may provide a useful measure of progress in psychotherapy. They have been clustered in six dimensions related to: I. Managing stress adequately; II. Dealing with experience attentively, openly, consistently and conventionally; III. Modulating affect pleasurably and sufficiently; IV. Using ideation effectively; V. Examining him/herself.; VI. Feeling comfortable in interpersonal relationships.

I. Managing stress adequately

Matilde appeared to be in a state of mild situational and chronic stimulus overload resulting from persistent difficulty in using psychological resources to cope with the demands being imposed on her by internal and external events in her life ($D = -1$ and $AdjD = -1$). The specific sources of stress in her life appeared to involve ongoing concerns and issues rather than merely situational or transient problems and worries. Although she showed a good amount of psychological resources for implementing deliberate strategies of resolving problematic situations (EA = 9), she seemed not to be able to use them in a consistent way to meet experience demands. Some of her stress appears to stem from painful internalized affects (C' = 7). They are probably due in part to self-critical attitudes that may be provoked by feelings of guilt and remorse or by regrets for ill-advised actions (V = 5). Because her adaptive capacities are not sufficient for her to manage the ideational and emotional stresses in her life without becoming upset by them, she is at risk for recurrent episodes of overt anxiety, tension, nervousness, and irritability. She is not immature in social situations also because the level of her chronic stimulus overload is quite mild, the usual extent of her subjectively felt distress is unlikely to result in any serious adjustment problems (CDI = 3).

II. Dealing with experience attentively, openly, consistently and conventionally

She showed an extratensive style (EB style) of functioning that means she used mostly affects and feelings to approach internal and external requests. She showed an overincorporating style of information processing (Zd = 8). Under time pressure Matilde could become anxious and feel dissatisfied with the products of her uncomfortably efforts. She might typically feel that she lacked sufficient information on which to base choices that need to be made. Her overincorporative style was also likely to contribute to her excessive involvement and limited detachment in considering the meaning of her experience, simply by virtue of bringing more information than most people ordinarily attempt to process to her attention. Moreover, she seemed to be overwhelmed by the complexity of the stimulus because, according to her way of functioning, she was not able to simplify the reality. Matilde showed an excessive openness to experience, characterized by an overly broad focus of attention, and she is likely to be highly sensitive to her experience and acutely aware of events in her life. She commonly welcomed and even sought out ambiguous and complex situations, and she tends to feel most comfortable in environments that are relatively unstructured and open-ended. On the other hand, she rarely dealt with situations in a simple, detached, or objective manner. Instead, she tends to become over involved in contemplating the underlying significance of events or sorting out her feelings about them. As a result, she might be inclined to make her ways of dealing with people and events more complicated than they need to be (L = .18).

Matilde demonstrated impairment of her reality testing abilities ($XA\%$ = .65 and $WDA\%$ = .73; $X+\%$ during high school years = .35 and $X-\%$ = .35). She tended to misperceive events and to form mistaken impressions of people and what their actions signify. Her failure to perceive people and events realistically occurred primarily at times when she responds to emotionally arousing situations and when she has difficulty in experiencing and expressing her feelings in ways that are comfortable for her.

III. Modulating affect pleasurably and sufficiently

Matilde gave evidence of being predisposed to affective maladjustment that could interfere with her being able to function consistently (*DEPI* = 5). She appeared to be as willing as most people to process emotional stimulation, whether or not she chose to make her own feelings known (*Afr* = .63). However, her openness to becoming engaged in affectively charged situations should contribute to her being reasonably comfortable in social situations, even when strong feelings are being expressed by her or others. Matilde seemed to have a great amount of affects at disposal, but she was inclined more toward formal and restrained expression of relatively stable affects than to casual and expansive expression of relatively transitory affects (*FC:CF+C* = 6:3). Matilde appeared to be experiencing considerable emotional stress that is interfering substantially with her pleasure in life and making her susceptible to becoming anxious and depressed. She might not be fully aware of having such feelings and may not display negatively toned affect, (*SumSh* > *Fm+m*). Her level of stress appeared to derive in part from negative feelings she experienced toward herself in relation to personal characteristics she regarded as undesirable or decisions she regarded as badly made. In specific Matilde experienced a great amount of self-blame (*V* = 5) and emotional constriction (*C'* = 7). The extent to which she internalized, rather than expresses, affect constituted a maladaptive emotional blockage.

IV. Using ideation effectively

Her ideation functioning seemed to be quite usual and consistent. Most of the time her thoughts seemed to be clear, logic and precise (*Sum6* = 4; *WSum6* = 11). Matilde showed some peculiarities in the ideational processing (*M-* = 1) due probably to some worries that could interfere with clarity of thought. For example a disconcerting awareness of needs that are not being met, or worrisome thoughts about being unable to prevent other people or events from determining her destiny.

V. Examining herself

Matilde seemed to have achieved a clear and stable sense of her personal identity. She demonstrated adaptive capacities to base her self-concept on social interactions she has actually experienced, rather than on imaginary encounters with people. Although Matilde did not pay sufficient attention to herself and might even be purposefully avoiding self-focusing (*FD* = 0). It seems that this attitude derives from a low esteem of her personal worth. Accordingly, she might be comparing herself unfavourably to other people, whom she regards as being more able, more attractive, more talented, and generally more worthwhile than she believes to be. She was likely to experience low self-esteem and might lack confidence in herself

$(3r+(2)/R = .15)$. She might experience chronic self-criticism and poor self-regard, and her negative attitudes toward herself were probably promoting a sense of personal dissatisfaction that could range from mild displeasure to self-disgust or even self-loathing.

VI. Feeling comfortable in interpersonal relationships

Matilde showed a hypervigilant personality style (HVI positive), which means that she keeps herself constantly alert for potential sources of threat to her safety and security. Such hypervigilance is associated with an approach to the world in which close interpersonal relationships are viewed with alarm and avoided in favour of keeping one's distance from others. Matilde carefully guarded the boundaries of one's personal space, taking pains to preserve her own privacy (T = 0). In her relationships Matilde gave evidence of being behaviourally passive and acquiescent in her interpersonal relationships. She seemed to subjugate her needs and wishes to those of others, to defer to whatever choices others prefer, and to accommodate their actions to satisfy the requests of those around her (a:p = 1:3). She seemed to be more comfortable being gregarious than leader, and she felt most comfortable when other people made decisions for her. She showed interest in other people and paid attention to what they say and do (H = 4 and $H:(H)+Hd+(Hd)$ = 4:3).

9.3 Therapy phase

A once-a-week therapy based mostly on supportive and not expressive (interpretative) therapist's interventions, was proposed to Matilde and accepted by her. The therapy was concluded after two years with a mutual reciprocal agreement between the patient and the therapist. At the beginning of the therapy, the therapist formulated some therapeutic goals to be reached with Matilde, following Bilhar and Carlson's (2001) suggestions. The goals were formulated on the base of the different tools administered in the assessment phase. As for affective functioning, the clinician thought it was important to provide Matilde with a psychic space to modulate affective expression, in particular concerning negative emotions. As for cognitive functioning, although Matilde in the interviews showed a good reality testing, the Rorschach test alerted the clinician of some difficulties. Above all it evidenced a decreasing of the reality testing in relation to answers in which a great primitive unexpressed anger has been shown (S-% = 33). The therapeutic goal could be to make her express and modulate the primitive rage, responsible to the lack of reality testing.

From the interpersonal point of view, Matilde tended to control herself and the situations in which is involved. But she tended to be submitted to the rules. Matilde lived this particular aspect as a limit. In this sense it was very important to help her to achieve flexibility and to explore and work on the ability to be in relation with other people. The goal could be to help Matilde to find pleasure in interpersonal relationships, supporting an adequate management of conflicts self perception. In this way she could learn to develop a way of changing which brings on a more realistic view of self, working on the perception of personal competence and ability, not only at cognitive level.

According to the therapist, the therapy process showed a good therapeutic alliance, a increasing flexibility in the defence structure and a more flexible and richer approach in interpersonal relationships. This was also confirmed by a quantitative evaluation of the alliance and of the defences (Lingiardi & Madeddu, 2002; Dazzi, Lingiardi, & Colli, 2006).

It is to be noted that during the therapy Matilde faced a very severe episode of solitude, abandonment, and separation anxiety. She was supported by the therapist, but she decided that the best way to deal with the situation was to go back home. Coming back to her parents represented for her the heaven of safety she had described in her AAP (like a nightmare which needed to be soothed by her mother). She came back more integrated and secure. We can hypothesize that in the therapy she could have faced in the transference some attachment segregated systems, which she was more able to integrate because of her secure pattern of attachment. According to clinical data emerged from AAP and therapeutic sessions, the Hypervigilance Index in the Rorschach could be explained in this particular clinical case such as a defence mechanism to better modulate and manage the presence of the Segregated System, by keeping a high level of distance and control from relationships. As explained before, she needed to return to her family, to the heaven of safety, and moving away from the therapy in a moment of deeper transference engagement, which probably had *opened the box* of the segregated system, to re-organize herself.

9.4 Post-assessment phase

The post assessment phase took place two months after the end of the two year therapy and was carried out by the same psychologist who met Matilde in test phase.

The post assessment phase included Rorschach, AAI, SCL-90 and GAF. In the post-assessment phase, the AAI was chosen to give information not only about Matilde's attachment pattern, but also on her attachment history and autobiographical experiences.

GAF

The therapist gave a score of 61 on the GAF at the second assessment: weak symptoms (depressive attitude) and some difficulties in social functioning (few friends but she seems to be interested in a boy). But it seems that her functioning is quite good (good at school and some true friends).

AAI: F2/Ds3

Matilde's AAI was scored *secure* with some restriction in feelings of attachment (F2 = somewhat dismissing or restricted in attachment; DS3 = restricted in feelings with some evidences of Lack of Memories). She was substantially free and fresh in exploring thoughts and feelings in the course of the AAI, even if she was partially defended at the beginning of the interview. But finally she was able to open herself to her experience of attachment.

Biographical information about the specific relationship with her mother and her father separately were highlighted. Matilde's mother was described in a very positive and loving way (loving), but Matilde was not always able to provide attachment related events supporting her words (idealization). Her father was depicted with more neutral and less emotional expressions, and less affectionate then her mother (rejection and pressure to achieve). Matilde appeared to be aware of the nature of experiences with her parents and about the effects of those experiences in her present state of mind and on her personality (metacognitive and coherence of mind). Although, she remained a little bit restricted in the emotional expressions, preferring to rationalize and sometime failing in recall episodes of her childhood (lack of memories).

The scores on the state of the mind scales and on the experience scales are shown in the following table.

Experience Scales				State of Mind			
	Mother	Father		Mother	Father		
Loving	7.0	5.0	Idealization	2.5	2.0	Lack of Memory	4.0
Neglect	1.0	1.5	Derogation	(2.0)	Brother	Preoccupied Anger	1
Rejection	1.5	1.5				Passivity	1
Pressure to achieve	1.0	2.5				Fear of Loss	3.0
Role Reversing	1.0	1.0				Metacognitive	3.5
						Coherency Transcript	6.0
						Coherency Mind	6.0

9.5 Comparison pre-post therapy

Managing stress adequately

Matilde maintained a consistent amount of psychological resources (EA = 8.5), but she still seemed to experience distress, both in situational and in chronic domains (D = -2 and $AdjD$ = -1). It is interesting how the pattern of stress changed from the beginning to the end of the therapy. In the assessment phase, Matilde showed a big amount of stress connected with a very fairly amount of self-blame (V = 5) and constriction (C' = 7), but she did not cognitively perceive any primitive needs (FM = 0). At the end of the therapy she became able to perceive primitive needs (FM = 5) and at the same time she was less stressed by self blame and emotional constriction (V = 2 and C' = 3).

I. Dealing with experience attentively, openly, consistently and conventionally

Two very specific unexpected patterns appeared at the end of the treatment: a shifting to a positive CDI and a shifting from an extratensive (3:6) to an ambient style (4:4.5). The positive CDI gave evidence of a cautious approach to interpersonal situations, which might contribute to a greater than average susceptibility to experiencing stress in social settings and in close involvements with others.

The ambitent style of functioning (EB) showed Matilde's lack of a consistent and well-defined coping style. At the end of the therapy she seemed to be more prone to go back and forth between expressive and ideational ways of dealing with her experience. It is possible that this feature will create in Matilde's coping style some difficulties in making decisions because she would probably pay attention both to her mind and to her feelings.

She was still overincorporator, making a great effort to grasp all details of reality, even if it seemed to be in a more limited and contained way (Zd).

One of the most important improvements regarded her approach to reality (post therapy L = .57). In the assessment phase she was overwhelmed by the complexity of reality and in the post-treatment phase she dealt with the complexity in a consistent and balanced way.

She improved also her reality testing. She seemed to be more accurate, although she continued to fail when she had to face very complicated situations ($X \% $ = .27).

II. Modulating affect pleasurably and sufficiently

About affective functioning, at the end of the treatment, Matilde still showed depressive features and some distress in term of emotions ($DEPI$ = 5).

Although at the end of the treatment Matilde tended to be basically less involved in emotional stimuli (Afr = .43), she became more able to be free in her

expression of emotions, to manage and modulate emotional material in a spontaneous and partially uncontrolled way . (*FC:CF+C* = 3:3).

Matilde appeared to continue to experience considerable emotional stress that
is interfering substantially with her pleasure in life and making her susceptible to
becoming anxious and distressed (*FM+m:SumSh* = 7:8). But the level of self-blame
(*V* = 2), and emotional constriction (*C'* = 3) appeared to be strongly diminished at
the end of the treatment. General anxiety is still present (*Y* = 3).

III. Using ideation effectively

Regarding ideational processes, Matilde showed the same well functioning
pattern both in the beginning and the end of treatment. Matilde ideational functioning appeared to be quite regular and consistent. There were no severe problems in her ideational processing: she seemed to be clear, logic and consistent
in her decision making procedures. In the post treatment test she showed a more
frequent use of fantasy as a defence mechanism to face challenging situations
(*Ma:Mp*).

IV. Examining oneself

At the end of treatment, Matilde showed a higher adaptive balance between
focusing on herself (*3r+(2)/R* = .33) and paying attention to others. She attended
to herself sufficiently but not excessively, neither avoiding self-focusing nor
becoming so self-absorbed (*Fr+rF* = 0) as to ignore what is going on in the lives
of other people.

Matilde was still not prone to be introspective (*FD* = 0). She continued to
experience chronic self-criticism and poor self-regard, and her negative attitudes
toward herself were probably promoting a sense of personal dissatisfaction.
However, when she looked at herself she was more able to see herself in a less
negative way.

V. Feeling comfortable in interpersonal relationships

Matilde still appeared to have limited ability to manage interpersonal relationships in a comfortable and rewarding manner. First, the permanence of her hypervigilant personality style (*HVI* positive) made her constantly be on alert for potential sources of threat to her safety and security. Such hypervigilance is associated
with an approach to the world in which close interpersonal relationships are viewed
with alarm and avoided in favour of keeping one's distance from others, carefully
guarding the boundaries of one's personal space, and taking pains to preserve one's
privacy (*T* = 0). She showed an interest in real people, but preferred to keep a safe
distance.

9.6 Conclusion

The different tools administered to Matilde at the beginning and at the end of her therapy gave a very complex picture of personality functioning and changes. The AAP and AAI showed a secure base from where Matilde could start to explore the word. But the AAP also showed a segregated system that unleashed in the treatment and that seemed to be integrated in the AAI discourse.

The Rorschach gave a lot of information that seemed to indicate that, although from the viewpoint of attachment Matilde was secure, something had happened to her personality structure, because she seemed to have some difficulty to deal with interpersonal relationships and with the involvement with the self. She was hypervigilant at the beginning of the treatment and remained hypervigilant at the end. Her desire for close intimate relationship is lacking. Self blame is an aspect quite present at the beginning of treatment and is still present at the end, however clearly reduced. One hypothesis for this picture can be that some primitive experience connected with segregated system could have influenced some basic feature of personality development.

10 LEGAL APPLICATION: THE ASSESSMENT OF *FUTURE PARENTS* AT THE BEGINNING OF THE ADOPTIVE PATH

S. Salcuni, A. Lis, M. Oliva

10.1 Introduction

This chapter includes some preliminary data of a wider research project focused on a specific aspect of adoption: early assessment of *future parents* who want to adopt a child (Salcuni, Ceccato, Di Riso, Lis, 2006; Salcuni, 2004).

We decided to focus on the early assessment of these *future* parents for at least two main reasons. First, from a psychological point of view, the early assessment of a parent-to-be in the adoption field has been scarcely analyzed in the existing literature; more attention has been given to assess parents and children after adoption. Second, both from psychological and forensic viewpoints, data from different countries, in which adoption is a common practice, showed a really elevated percentage of adoptive failures when the child enters the family (Levy & Orlans, 2003). Moreover, when early assessment is taken into account, procedures of assessment are not always included in a meaningful theoretical-methodological project, at least in Italy.

In Italy there are many different psychological procedures to assess the fitness or suitability to become adoptive parents, but only seldom a *multi-method* approach has been used. The use of different instruments, based on specific theories, allows the ability to transform theoretical concepts into quantitative and concrete variables, which, then, can lead to the development of both theoretical speculation and methodological applications. The psychological evaluation of parents-to-be is strictly connected to the forensic concern of gaining a best fit for the adoption. This is one of the main fields in which psychological assessment and legal concerns are linked with a non clinical population, regarding a prevention issue.

The specific purpose of this chapter is to contribute to the assessment of *adoptive future parents* at the beginning of their adoptive path, when they have to obtain the certificate of fitness to be an adoptive parent (as requested by the Italian law) and to verify how this assessment will result in the adoptive process when the child enters the family. We propose some guidelines and assessment methods related to concrete procedures that could give, in the future and after some follow-up studies, important clinical-diagnostic ability to select subjects who want to adopt, with the aim to guarantee a good resolution of the adoption.

After the presentation of the general structure of the study, we will compare two couples of parents-to-be from a qualitative clinical point of view: one of the prototypical couples who obtained the *fitness to adoption*, and one who failed to obtain it.

Comments and conclusions will be gathered analyzing the usefulness of psychological assessment in forensic evaluation of adoptive fitness, comparing qualitatively these two couples.

10.2 Background: Natural and adoptive parenthood

Transition to parenthood is a complex period in the life span, both for natural and for adoptive parents-to-be. Many authors highlighted some similarities and some differences in these two conditions (Belsky, 1984; Belsky, Herzog & Rovine, 1985; Feldman & Nash, 1985; Levy-Shiff, Bar, & Har-Even, 1990; Levy-Shiff et al., 1991; Noy-Sharav, 2002; Levy & Orlans, 2003; Johnson & Whiffen, 2003; Zavattini 2006). Many studies about transition to parenthood focused on the study of the Internal Working Models, coping and adjustment style, expression and modulation of affects, ability to mentalize (Fonagy, ANNO) and detect feelings and thoughts of self and others. Specifically for adoptive couples, studies have focused on the possibility to give to the child a real sense of belonging in the adoptive family (Levy & Orlans, 2003), and the presence of a family-social environment able to facilitate and accept the child's diversity (Kadushin, 1964, 1980). Many of these personality characteristics are theoretically linked to the early care giving experiences of nurturance parents-to-be experienced in their infancy. Consequently, many studies were conducted with respect to evaluation of attachment and transition to natural or adoptive parenthood.

Main topics concerning adoptive parenthood were carried out studied in the literature, such as conceptualization of adoption in the family life-span context (Carter & McGoldrick, 1980; Duvall, 1977); the analysis of specific stressors linked with this path (Brodzinsky, Lang & Smith,1995); its particular developmental goals and complexity (Brodzinsky, 1987; Hajal & Rosemberg, 1991) and the relevance of this choice as a *second chance* (Kirk, 1964) derived by infertility and, consequently, its bond with narcissistic features (Shapiro, 1988; Noy-Sharav, 2002).

The importance of an early assessment has been stressed and many studies were conducted on exclusion criteria and risk factors in the adoption path, such as psychopathological aspects of both individuals and couples (Rosenthal, Schmidt & Conner, 1988), and early losses, separation and divorces in parents' families (Hoopes, 1982; Kraus, 1978; Brodzinsky & Brodzinsky, 1992; Kaye, 1990; Brodzinsky et al., 1993; Cadoret, 1990; Rosenthal, Schmidt, & Conner, 1988). However, scarce attention was paid to studies related to individual's personality characteristics, with specific attention on cognitive, affective and relational strengths and resources needed to guarantee a good outcome of adoption (Belsky, 1984; Belsky, Herzog & Rovine, 1985; Feldman & Nash, 1985; Johnson & Whiffen, 2003). Only very few studies used the Rorschach to investigate the personality structure (Noy-Sharav, 2002).

Research had revealed an important role the family can play in helping or provoking pathological reaction to environment adjustment. This is a very important topic in the adoption field because of the significant distress often adopted children had. Of particular relevance to development of psychosis or relational psychopathology is the level of *expressed emotion* (yelling, shouting, fighting, or critical or hostile comments) and stress that is in the environment (Stubbe, Zahnen, Goldstein & Leckman, 1993). Research has demonstrated that individuals from families with high *expressed emotion* are 3.7 times more likely to relapse than those in families with a low level of expressed emotion. Family members's attitudes can affect the level of good or bad adjustment (Vostanis et al., 1994). Neither the tendency to become critical or actively hostile towards the individuals belonging to the family (child included), or to become very upset and emotionally over- involved, are desirable. Either or both of these attitudes in caregivers (i.e. criticism or over- involvement) have been described as *high expressed emotion*. If they become extreme, they have been found to lead to poorer outcome both in psychopathological rehabilitation and in adoptive field, and to increase psychotic experiences. In contrast, people living in more supportive, tolerant, low expressed emotion environments tend to have a lower development of psychotic experiences, better social functioning, and better outcome (Magana, 1986; Weiss, 2002).

10.3 Plan of Research: Phases and aims

The aim of this research is to identify in *future adoptive parents* factors that can favor or prevent an adequate transition to adoptive parenthood.

A first step was to build up a theoretical profile based on the existing literature and previous data (Salcuni & Lis, 2004). Then, through a comparison between a theoretical profile and a real profile taken from an experimental procedure of assessment of adoptive parent-to-be, we were able to identify some concrete guidelines for fitness to adopt. Personality characteristics based on theoretical and empirical formulations can delineate a good *baseline* to detect adoptive future parents who are "good enough", that is full of psychological resources, emotionally stable and free in attachment to be able to adequately receive these children.

First, we studied the existing literature on adoptive parenthood and the adoptive family, with the aim of highlighting some basic characteristics of the *adequate adoptive parent*. Following Bihlar and Carlsson's guidelines (2001), we have chosen some structural personality variables that seem to define a good baseline to the adoptive task (Noy-Sharav, 2002; Brodzinsky & Huffman, 1988; Levy-Shiff, Bar, & Har-Even, 1990; Levy-Shiff et al., 1991; American Academy of Pediatric, 1999; Brodzinsky & Schechter, 1990; Levy & Orlans, 2003). Based on the international literature, we also chose to analyze fantasies, levels of expressed emotions and state of mind regarding attachment. It is important to emphasize that our aim was not to flatten inter-subjects differences, creating a completely homogeneous profile for all of them. Instead, we tried to find theoretically a common personality background, which can identify some fundamental characteristics for a good adoptive parenthood. Within this basic profile subjects will be able to express their own peculiarities. At the end of the literature review, the theoretical *good adoptive parent* profile that emerged was a *good enough parent* (Winnicott, 1960; Lichtenberg, 1989; Russek & Schwartz, 1997), who is able to recognize and to respect the new child's specific identity and problems (Fonagy & Target, 2001). He/She might show a low level of idealization, a free attachment pattern to propose him/her self as a secure base (Bowlby, 1969), low idealization and few exaggerate positive fantasies, low level of expressed emotion (Alpert, Richardson & Fodasky, 1983; Hopkins, Marcus & Campbell, 1984; Tessier, Piche, Tarabulsy & Muckle, 1992), no pathological features and better abilities in relationships, affective modulation and self perception (Noy-Sharav, 2002; Greenberg & Mitchell, 1983) than the natural parents.

The second phase of the study, through a multi-method approach, was to empirically estimate personality characteristics, attitudes, fantasies about the possible future child and the state of the mind regarding attachment, of real couples wishing to become adoptive parents. There were 40 recruited couples (males mean age 42.13, SD = 6.05; females mean age 41.98, SD = 6.45; years of marriage 10.09 ys, SD = 7.00; Hollingshead's SES = 5.03) in three Italian Services in which specialized teams worked to assess their fitness to become adoptive parents. At the beginning of the process, all applicants were assessed using the research assessment instruments for their fitness to adopt. Some important data on 29 of these couples showed the following: a partial sterility in 62% of them with 5 couples totally sterile; the presence of natural sons in 5 couples (8%); history of pharmacological interventions (62%) and natural abortions (4 couples, 10%). These anamnesis data were very similar to data found in literature (Levy-Shiff, Bar, & Har-Even, 1990; Levy-Shiff et al., 1991; Noy-Sharav, 2002).

We administered different instruments in two separated sessions. In the first session, we administered a brief shedule to the couples about how and why they had decided to adopt, the level of their motivation to adopt and some characteristics of the couple itself. The Semantic Differential (SD), titled *My Child* (Lis & Zennaro, 1997) and the Five-Minute-Speech-Sample (FMSS; Magaña, 2000) were given to each parent separately, in order to evaluate fantasies, representations of the future child and the level of *expressed emotion* in the family environment. In the second session, the Adult Attachment Interview (AAI; George et al., 1984, 1985, 1996; Main & Goldwyn, 1998) and the Rorschach test, according to Exner's Comprehensive System (RCS; 1991, 1993) were administered to each parent separately, in order to estimate the state of the mind regarding adult attachment and the structure of personality. The reliability in administration and scoring for each tool was given, according to the author's guidelines.

At the end of the experimental phase, all the data were processed and discussed at a quantitative and qualitative level. Specific attention was given to the comparison between the basic characteristics of the theoretically adequate adoptive parents' profile, which has emerged from the literature (Phase One), and the real adoptive parents' profile (Phase Two).

10.4 Results

The adoptive couples showed higher level of idealization and no differences in four factors of Semantic Differential between adoptive mothers and fathers (Activity and dauntlessness; Pleasure of aroused emotions; Expected Satisfaction; Personality strength). This finding is in contrast with couples eith natural pregnancy (Zennaro and al., 1997), who always indicated a higher level of positive fantasies than the adoptive parents-to-be: this could pose a problem, because the child will bring his problematic background into the new family, creating a big difference from these idealized representations.

The results on our 40 couples showed, as expected, that a low percentage of subjects had a pathological level of expressed emotion in FMSS: only five people showed a *high expressed emotion*, which is clinically linked to a higher risk of developing psychopathology, worse social functioning, and a worse outcome of adoption.

With respect with attachment patterns distribution of AAI, we found 47,5% (N = 38) of subjects were Free, 30% (N = 24) Dismissing, 17.5% (N = 14) Entangled and 5% (N = 4) with Unresolved Losses.

The matching of the couples, with respect to attachment patterns, showed many different combinations. Eight couples were Free individuals (F-F 20%); fourteen couples were Free and Dismissing individuals (F-DS 35%) and six couples were Free and Entangled subjects (F-E 15%). Two couples were Free and Unresolved people (F-U 5%). Three couples were Entangled subjects (E-E 7.5) and other three couples were Dismissing subjects (DS-DS 7.5). Two couples were Dismissing and Entangled (DS-E 5%) and two couples were Dismissing and Unresolved (DS-U 5%).

The Rorschach profile of our 80 future adoptive parents was not very different from the normative Italian population (Salcuni, 2004; Salcuni, et. al., 2006). They showed: strong motivation to adopt (*W:M*); strong and particular individuality (high *Xu%*); good affective modulation and average stress tolerance; high presence of painful affect (Sum*V* and Sum*C'*); good introspective capacity (*FD*), and normal flexibility to adaptation. They also showed a normal capacity in self-perception and in relationship abilities. The subjects didn't have either a *special* ability in relationships or in Ego strength, but they showed a particular capacity to be introspective, maybe for their infertility problems had brought them to think about their own affective state and capacity to create life.

Comparing the *theoretical* profile and *real* profile of adoptive future parents, we noticed that these parents were very similar to the normative population regarding FMSS trend and the Rorschach profile. Most of our group met our theoretical standard regarding adaptation and absence of psychopathology (Rorschach), affective modulation and low level of expressed emotions (FMSS, Rorschach) and Free AAI's IWM.

On the other hand, a few couples (specifically in their matching as couple, such as DS-E or DS-U) did not show an adequate amount of capacities that we hypothesized would be useful to become adoptive-parent-to-be.

The results of the psychological profiles of these following two couples (the most adequate and the less adequate) went in the same direction as the forensic legal decision to give or not give them the fitness for adoption.

10.4.1 Mr. and Mrs. A: a couple that was successfully considered fit for adoption

Mr. A was a 37 year old man, who worked as bank employee. He was married to Mrs. A, a 35 year old woman, who worked as shop assistant. They married six years before the assessment. They decided to begin the adoption path because they wished to adopt a child, because of their infertility. They had a very nice family environment, which created a strong net around them and their problems. Neither of them was in psychotherapy.

Mr. A's Semantic Differential

Globally, the profile of Mr. A's SD indicates a tendency to idealize the future child, as always happens with adoptive couples. Mr. A compared with the normative group of natural fathers-to-be during pregnancy period described a fantasy child as not too active, strong in personality, expressing emotion and pleasure, and satisfying.

Mr. A's Five Minutes Speech Sample

Low Expressed Emotion.

Mr. A's Adult Attachment Interview

Mr. A's AAI was scored prototypically continuous secure/autonomous (F3a). In addition to a marked overall coherence of transcript, he rarely manifested even low levels of idealization of the parents. He always exhibited good memories of his childhood's episodes in a clear and objective way, with high levels of straightforward spontaneity and flexibility. He was substantially free and fresh in exploring thoughts and feelings in the course of the AAI, and he was able to open himself to his experience of attachment. Although in some episodes reported parents had negative neglecting features, he was able to describe them clearly, without any discourse derogations or angrily preoccupied expressions.

Biographical information about his relationship with his mother and father was highlighted. He described his mother in a very positive and loving way, and he was able to explain and forgive her for some neglecting episodes in childhood, with high levels of metacognitive monitoring about the reasons of her behaviours. The relationship with his father was very collaborative, affective and caring and he could keep in his mind this caregiving figure as the most important and present in his childhood. He appeared to be aware of the nature of experiences with his parents and about the effects of those experiences in his present state of mind and on his personality, and he felt very grateful even if he could recognized that they were not perfect.

Mr. A's Rorschach

Mr. A gave a valid protocol that provided reliable information and supported valid interpretation. He did not present any positive psychopathological features, such as Perceptual Thinking Index, or Depression Index or Coping Deficit Index. The key variables from which we started the interpretation are the following: (a) $D < AdjD$, (b) $SumSh > Fm+m$.

These indexes gave us basic initial information we needed to pay attention to, during the entire Rorschach analysis. He seemed to have a big amount of resources, good quality reality testing, good interpersonal perception, but he showed some liabilities in situational stress management (*D*) and he experienced a certain degree of distress (*SumSb>Fm+m*). His interpretative search strategy was: Controls - Situation stress - affect - self perception –interpersonal perception - processing - mediation - ideation.

Controls

Mr. A showed an ambitent style of functioning (*EB*): he did not have a specific and clear way to deal with both internal and external demands when managing his experience. He went back and forth between emotional and ideational resources. He was quite overwhelmed by the complexity of reality (*L*) although he had a good amount of psychological resources (*EA*) that did allow him to manage chronicle stress (*AdjD*). On the other hand Mr. A showed some difficulties to manage situational stress (D) at which he used to react with situational anxiety (*Y*).

Affect

Mr. A seemed to be able to recognize affective issues, but he showed some problems in emotional expression (*SumC'>WsumC*): in fact, he experienced some amount of distress (*SumSb>FM+M*), seemed to be constricting his emotional expression (*C'*) and, according to this emotional pattern, he seemed to be concerned about maintaining a personal space (*T*). When he tried to express his emotional internal world, he modulated it excessively (*FC>Cf+C*). This means that he did not become easily engaged in affectively charged situations (*Afr*). This aspect did not necessarily preclude Mr. A's being interested in interactions, but when strong feelings would come up in the relationships, he would often tend to break off. Mr. A showed some evidence of oppositional tendencies (*S*).

Self-Perception

Mr. A's identity did seem to be based on realistic identification but he was not really focused on his self (*EgoIndex*): it means that he didn't usually pay much attention to his personal value (*Fr+rF*) or his negative or disphoric features (*MOR* and *V*). He was usually concerned about physical issues (*An+Xy*), although he seemed to have a good introspective capacity (*FD*). This could be interpreted as a good prognostic indicator in order to start a psychotherapeutic program.

Interpersonal Perception

Mr. A seemed to consider interpersonal relationships as a meaningful dimension of his experience (Isolation Index); specifically he usually had a representation of interactions both good and cooperative (*COP* and *AG*). He seemed to be adapted in his interpersonal relations (*GHR:PHR*), although he often showed a tendency to have an unclear idea of others, about who they are and what they thought (*H*). Although he did not seem to engage in relationship with others in a passive or dependent way (*a:p* and Food), he used a defensive way in approaching others: he had the tendency to demonstrate his knowledge with the aim of reassuring himself (*PER*). As a consequence, he seemed to preserve his personal space during the interactions (*T*).

Processing

Mr. A showed a consistent pattern of processing that means he usually balanced the processing of meaningful and useless details (*Zd*). Although he showed a strong achievement orientation, he was not able to balance resources at his disposal with his goals (*W:M*). Moreover, in dealing with processing experience he made a huge effort to put together and integrate different parts of the stimulus (*Zf*, *W:D:Dd*). As a consequence, most of the time Mr. A did not show an efficient processing quality especially in complex situations (*DQ+* and *DQv*).

Mediation

Mr. A's reality testing is good and consistent (*X-%* and *S-%*), he seemed to strive to analyze reality as accurate as he could (*WDA%*, *XA%*). However, she seemed to have an original way to perceive people and events (*Xu%*) and he read reality in a subjective and more individualistic way (*P*).

Ideation

Mr. A showed a good and consistent ideational organization. First, he seemed to be flexible in his ideational production (*a:p*) and his thoughts seemed to be clear, logic and precise (*Sum6*, *WSum6*, *Lvl-2*). In his ideational functioning Mr. A did not use defences such as intellectualization in order to neutralize emotional content (*Intellectual Index*) or escaping into a fantasy world in order to avoid fearful aspects of reality (*Ma:Mp*).

Mrs. A's Semantic Differential

Globally, the profile of Mrs. A's SD indicates a tendency to idealize the future child, as always happens with adoptive couples. Compared with the normative group of natural mothers-to-be during pregnancy period, Mrs. A described a fantasy child as not too much active, strong in personality, expressing emotion and pleasure, and satisfying.

Mrs. A's Five Minutes Speech Sample

Low Expressed Emotion.

Mrs. A's Adult Attachment Interview

Mrs. A's AAI was scored secure with some restriction in feelings of attachment (F2). She presented a moderate lack of memories of her childhood, moderate idealization of her father and some evidence of fear of loss of a child through death. However, she was ultimately characterized by expressions of affection, compassion, humour and forgiveness that gave her the ability to value the importance of attachment relationships. Although she was partially defended at the beginning of the interview, she finally was able to open up about herself to her experience of attachment.

Biographical information about the specific relationship with her mother and her father separately was highlighted. Her mother was described in a very positive and loving way, her memories had intense and clear episodes. Her father was depicted quite idealized, but the episodes showed he had some neutral and less affectionate expression than her mother (some neglecting and pressure to achieve). She appeared to be aware of the nature of experiences with her parents and about the effects of those experiences in her present state of mind and on her personality, but she remained a little restricted in her emotional expressions, preferring to rationalize and sometime failing to recall episodes of her childhood.

Mrs. A's Rorschach

Mrs. A gave a valid protocol that provides reliable information and supports valid interpretation. She did not present any positive psychopathological features. The key variables from which we started the interpretation are the following: (a) $D < AdjD$, (b) $L > .99$.

These indexes gave us basic initial information we needed to pay attention to during the Rorschach analysis: Mrs. A presented some problems related to a contingent stress situation an, as a strategy to manage life complexity, she tended to oversimplify reality ($L > .99$).

Mrs. A interpretative search strategy was: Controls – Processing – Mediation – Ideation –Affect - Self perception - Interpersonal perception.

Controls

Mrs. A had a good amount of psychological resources (EA) that allow her to manage both situational and chronic stress (D and $AdjD$), but she showed an ambient style of functioning (EB): she did not have a specific and clear way of facing both internal and external demands in dealing with her experiences. She went back and forth between emotional and ideational resources. It is very important to note that Mrs. A showed an avoiding style when facing reality, which means that she had a tendency to oversimplify the complexity of reality. As a consequence she did not seem to experience a significant amount of distress (es and $Adjes$) and she did not pay attention to her unsatisfied needs (FM). This flat profile seemed to justify the apparent adjusted stress management (D and $AdjD$). However, she had a situational peripheral ideation (m) that could interfere with concentration and attention.

Processing

Mrs. A showed a overincorporating processing style, which means that she had a tendency to pay a lot of attention to all the details of reality (Zd). In order to maintain such a style, she made a great affort (Zf), but with some difficulties, to integrate the different aspects of reality, showing a very economical way of processing ($W:D:Dd$) and a quite simple quality of processing ($DQ+$).

Mediation

Mrs. A's reality testing was good and consistent ($WDA\%$ e $XA\%$) but sometimes she failed in preciseness and accuracy: especially if she had to manage emotions of anger, she could show a less precise mediation pattern.

Ideation

Mrs. A did not show a very good and consistent ideational organization. Her thoughts were not always clear, logic and precise in decision making and judgment capacity ($Sum6$, $WSum6$, $M-$). Her ideational functioning seemed to be flexible ($a{:}p$) and she tended to fly to fantasy in order to avoid the fearful aspects of reality ($Ma{:}Mp$).

Affect

Mrs. A seemed to be able to recognize affective material and she was able to express it in a fresh and lively way ($FC{:}CF+C$). She easily engaged in emotionally charged situations (Afr) and she did not show problems in emotional expression ($SumC'<WsumC$). Although she showed some evidences of oppositional tendencies (S).

Self-Perception

Mrs. A's identity seemed to be based on realistic identifications ($H>(H)+Hd+(Hd)$). But she preferred to focus on other people than on herself ($EgoIndex$) and, as a consequence, she did not seem to have a good introspective capacity (FD). Moreover, she usually didn't pay attention to her personal value ($Fr+rF$) or her negative or dysphonic features about her internal world and body (MOR and V, $An+Xy$).

Interpersonal Perception

Mrs. A seemed to consider interpersonal relationships as a meaningful dimension of her experience and she usually had a good and cooperative representation of interactions (*COP* and *AG*). She seemed to be adapted in his interpersonal relations (*GHR:PHR*), and showed a tendency to have a clear idea of others, and about who they were and what they thought (*H*). She did not seem to engage in relations with others in a passive or dependent way (*a:p* and *food*), although he used a slightly defensive approach to others, and she sometimes had the tendency to demonstrate her knowledge trying to reassure herself (*PER*). As a consequence, she showed the need to preserve her personal space during the interactions (*T*).

10.4.2 Mr. and Mrs. B: a couple that did not qualify fit for adoption

Mr. B was a 42 year old man, who worked as a paramedic. He was married with Mrs. B, a 38 year old woman, who was a teacher in high school. They got married 12 years before the evaluation. They decided to begin the adoptive path after many failed medical trials, such as hormonal therapy and artificial insemination, with the result of several abortions. They had a very nice family environment, which created a strong net around them and their problems. Neither of them was in psychotherapy.

Mr. B's Semantic Differential

Globally, the profile of Mr. B's SD indicates a tendency to idealize the future child, as always happens with adoptive couples. In fact, compared with the normative group of natural fathers-to-be, during the pregnancy period Mr. B showed a fantasy child as not too much active, strong in personality, expressing emotion and pleasure, and satisfying.

Mr. B's Five Minutes Speech Sample

Mr. B's FMSS was scored High Expressed Emotion, because of the presence of significant over-involvement and self-sacrifice attitude. This finding is clinically linked to a higher risk of developing psychopathology, worse social functioning, and worse outcome of adoption.

Mr. B's Adult Attachment Interview

Mr. B's AAI was coded angry/conflicted attachment (E2). He was unable to go beyond the topic addressed by the interviewer in order to detail difficulties with mother and father, recounting specific incidents which continually troubled him and his own reactions of distress and anger.

Episodes were very general and unspecific for both mother and father. Current active resentment toward parents (*mother anger* and *father anger*) was found and he seemed to be unable to distinguish between them. Parents were extensive blamed for their past and present behaviours and his relationship with them was mostly described such as conflictual at the present moment. Many features of passive and rambling attachment-related discourse (*passivity*) were found, such as run on sentences off the topic, psychobabble, and jargon to describe and analyze his relationships. No awareness, forgiveness or metacognitive monitoring of the nature of his experiences with parents and about the effects of those experiences in the present state of mind and on his personality, were detected.

Mr. B's Rorschach

Mr. B gave a valid protocol that provides reliable information and supports valid interpretation. He presented one positive affective psychopathological key entry, the Depression Index. This index gave us basic initial information we should pay attention to, during the Rorschach analysis: Mr. B gave evidence of a significant affective disturbance, which was likely to be associated with either a Major Depression Disorder or a chronic disposition to becoming depressed. He's interpretative search strategy was: Affect – Controls - Situational stress - Self perception – Interpersonal perception - Processing - Mediation - Ideation.

Affect

Mr. B seemed to be able to recognize affective material, and did not show any problems in emotional expression ($SumC'<WsumC$) even though some constriction appeared (C'). In spite of this, he experienced a big amount of distress ($SumSh>FM+M$), and showed as a defence mechanism a tendency to control and deny all his primitive needs (FM), and the need to maintain a personal space (T). He often became excessively engaged in affectively charged situations (Afr) and when it happened, he excessively modulated his emotional internal world ($FC>Cf+C$), experiencing a very intense situational anxiety (Y). Mr. B showed some evidence of oppositional tendencies (S) and his rage always made him lose his reality testing functioning (S-).

Controls

Mr. B showed an ambitent style of functioning (EB): he did not have a specific and clear way in coping with both internal and external demands while dealing with his experiences. He went back and forth between emotional and ideational resources. He used a strategy to oversimplify the complexity of reality (L) although he had a normal amount of psychological resources (EA) that did allow him to manage situational (D) and chronic stress ($AdjD$).

Self-Perception

Mr. B's identity did not seem to be based on realistic identifications and he did not focus on himself ($EgoIndex$): This means that he didn't usually pay attention to his personal value ($Fr+rF$) and when he did paid attention, he considered himself having negatives features (V). He usually was concerned about physical issues ($An+Xy$). He did not have a good introspective capacity (absence of FD).

Interpersonal Perception

Mr. B seemed to consider interpersonal relationships as a meaningful dimension of his experience (*Isol.Index*), but he was not able to give a particular quality to interactions, neither as cooperative or aggressive representations (absence of *COP* and *AG*). He seemed to be adapted in his interpersonal relations (*GHR:PHR*), although he often had a tendency to not have a clear idea of others, or about who they were and what they thought (*H*). He used a defensive manner in approaching others and he showed the tendency to emphasize his knowledge as a way to reassure himself (*PER*). As a consequence, he seemed to preserve his personal space during the interactions (*T*).

Processing

Mr. B showed a very poor and impulsive processing pattern (underincorporator style) which means he was not able to balance the processing of meaningful and useless details (*Zd*), and he gave responses without thinking. Although he showed a strong achievement orientation, he was not able to balance resources at his disposal with his goals (*W:M*). Most of the time, Mr. B did not show an efficient processing quality, especially in complex situations (*DQv*).

Mediation

Mr. B's reality testing was mildly good (*WDA%, XA%*). He seemed to have an original way to perceive people and events (*Xu%*). Every time he became angry he felt unable to cope with it and his reality testing deteriorated greatly (*X-%* and *S-%*). He read reality in a subjective and very individualistic way (*P*).

Ideation

Mr. B showed a good and consistent ideational functioning. He was quite flexible in his ideational production (*a:p*) and his thoughts seemed to be enough logical and precise (*Sum6, WSum6, Lvl-2*). In his ideational functioning Mr. B did not use any kind of defence, such as intellectualization in order to neutralize emotional content (*Intellectual Index*) or escape into a fantasy world in order to avoid reality's fearful aspects (*Ma:Mp*).

Mrs. B's Semantic Differential

Globally, the profile of Mrs. B's SD indicates some tendency to idealize the future child, as always happens with adoptive couples. In fact, compared with the normative group of natural mothers-to-be, during pregnancy period, Mrs. B's fantasy child was not too active, strong in personality, expressing emotion and pleasure, and satisfying.

Mrs. B's Five Minutes Speech Sample

Low Expressed Emotion.

Mrs. B's Adult Attachment Interview

Mrs. B's AAI was scored Dismissing of attachment (DS1). In her Experience scales, she presented low levels of Loving experiences, both from mother and father. No real affective comfort, care, protection and loving physical contact with parents during childhood were described and, if present, they were functional only to satisfy concrete needs. Rejection and neglecting scales were very high for her father's behaviours of refusal and avoidance, and her experiences of her mother's behaviours underlined a highly neglecting attitude. Ultimately, she completely endorsed both of them, and even though some resentment was present it was total-ly unexpressed. No Involving/Role-Reversing aspects were found. The inability to recall events from childhood (*lack of memory*) was very present and she showed a strong tendency to idealize her mother, and to normalize and minimize childhood experiences with her father. The overall scoring for coherence in the transcript was very low: the interview on the whole appeared unemotional, planned and she emphasized herself and her family as normal.

Mrs. B's Rorschach

Mrs. B gave a valid protocol that provided reliable information and allowed a valid interpretation. The key variable from which we begun the interpretation was *CDI > 3*.

This index gave us an initial information from which to organize the whole Rorschach analysis: Mrs. B seemed to have some interpersonal coping deficits and difficulties. Her interpretative strategy was: Controls - Interpersonal Perception - Self Perception - Affect - Processing - Mediation - Ideation

Controls

Mrs. B showed an ambient style of functioning (*EB*): she did not have a spe-cific and clear way to cope with both internal and external demands when dealing with her experiences. She went back and forth between emotional and ideational resources, which were sparse (*EA*). The most meaningful feature of her approach seemed to be that she oversimplified her reality analysis: This means she was unable to pay attention to different aspects of reality at once (*L*). She had a tenden-cy to ignore external and internal demands and as a consequence she did not seem to experience any kind of stress (*D* and *AdjD*) or dysphonic feelings (*V, C'*).

Interpersonal Perception

Although Mrs. B did not seem to be isolated (Isolation Index), she did not consider interpersonal relationships as a fundamental and meaningful part of her experience (absence of *COP* and *AG*). During her interpersonal exchanges she had a tendency to assume a passive role (*a:p*), conforming to others point of view, but at the same time she seemed to preserve her personal space showing clear difficulties in deep and intimate relationships (*T*).

Self-Perception

Mrs. B's identity seemed to be based on unrealistic identification (*H<(H)+Hd+(Hd)*) and she was not really focused on herself at all (*EgoIndex*). She presented a lack of introspective capacity (*FD*) and as a consequence she didn't usually pay attention about herself, but when this happened, she felt feelings of blame (*V*). She usually concerned about physical issues (*An+Xy*).

Affect

Mrs. B's emotional world seemed to be very poor, and she had the tendency to express her feelings in an unmodulated way (*FC<CF+C*). As a matter of fact she felt a great amount of rage and an oppositional attitude (*S*).

Processing

Mrs. B showed a very economical processing pattern that means she usually was not able to take into consideration all the useful details of reality (*W:D:Dd*). In her information processing she did not seem to be able to discriminate the fundamental aspects of reality, paying attention to unusual elements (*Dd*). As a consequence, most of the time Mrs. B did not show an efficient processing quality, especially in complex situations (*DQ+* and *DQv*).

Mediation

Mrs. B's reality testing was usually good and consistent (*X-%* and *S-%*), but sometimes she seemed to fail in her usual perceptual accuracy and preciseness (*X+%* and *Xu%*). She preferred an original way to perceive people and events (*Xu%*) and seemed to read the reality in a very subjective and highly individualistic way even in simple and well-defined situation, without paying attention to social expectations (*P*).

Ideation

Mrs. B showed a good and consistent ideational functioning. She seemed to be flexible in her ideational production (*a:p*) and her thoughts seemed to be clear, logic and precise (*Sum6, WSum6, Lvl-2*). In her ideational functioning Mrs. B did not use any kind of defence, such as intellectualization in order to neutralize emotional content (*Intellectual index*) or by escaping into a fantasy world in order to avoid the fearful aspects of reality (*Ma:Mp*).

Summary table: Results on tools for two couples.

	Couple A		Couple B	
Tools	Mr. A	Mrs. A	Mr. B	Mrs.B
SD	Idealize	Idealize	Idealize	Idealize
FMSS	Low Expressed Emotion	Low Expressed Emotion	High Expressed Emotion (hyper involvement and criticism)	Low Expressed Emotion
AAI	F3a. Prototypical secure autonomous	F2. Secure with some restriction in feelings of attachment	E2. Angrily and conflict-ed preoccupied	DS1. Dismissing of attachment
Rorschach CS	D < AdjD SumSh>Fm+m	D < AdjD, (b) L>.99,	DEPI positive	CDI>3
Fitness	Yes		No	

10.5 Conclusions

In the Italian Services involved in the procedures to determine *fitness to adopt*, a high percentage of our couples reached the standard to adopt: two out of 40 couples abandoned the research; 11 couples had not finished their assessment process yet; and of the 38 remaining couples, 22 were accepted as fit to adopt; only five were not accepted.

A good resolution of adoption is a very complex and difficult goal to reach, because of the many variables (child, couple, single parents, age, special needs...) involved.

Looking at the two couples we used as examples, it is easy to notice that only few characteristics distinguish the couple who was given permission for adoption fitness from the couple who wasn't. They both present almost similar trends in SD variables, showing a tendency to idealize in their fantasy about the qualities of the future child, and are similar to natural parents during pregnancy.

With respect to the other tools, the couple A, who was allowed to adopt, showed a substantially Free attachment pattern, a definitively low level of Expressed

Emotion in the family environment and no psychopathological features in the Rorschach. In contrast, couple B showed a insecure matching of attachment (E-DS), higher Expressed Emotion, and both the Rorschach protocols showed psychopathological elements.

It is very interesting to compare the Rorschach protocols of couple A and couple B. Even if couple A did not present psychopathological features, they are not *perfect*. They present several small problems in controls, specifically in relation to manage situational stress. These features ($D < AdjD$, with $AdjD = 0$) were a common finding in the couples we tested during our research, and it is possible to hypothesize that this might be linked with the adoptive process itself. Couple A was differentiated from couple B by their better interpersonal abilities and the self perception features they presented. Even if they are not perfect people, they are *good enough* to be considered fit to adopt, in contrast to couple B who presented more difficulties, in both affective and relational coping features.

It seems that, in the Italian Services, the trend is *better two average parents than no parents at all*, thereby only excluding strong relational and personality psychopathology.

The use of a multi-method assessment, combining a self-report questionnaire with personality and attachment tools, seems to provide the best profile in order to discriminate and predict both the parent-to-be capacity in the future relationship with the adoptive child, and a forensic decision on the adoptive fitness. As shown, only SD self-reports were unable to distinguish between couple A and couple B. The FMSS gave a more accurate view of emotional reaction and management, and, above all, AAI and the Rorschach were able to give an adequate and deep profile.

The data are encouraging and supports the carrying out of this research and to use a combination of different and complex measures of the personality. With this multi-method approach, we are able to find better strategies and interventions, based on a solid research ground, to assist people during the transition to adoptive parenthood and during the adoptive process itself.

CONCLUSIONS

A.Lis, C. Mazzeschi, S. Salcuni, D. Di Riso

The aim of this volume was to describe how attachment can be useful in clinical setting. The first part of the volume was devoted to a description of Bowlby's model, stressing the importance of attachment for mental health development and personality. Bowlby's concepts originated many different pathways of research and clinical studies. Although we briefly mentioned some of them, our attention was focused on two main topics: psychopathology and psychotherapy outcome, and attachment measures. We presented a brief review of empirical studies carried out on attachment and DSM categorizations, distinguishing between Axis I and Axis II and according to measures of attachment pattern and measures of attachment status. We thought it is very important to provide clinicians with an overview of how many studies have been carried out on the topic. However we would like to stress how much attention in these studies are based on a nomothetic association between attachment and psychopathology. Most of them still were able to confirm an association between insecurity of attachment and psychopathology.

In the second part of this volume two chapters are devoted to a detailed description of two measures of attachment pattern: the *golden standard way* to measure attachment patterns, the AAI, and a new measure, the AAP. The AAI and the AAP lead to a classification of attachment according to Bowlby categorization. However, from a clinician perspective, both instruments share two clear disadvantages:

a) They cannot be considered as *neutral* instruments. The AAI involves the individual in a revision of the history of his personal early experiences; the AAP allows the individual, although not directly autobiographically, to face themes of separation, sickness and death. All these elements are highly emotionally involving and potentially stressful. Administering the AAI or the AAP means to accompany the patients in a very dynamically involved process, very different from the one displayed by the items of a self-report questionnaire on attachment. We think anyway that this is very rewarding for the patient and the clinician, as we hope has been demonstrated in the third part of the volume.

b) Although the final classification is very simple, to reach the classification requires following a complicated pathway which requires a specific and complex training (with the acquisition of reliability) for the scoring. Moreover it requires a clinical comprehension of the dynamics of attachment to really understand the protocol.

The other two instruments to which we have devoted space were the MMPI and the Rorschach. The MMPI is the only *descriptive* instrument in this volume. We proposed it because it is a personality inventory so well known and frequently used. As we have seen, few studies have been devoted to the relationship between MMPI and attachment. Their aim was to find associations between personality profiles and attachment. They were nomothetic studies. We ought to have more of them.

In the literature more attention was given to *Rorschach and attachment*. In our review we have made a distinction between three categories of studies: AAI and Rorschach variables, questionnaires on attachment and Rorschach variables, and attachment variables in the Rorschach. About attachment variables in the Rorschach we think that, on the one hand it is important to detect variables connected with interpersonal and self perception and to see if they can be connected with attachment, but we would like to stress that this could offer a very weak connection with attachment that, as we have seen is a very specific kind of tie. Further research is needed: a) to clarify construct and concept of attachment and how can be measured with the Rorschach; b) to develop an attachment measure that is more finely-tuned and efficient in making differentiations among attachment styles; c) to understand, if possible, how attachment theory and attachment measures can be integrated into a psychological assessment battery.

Attachment theory, as we have stressed in our first chapter, is not a vague theory about relatedness, even if there are consequences for interpersonal relationships. Research studies need to make more explicit their theoretic constructs and the variables that mediate or not the resulting correlations. For instance, we need more explicit hypotheses such as that supported by Priel (2001) who assumed that, while conceptualizations of attachment behavior and internal working models grasp the early patterns of interpersonal relationships and affect regulations, object representations indicate current transformations of these patterns in an individual's internal world.

The studies we have reviewed in the first two parts of this volume are mostly correlational. They focus in establishing correlations between attachment and psychopathology. In this approach, the data derived from one instrument are treated out of context from the data derived from other instruments and sources of information. Such a strategy is perfect for validation studies. However such a strategy does not help the assessment clinician who is never concerned with just a single scale. Rather, an assessment clinician works ideographically (focused on the uniqueness of the person) and tries to find a meaningful pattern of information within the data generated by many scales, drawn from several testing methods, along with observations of the patient and information drawn from his or her history. Beside nomothetic relationships between different measures of attachment patterns and styles, ideographic relationships can be found and are useful to a better assessment of each single patient.

The aim of the third part of the book was to introduce a model of multi-method ideographic approach to assessment in which attachment is meant to play a basic role. We are aware that our clinical examples do not cover a wide range of psychopathology or clinical relevance.

Our approach was carried out mostly using measures of patterns and instruments based on personality performance (Rorschach).

As Miller (1987) and others (Handler and Meyer) have articulated, unstructured interviews elicit information relevant to thematic life narratives; structured instruments elicit information relevant to conscious self-schema; performance based personality tests (e.g. Rorschach and Thematic Apperception Test (TAT)) elicit information relevant to implicit dynamics and underlying templates of perception and motivation; and observer ratings elicit perceptions of behavior that are bound by the parameters of particular observational settings. As suggested by Handler and Meyer, scholars in personality assessment should understand the distinction among these methods and should be duly instructed in ways to explore these distinctions in order to obtain qualitatively unique arrays of information from each method, so to more fully understand the complexity of the different personality dimensions of the subjects under investigation.

REFERENCES

ABER, J. L., SLADE, A., BERGER, B., BRESGI, I., & KAPLAN, M. (1985). *The parent development interview: Manual and administration procedures.* New York: Barnard College, Department of Psychology.

ACKERMAN, S., HILSENROTH, M., BAITY, M., & BLAGYS, M. (2000). Interaction of Therapeutic Process and Alliance During Psychological Assessment. *Journal of Personality Assessment, 75(1),* 82–109.

ADAM, K. S., SHELDON-KELLER, A. E., & WEST, M. (1996). Attachment organization and history of suicidal behavior in clinical adolescents. *Journal of Consulting and Clinical PsycholoOgy, 64(2),* 264-272.

ADDIS, M. E., & JACOBSON, N. (1996). Reasons for depression and the process and outcome of cognitive-behavioral psychotherapies. *Journal of Consulting and Clinical Psychology, 64(6),* 1417-1424.

AGRAWAL, H. R., GUNDERSON, J., HOLMES, B. M., & LYONS-RUTH, K. (2004). Attachment studies with borderline patients: A review. *Harvard Review of Psychiatry, 12(2),* 94-104.

AINSWORTH, M. D. (1962). *The development of infant-mother interaction among the Ganda.* In: B. Foss (ed.) Determinants of infant behaviour II. London, Methuen, New York, Wiley Pp.67-112.

AINSWORTH, M. D. S. (1963). The development of infant-mother interaction among the Ganda. In B.M. Floss determinants of infant Behavior, (eds.) New York: Wiley (pp. 67-104).

AINSWORTH, M. D. S. (1967). *Infancy in Uganda: Infant care and the growth of love. Infancy in Uganda: Infant care and the growth of love.* (pp.471)Oxford, England: Johns Hopkins Press.

AINSWORTH, M. D. S., BLEHAR, M.C., WATERS, E., & WALL, S. (1978). *Patterns of attachment: A psychological study of the strange situation.* Oxford, England: Lawrence Erlbaum.

AINSWORTH, M. D. S., & BOWLBY, J., (1991). An ethological approach to personality development. *American-Psychologist, 46*, 333-341.

AINSWORTH, M. S. (1979). Infant-mother attachment. *American-Psychologist, 34(10)*, 932-937.

ALDEN, L.E., WIGGINS, J.S., & PINCUS, A.L. (1990). Construction of circumplex scales for the Inventory of Interpersonal Problems. *Journal of Personality Assessment, 55(3-4)*, 521-536.

ALLEN, J.P., HAUSER, S. T., EICKHOLT, C., BELL, K. L., & AL. (1994). Autonomy and relatedness in family interactions as predictors of expressions of negative adolescent affect. *Journal of Research on Adolescence, 4(4)*, 535-552.

ALLEN, J.P., HAUSER, S.T., & BORMAN-SPURRELL, E. (1996). Attachment theory as a framework for understanding sequelae of severe adolescent psychopathology: An 11-year follow-up study. *Journal of Consulting and Clinical Psychology, 64(2)*, 254-263

ALLEN, J. (2002). Assessment training for practice in American Indian and Alaska native setting. *Journal of Personality Assessment, 79(2)*, 216-255

ALLEN, J.P., PORTER, M., McFARLAND, C., McELHANEY, K.B., & MARSH, P. (2007). The relation of attachment security to adolescents' paternal and peer relationships, depression, and externalizing behavior. *Child Development*, 78, 1222-1239.

ALPERT, J.L., & RICHARDSON, M.S., & FODASKY, L. (1983). Onset of parenting and stressful events. *Journal of Primary Prevention, 3(3)*, 149-159.

AMERICAN ACADEMY OF PEDIATRICS (1999). *Adoption: guideline for parents.* Elk Grove Village, IL: Author.

AMERICAN PSYCHIATRIC ASSOCIATION. (1994). *Diagnostic and statistical manual of Mental disorders (4th ed.)*. Washington, DC: Author.

ANDREWS, C. B.(2004). The relationship of therapists' attachment style, object representations, and narcissism to their experiences of patient termination from long-term psychodynamic therapy. *Dissertation Abstracts International: Section B: The Sciences and Engineering, 64(9-B)*, 4603.

ARMSDEN, G. C., & GREENBERG, M. T. (1987). The Inventory of Parent and Peer Attachment: Individual differences and their relationship to psychological well being in adolescence. *Journal of Youth and Adolescence., 16(5)*, 427 454.

BAGBY, R.M., PARKER, J. D., & TAYLOR, G. J. (1997). The Twenty-Item Toronto Alexithymia Scale: I. Item selection and cross-validation of the factor structure. *Journal of Psychosomatic Research, 38*, 23-32.

BAKERMANS-KRANENBURG, M. J., & VAN IJZENDOORN, M. H. (1993). A psychometric study of the Adult Attachment Interview: Reliability and discriminant validity. *Developmental Psychology, 29*, 870–879

BARBER, J. P., & MUENZ, L. R. (1996). The role of avoidance and obsessiveness in matching patients to cognitive and interpersonal psychotherapy: Empirical findings from the Treatment for Depression Collaborative Research Program. *Journal of Consulting and Clinical Psychology, 64(5)*, 951-958.

BARONE, L. (2003). Developmental protective and risk factors in borderline personality disorder: A study using the Adult Attachment Interview. *Attachment and Human Development, 5(1)*, 64-77.

BARTHOLOMEW, K. (1990). Avoidance of intimacy: An attachment perspective. *Journal of Social and Personal Relationships. Vol 7(2) May 1990*, 147-178.

BARTHOLOMEW, K., & HOROWITZ, L. M. (1991). Attachment styles among young adults: A test of a four category model. *Journal of Personality and Social Psychology, 61*, 226 243.

BARTHOLOMEW, K., & HOROWITZ, L. (1991). Attachment styles among young adults: A test of a four-category model. *Journal of Personality and Social Psychology, 61(2)*, 226-244.

BATTLE, C.C., IMBER, S.D., HOEHN-SARIC, R.H., STONE, A.R., MASH E.R., & FRANK, J.D. (1966). Target Complaints as criteria of improvement. *Am J Psychother 20*, 184–192.

BECK, A. T., & STEER, R. A. (1984). Internal consistencies of the original and revised Beck Depression Inventory. *Journal of Clinical Psychology, 40(6)*, 1365-1367.

BELL, M. D. (1995). *Bell Object Relations and Reality Testing Inventory (BORRTI)* Manual. Los Angeles CA: Western Psychological Services.

BELSKY, J. (1984). The determinant of parenting: A process model. *Child Development, 55*, 83-96.

BELSKY, J., HERZOG, C., ROVINE, M. (1985). *A path analysis of multiple determinants of parenting.* Paper presented at the biannual meetings of the Society for research in child development, Boston.

BENJAMIN, L. S. (1988). *Intrex users manual. Madison*, WI: Intrex Interpersonal Institute.

BENNETT, C.S. (2006). Attachment theory and research applied to the conceptualization and treatment of pathological narcissism. *Clinical Social Work Journal, 34(1)*, 45-60.

BERANT, E., MIKULINCER, M., SHAVER, P. R., & SEGAL, Y. (2005) Rorschach Correlates of Self-Reported Attachment Dimensions: Dynamic Manifestations of Hyperactivating and Deactivating Strategies. *Journal of Personality Assessment,84(1)*, 70-81.

BIHLAR, B., & CARLSSON, A. M. (2001). Planned and actual goals in psychodynamic psychotherapies: Do patients' personality characteristics relate to agreement? *Psychotherapy-Research, 11(4)*, 383-400.

BIHLAR, B., CARLSSON, A. M. (2000). An exploratory study of agreement between therapists' goals and patients' problems revealed by the Rorschach. *Psychotherapy Research*, 10(2), 196-213.

BISCOGLIO, R. L. (2005). Patient and therapist personality, therapeutic alliance, and overall outcome in Brief Relational Therapy. *Dissertation Abstracts International: Section B: The Sciences and Engineering, 65(12-B)*, 6642.

BLATT, S. J., BRENNEIS, C. B., SCHIMEK, J. G., & GLICK, M. (1976a). Normal development and psychopathological impairment of the concept of the object on the Rorschach. *Journal of Abnormal Psychology, 35*, 364 373.

BLATT, S. J., BRENNEIS, C.B., SCHIMEK, J.G., & GLICK, M. (1976). Normal development and psychopathological impairment of the concept of the object on the Rorschach. *Journal of Abnormal Psychology, 85(4)*, 364-373.

BLATT, S. J., & LERNER, H.D. (1983a). Investigations on the psychoanalytic theory of object relations and object representations. In: J. Masling (Eds.), *Empirical studies of psychoanalytic theories, Vol. 1* (pp. 189-249). Hillsdale: NJ: Analytic Press.

BLATT, S. J., & LERNER, H.D. (1983b). The psychological assessment of object representation. *Journal of Personality Assessment, 47*, 7-28.

BLATT, S. J., & LERNER, H. (1991). Psychoanalytic perspectives on personality theory. In: M. Hersen, A. Bellack, J.A.E. Kazdin (Eds.), *Handbook of Clinical Psychology, Revised Edition* (pp. 147-169). New York: Pergamon Press.

BLATT, S. J. & FORD. R.Q. (1994). *Therapeutic Change: An Object Relations Perspective.* New York: Plenum.

BOLTON-OETZEL, K. (2006). Attachment as an indicator of adolescent substance abuse treatment outcome: A study of autonomy and relatedness. *Dissertation Abstracts International Section A: Humanities and Social Sciences, 66(8-A),* 2838.

BOWLBY, J. (1951). Maternal care and mental health. *Bulletin-of-the-World-Health-Organization, 3,* 355-533.

BOWLBY, J. (1958). The Nature of the Child's Tie to His Mother. *International Journal of Psycho-Analysis, 39,* 350-373.

BOWLBY, J. (1960). Grief and Mourning in Infancy and Early Childhood. *Psychoanal. St. Child, 15:*9-52.

BOWLBY, J. (1960). Separation anxiety. *International Journal of Psycho Analysis, 41,* 89-113.

BOWLBY, J. (1969). *Attachment and Loss. Vol. 1: Attachment.* London: Hogarth *Press (2nd ed.: New York: Viking Penguin, 1984) (trad. it.: Attaccamento e perdita. Vol. 1: L'attaccamento alla madre.* Torino: Boringhieri, 1976 [1a ed.], 1989 [2a ed.]).

BOLWBY, J. (1969). *Attachment and loss: Vol. 1. Attachment.* New York: Basic Books.

BOWLBY, J. (1969). Disruption of affectional bonds and its effects on behavior. *Canada's-Mental-Health-Supplement, 59,* 12.

BOWLBY, J. (1973). *Attachment and Loss. Vol. 2: Separation: Anxiety and Anger.* London: Hogarth Press (trad. it.: *Attaccamento e perdita. Vol. 2: La separazione dalla madre.* Torino: Boringhieri, 1978).

BOWLBY, J. (1976). Human personality development in an ethological light. In Kling, A. (Ed); Serban, G. (Ed). (1976). *Animal models in human psychobiology.* (pp. 27-36). New York, NY, US: Plenum Press. XIV, 297 pp.

BOWLBY, J. (1977). *Costruzione e rottura dei legami affettivi.* (Tr. it. Milano: Raffaello Cortina Editore, 1982).

BOWLBY, J (1978). Attachment theory and its therapeutic implications. *Adolescent Psychiatry, 6,* 5-33.

BOWLBY, J. (1980). *Attachment and Loss. Vol. 3: Loss: Sadness and Depression.* London: Hogarth Press (trad. it.: *Attaccamento e perdita. Vol. 3: La perdita della madre.* Torino: Boringhieri, 1983).

BOWLBY, J. (1982). Attachment and loss: Retrospect and prospect. *American Journal of Orthopsychiatry, 52,* 664-678

BOWLBY, J. (1986). *The nature of the child's tie to his mother.* Buckley, P. (Ed). *Essential papers on object relations.* (pp. 153-199). New York, NY, US: New York University Press. xxv, 477 pp.

BOWLBY, J. (1988). *A Secure Base: Parent-child Attachment and Health Human Development.* New York. Tr. It. *Una base sicura.* Milano: Raffaello Cortina Editore.

BOWLBY, J. (1991). Ethological light on psychoanalytical problems. In Bateson, P. (Ed). *The development and integration of behaviour: Essays in honour of Robert Hinde.* (pp. 301-313). New York, NY, US: Cambridge University Press. x, 506 pp.

BOWMAN,-M.J. (2000). Emotional eating and parental attachment as predictors of eating disorder symptoms in a non-clinical college population. *Dissertation Abstracts International: Section B: The Sciences and Engineering, 60(7-B),* 3557.

BORNSTEIN, R.F. (2005). *The dependent patient: A practitioner's guide.* Washington, DC: American Psychological Association.

BRETHERTON, I. (1985). Attachment theory: Retrospect and prospect. *Monographs of the Society for Research in Child Development, 50,* 3-35.

BRETHERTON, I., BIRINGEN, Z., RIDGEWAY, D., & MASLIN, C. (1989). Attachment: The parental perspective. *Infant Mental Health Journal, 10(3),* 203-221.

BRETHERTON, I. (1991). *The roots and growing points of attachment theory.* Marris, Peter (Ed); Parkes, Colin Murray (Ed); Stevenson-Hinde, Joan (Ed). *Attachment across the life cycle.* (pp. 9-32). New York, NY, US: Tavistock/Routledge. viii, 307 pp.

BRETHERTON, I. (1992). Attachment and bonding. Perspectives in developmental psychology. In Hersen, Michel (Ed); Van Hasselt, Vincent B (Ed). *Handbook of social development: A lifespan perspective.* (pp. 133-155). New York, NY, US: Plenum Press, 608 pp.

BRETHERTON. I, (2005). In Pursuit of the Internal Working Model Construct and Its Relevance to Attachment Relationships. In E. Waters, (Ed); K. E. Grossmann, (Ed). *Attachment from infancy to adulthood: The major longitudinal studies.* (pp. 13-47). New York, NY, US: Guilford Publications. xiv, 332 pp.

BRIDGES, M.R., WILSON, J.S., & GACONO, C. B. (1998). A Rorschach investigation of defensiveness, self perception, interpersonal relations, and affective states in incarcerated pedophiles. *Journal of Personality Assessment, 70(2):* 365 385.

BRODZINSKY, D. M. (1987). Adjustment to adoption: A psychosocial perspective. *Clinical Psychology Review, 7,* 25-47.

BRODZINSKY, D. M., HUFFMAN, L. (1988). Transition to adoptive parenthood. *Marriage and Family Review, 6,* 267-286.

BRODZINSKY, D. M., SCHECHTER, M. D. (1990). *The psychology of adoption.* New York: Oxford University Press.

BRODZINSKY, D. M., BRODZINSKY, A. B. (1992). The impact of family structure on the adjustment of adopted children. *Child Welfare, 71, 69-75.*

BRODZINSKY, D. M., HITT J. C., SMITH, D. (1993). Impact of parental separation and divorce on adopted and nonadopted children. *American Journal of Orthopsychiatry, 63,* 451-461.

BRODZINSKY, D. M., LANG, R., SMITH, D. W. (1995). *Parenting adopted children. Handbook of parenting, Vol. 3: Status and social conditions of parenting.* (pp. 209-232). Hillsdale, NJ, England: Lawrence Erlbaum Associates, Inc. xxvi, 595 pp.

BROWN, W.R., & McGUIRE, J.M. (1976). Current psychological assessment practices. *Professional Psychology, 7(4),* 475-484.

BUCHHEIM, A., & KACHELE, H. (2001). Adult Attachment Interview einer Personlichkeitsstorung Eine Einzelfallstudie zur Synopsis von psychoanalytis- cher und bindungstheoretischer Perspektive / Addult Attachment Interview of a patient with a borderlinepersonality organization: a single case study inte- grating attachment and psychoanalytic perspective. *Personlichkeitsstorungen Theorie und Therapie, 5,* 113-130.

BUCHHEIM, A. (2005). Mein Hund stirbt heute": Bindungsnarrative und psychoana- lytische Interpretation eines Erstinterviews / "My dog dies today". Attachment narratives and the psychoanalytic interpretation of a first interview. *Zeitschrift- fur-Psychoanalyse-und-ihre-Anwendungen, 59,* 35-50.

BUCHHEIM, A., ERK, S., GEORGE, C., KAEKELE, H., RUCHSOW, M., SPITZER, M., KIRCHER, T. & WALTER, H. (2006). Measuring Attachment Representation in an fMRI Environment: A Pilot Study. *Psychopathology, 39(3),* 144-152.

BURNS, B., & VIGLIONE, D.J. (1996). The Rorschach Human Experience Variable, interpersonal relatedness, and object representations in nonpatients": Correction. *Psychological Assessment, 9(2),* 82.

BURNS, B., & VIGLIONE, D.JR (1996). "The Rorschach Human Experience Variable, interpersonal relatedness, and object representations in nonpatients": Correction. *PsychologicalAssessment, 8(1),* 92-99.

BUTCHER, J., DAHLSTROM, W., GRAHAM, J., TELLEGEN, A., & KAEMMER, B. (1989). *Minnesota Multiphasic Personality Invertory-2 (MMPI-2): Manual for administation and scoring.* Minneapolis: Univeristy of Minneapolis Press.

BYERS,C. (2002). Chronicle of a collaborative assessment: A Rorschach letter. *The Humanistic Psychologist, Vol 30(1-2),* 63-74.

CADORET, (1990). Biologic perspective of adoptee adjustment. In D. Brodzinsky & M. Shecther (eds.), *The psychology of adoption* (pp. 25-41). New York: Oxford University Press.

CAMPOS, R. C. (2002). Manifestations of dependent and self critical personality styles in Rorschach: An exploratory study. *Journal of Projective Psychology and Mental Health, 9(2),* 93 104.

CARLSON, E. A., & SROUFE, L. A. (1995). *Contribution of attachment theory to developmental psychopathology.* Cohen, D. J. (Ed); Cicchetti, D. (Ed). (1995). *Developmental psychopathology, Vol. 1: Theory and methods.* (pp. 581-617). Oxford, England: John Wiley & Sons. xx, 787 pp.

CARLSON, V., CICCHETTI, D., BARNETT, D., & BRAUNWALD, K. (1989). Disorganized/disoriented attachment relationships in maltreated infants. *Developmental-Psychology, 25(4),* 525-531.

CARTER, E.A., & MCGOLDRICK, M. (Eds.). (1980). *The family life cycle.* New York: Gardner Press.

CASSELLA, M. J. (1999). The Rorschach texture response: A conceptual validation study. (attachment). *Dissertation Abstracts International: Section B: The Sciences and Engineering, 60(5 B),* 2405.

CASSIDY, J., & KOBAK, R. R. (1988). Avoidance and its relation to other defensive processes. Child psychology. In Nezworski, Teresa (Eds); Belsky, Jay (Eds). *Clinical implications of attachment.* (pp. 300-323). Hillsdale, NJ, England: Lawrence Erlbaum Associates, Inc. XVII, 440 pp.

CASSIDY, J., & SHAVER, P. (1999). *Handbook of attachment: Theory, research, and clinical applications. Handbook of attachment: Theory, research, and clinical applications.* New York, NY, US: Guilford Press.

CAVIGLIA, G., FIOCCO, B., & DAZZI, N. (2004). La Trasmissione Intergenerazionale del Trauma della Shoa: Uno Studio Condotto Con L'Adult Attachment Interview / Intergenerational Transmission of the Trauma of Shoa: A Study Conducted by the Adult Attachment Interview. *Ricerca in Psicoterapia, 7(1),* 67-83.

CHABERT C. (1983). *Le Rorschach en clinique adulte. Interpretation psychoanalytique.* Paris: Dunod.

CICCHETTI, D., CUMMINGS, E. M., GREENBERG, M.T., & MARVIN, R.S. (1990). An organizational perspective on attachment beyond infancy: Implications for theory, measurement, and research.In E. M. Cummings, (Ed); M.T. Greenberg, (Ed); D. Cicchetti, (Ed). *Attachment in the preschool years: Theory, research, and intervention.* (pp. 3-49). Chicago, IL, US: University of Chicago Press. XIX, 507 pp.

CICCHETTI, D., & COHEN, D.J. (1995). *Developmental psychopathology, Vol. 1: Theory and methods.* Oxford, England: John Wiley & Sons. XX, 787 pp.

COLE-DETKE, H. (1998). Depression and eating disorder: A comparison of the roles of attachment organization, personality, field dependence, and coping strategies. *Dissertation Abstracts International: Section B: The Sciences and Engineering, 58(12-B),* 6803.

COLLINS, N. L., & READ, S. J. (1990). Adult attachment, working models, and relationship quality in dating couples. *Journal of Personality and Social Psychology, 58(4),* 644 663.

CRAIK, K. (1943). *The nature of explanation.* Cambridge, England: Cambridge University Press.

CRITTENDEN, M.P. (1992). Children's strategies for coping with adverse home environments: An interpretation using attachment theory. *Child Abuse and Neglect, 16(3),* 329-343.

CRITTENDEN, P.M. (1994). *Peering into the black box: An exploratory treatise on the development of self in young children.* Rochester: University of Rochester Press.

CRITTENDEN, P. M. (1998). *Dangerous behavior and dangerous contexts: A 35-year perspective on research on the developmental effects of child physical abuse.* Schellenbach, C. J. (Ed); Trickett, P. K. (Ed). *Violence against children in the family and the community.* (pp. 11-38). Washington, DC, US.

CROWELL, J.A. (1990). *Separation anxiety.* New York: Plenum Press.

CROWELL, J. A., & TREBOUX, D. (1995). A review of adult attachment measures: Implications for theory and research. *Social-Development, 4(3)*, 294-327.

CROWELL, J. A., FRALEY, R. C., SHAVER, P.R. (1999). *Measurement of individual differences in adolescent and adult attachment*. Shaver, P. (Ed); Cassidy, J. (Ed). Handbook of attachment: Theory, research, and clinical applications. (pp. 434-465). New York, NY, US: Guilford Press. XVII, 925 pp.

DAHLBENDER, R., BUCHHEIM, A., & DOERING, S. (2004). OPD und AAI: integrative Diagnostik von Struktur, Konflikt und Bindungsreprasentation / OPD and AAI: integrative diagnostics of structure, conflict and attachment representation. *Personlichkeitsstorungen-Theorie-und-Therapie, 8*, 251-261.

DAVIS, M.H. (1983). Measuring individual differences in empathy: Evidence for a multidimensional approach. *Journal of Personality and Social Psychology, 44(1)*, 113-126.

DAZZI N., LINGIARDI, V., & COLLI A. (2006) (a cura di). *La ricerca in psicoterapia. Modelli e strumenti*. Milano: Raffaello Cortina, pp. 919.

DECLERCQ, F., & PALMANS, VICKY. (2006). Two subjective factors as moderators between critical incidents and the occurrence of post traumatic stress disorders: Adult attachment and perception of social support. *Psychology and Psychotherapy: Theory, Research and Practice, 79(3)*, 323-337.

DELUCAS, A. L. (1997). *The quality of parental attachment and violent behaviors: A Rorschach study of convicted military offenders* (Doctoral dissertation, California School of Professional Psychology, San Diego, 1997, Dissertation Abstracts International, 58, 2115B.

DEROGATIS, L. R. (1983). SCL-90-R Administration, Scoring & Procedures, Manual-II. Towson, MD. *Clinical Psychometrical Research, 14,* 15.

DEROGATIS, L.R. (1994). *SCL-90-R, Brief Symptom Inventory, and matching clinical rating scales*. Hillsdale, NJ, England: Lawrence Erlbaum Associates, Inc.

DIAMOND, D., STOVALL-MCCLOUGH, C., CLARKIN, J. F., & LEVY, K. N. (2003). Patient-therapist attachment in the treatment of borderline personality disorder. *Bulletin of the Menninger Clinic, 67(3)*, 227-259.

DIEPERINK, M., LESKELA, J., THURAS, P., & ENGDAHL, B. (2001). Attachment style classification and posttraumatic stress disorder in former prisoners of war. *American Journal of Orthopsychiatry, 71(3)*, 374-378.

DUBERSTEIN, P. R., & TALBOT, N. L. (1993). Rorschach oral imagery, attachment style, and interpersonal relatedness. *Journal of Personality Assessment, 61(2)*, 294 310.

DUVALL, E. (1977). *Marriage and family development (5ᵃ ed.)*. Philadelphia: Lippincott.

EAGLE, M. (1997). Attachment and psychoanalysis*British. Journal of Medical Psychology, 70*, 217-229.

EGELAND, B., CARLSON, E. A., & COLLINS, W. A. (2005). *The development of the person: The*

EGOZI, P., & VIRGINIA, L. (1999) A comparison of the Roemer and the Rorschach tests as tools for distinguishing characteristics of psychopathy. *Dissertation Abstracts International: Section B: The Sciences and Engineering, 60(3-B)*, 1345.

ENDICOTT, J., SPITZER, R. L., FLEISS, J.L., & COHEN, J. (1976). The global assessment scale. A procedure for measuring overall severity of psychiatric disturbance. *Archives of General Psychiatry, 33(6)*, 766-771.

ENG, W. (2004). An examination of the interpersonal problems associated with symptoms of generalized anxiety disorder. *Dissertation Abstracts International: Section B: The Sciences and Engineering, 64(11-B)*, 5778.

ENG,-W., & HEIMBERG,-R.G. (2006). Interpersonal correlates of generalized anxiety disorder: Self versus other perception. *Journal of Anxiety Disorders, 20(3)*, 380-387.

ENGELMAN, D. H., & FRANKEL, S. A. (2002). The three person field: Collaborative consultation to psychotherapy. *Humanistic Psychologist,30(1-2)*, 49-62.

EPSTEIN, N. B., BALDWIN, L. M., & BISHOP, D. S. (1982). The McMaster Family Assessment Device. *Journal of Marital and Family Therapy, 9(2)*, 171-180.

EXNER, J.E. JR. (1991). *The Rorschach: A comprehensive system, Vol. 2: Interpretation (2nd ed.)*. Oxford, England: John Wiley and Sons.

EXNER, J.E. JR. (1993). *The Rorschach: A comprehensive system, Vol. 1: Basic foundations (3rd ed.)*. Oxford, England: John Wiley and Sons.

EXNER, J.E. JR. (1995). *Issues and methods in Rorschach research*. Hillsdale, England: Lawrence Erlbaum Associates, Inc.

EXNER, J.E. JR., & WEINER, I.B. (1995). *The Rorschach: A comprehensive system, Vol. 3: Assessment of children and adolescents (2nd ed)*. Oxford, England: John Wiley and Sons.

FARRAR, V. (1996). Object relations of incest survivors. *Dissertation-Abstracts-International:-Section-B:-The-Sciences-and-Engineering, 57(2-B)*.

FEINTUCH, B. (1999). Adult attachment, narcissism, shame, and defensiveness. *Dissertation Abstracts International: Section B: The Sciences and Engineering, 59(10-B)*, 5575.

FELDMAN, S.S., & NASH, S.C. (1984). The transition from expectancy to parenthood: Impact of the firstborn child on men and women. *Sex-Roles,11(1-2)*, 61-78.

FINN, S. (1996). *A manual for using MMPI-2 as a therapeutic intervention.* Minneapolis: University of Minneapolis Press.

FINN, S., & TONSAGER, M. (1992). Therapeutic effects of providing MMPI-2 test feedback to college students awaiting therapy. *Psychological Assessment, 4(3)*, 278–287.

FINN, S., SCHROEDER, D., & TONSAGER, M. (1995). *Assessment Questionnaire-2 (AQ-2): a measure of clients's experience with Psychological Assessment*, Unpublished Manuscript.

FINN, S. (1996). Assessment Feedback Integrating MMPI-2 and Rorschach Findings. *Journal of Personality Assessment, 67(3)*, 543–557.

FINN, S. E., & FISCHER, C. (1997) *Therapeutic psychological assessment: Illustration and analysis of philosophical assumptions.* Presented at annual meeting of the American Psychological Association, August 18, 1997.

FINN, S., & TONSAGER, M. (1997). Information-Gathering and Therapeutic Model of Assessment Assessment: Complementary Paradigms. *Psychological Assessment, 9(4)*, 374–385.

FINN, S., & MARTIN, H. (1997). Therapeutic Assessment with the MMPI-2 in managed health care. In J. Butcher, (Eds.), *Objective psychological assessment in managed health care: A Practitioner's guide.* New York: Oxford Univerity Press.

FINN, S.E. (1998). Teaching Therapeutic Assesssment in a required graduate course. *The LEA series in personality and clinical psychology.* Mahwah, NJ: Lawrence Erlbaum Associates Publishers.

FINN, S. E. (2003). Therapeutic assessment of a man with "ADD". *Journal of Personality Assessment, 80(2)*, 115-129.

FIRST, M. B., GIBBON, M., SPITZER, R. L., WILLIAMS, J. B., & BENJAMIN, L. S. (1997). *Structured clinical interview for DSM-IV, axis 2, personality disorders (SCID-II).* Washington, DC: American Psychiatric Press.

FLAVELL, J.H., GREEN, F.L., & FLAVELL, E. (1986). Development of knowledge about the appearance-reality distinction. *Monographs of the Society for Research in Child Development, 51(1)*, 1-68.

FONAGY, P., STEELE, H., STEELE, M. (1991). Maternal representations of attachment during pregnancy predict the organization of infant-mother attachment at one year of age. *Child Development, 62(5)*, 891-905.

FONAGY, P., STEELE, M., STEELE, H., LEIGH, T., KENNEDY, R., MATTOON, G., & TARGET, M. (1995). *Attachment, the reflective self, and borderline states: The predictive specificity of the Adult Attachment Interview and pathological emotional development*. Hillsdale, England: Analytic Press Inc.

FONAGY, P. (1996). The significance of the development of metacognitive control over mental representations in parenting and infant development. *Journal of Clinical Psychoanalysis, 5(1)*, 67-86.

FONAGY, P., LEIGH, T., STEELE, M., STEELE, H., & KENNEDY, R. (1996). Mattoon, Gretta; Target, Mary; Gerber, Andrew .The relation of attachment status, psychiatric classification, and response to psychotherapy. *Journal of Consulting and Clinical Psychology, 64(1)*, 22-31.

FONAGY, P., TARGET, M. (2001). *Attaccamento e funzione riflessiva*. Milano: Raffaello Cortina Editore.

FOSSATI, A., DONATI, D., DONINI, M., NOVELLA, L., BAGNATO, M., & MAFFEI, C. (2001). Temperament, character, and attachment patterns in borderline personality disorder. *Journal of Personality Disorders, 15(5)*, 390-402.

FOSSATI, A., FEENEY, J. A., CARRETTA, I., GRAZIOLI, F., MILESI, R., LEONARDI, B., & MAFFEI, C. (2005). Modeling the relationships between adult attachment patterns and borderline personality disorder: The role of impulsivity and aggressiveness. *Journal of Social and Clinical Psychology, 24(4)*, 520-537.

FOWLER, J.C., BRUNNSCHWEILER, B., SWALES, S., & BROCK, J. (2005). Assessment of Rorschach Dependency Measures in Female Inpatients Diagnosed With Borderline Disorder. *Journal of Personality-Assessment, 85(2)*, 146-153.

FRALEY, R. C., & SHAVER, P. R. (2000). Adult romantic attachment: Theoretical developments, emerging controversies, and unanswered questions. *Review of General Psychology, 4(2)*, 132-154.

FRANK, M. A., TUBER, S. B., SLADE, A., & GARROD, E. (1994). Mothers' fantasy representations and infant security attachment: A Rorschach study of first pregnancy. *Psychoanalytic Psychology, 11(4)*, 475-490.

FRANK, J. P. (2001). Adult attachment and its association with substance dependence treatment outcome. *Dissertation Abstracts International: Section B: The Sciences and Engineering. Vol 62(5 B)*, 2482.

FRODI, A., DERNEVIK, M., SEPA, A., PHILIPSON, J., & BRAGESJO, M., (2001). Current attachment representations of incarcerated offenders varying in degree of psychopathy. *Attachment and Human Development, 3(3)*, 269-283.

FUNDER, D. C. (1997). *The personality puzzle*. New York, NY, US: W. Norton & Co.

GACONO, C. B., & MELOY, J. T. (1991). A Rorschach investigation of attachment and anxiety in antisocial personality disorder. *Journal of Nervous and Mental Disease, 179(9)*, 546-552.

GACONO, C. B., & MELOY, J. T. (1991). A Rorschach investigation of attachment and anxiety in antisocial personality disorder. *Journal of Nervous and Mental Disease, 179(9)*, 546-552.

GACONO, C. B., MELOY, J. R., & BERG, J. L. (1992). Object relations, defensive operations, and affective states in narcissistic, borderline, and antisocial personality disorder. *Journal of Personality Assessment, 59(1)*, 32-49.

GACONO, C.B., & MELOY, J. R. (1994). The aggression response. In C.B. Gacono, & Meloy, J.R. (Eds.), *The Rorschach assessment of aggressive and psychopathic personalities* (pp.259-278). Hillsdale, NJ: Lawrewnce Erlbaum Associates, Inc.

GACONO, C. B., MELOY, J. R., & BRIDGES, M. R. (2000). A Rorschach comparison of psychopaths, sexual homicide perpetrators, and nonviolent pedophiles: Where angels fear to tread. *Journal of Clinical Psychology, 56(6)*, 757-777.

GACONO, C. B., LOVING, J. L., & BODHOLDT, R. H. (2001). The Rorschach and psychopathy: Toward a more accurate understanding of the research findings. *Journal-of-Personality-Assessment, 77(1)*, 16-38.

GEORGE, C., KAPLAN, N., & MAIN, M. (1984). *Adult Attachment interview for adults*. Manoscritto non pubblicato, University of California, Berkeley, 1984.

GEORGE, C., KAPLAN, N., & MAIN, M. (1984-1985-1996). *The Adult Attachment Interview* Unpublished manuscript, University of California at Berkeley.

GEORGE, C., KAPLAN, N., MAIN, M. (1984). *Adult Attachment Interview*. Unpublished Manuscript, University of California: Berkeley.

GEORGE, C., KAPLAN, N., MAIN, M. (1985). *Adult Attachment Interview (2nd Ed)*. Unpublished Manuscript, University of California: Berkeley.

GEORGE, C., KAPLAN, N., MAIN, M. (1996). *Adult Attachment Interview (3rd Ed)*. Unpublished Manuscript, University of California: Berkeley.

GEORGE, C., & SOLOMON, J. (1989). Internal working models of caregiving and security of attachment at age six. *Infant Mental Health Journal, 10(3)*, 222-237.

GEORGE, C., & SOLOMON, J. (1996). Representational models of relationships: Links between caregiving and attachment. *Infant-Mental-Health-Journal, 17(3)*, 198-216.

GEORGE, C., & SOLOMON, J. (1996). Defining the caregiving system: Toward a theory of caregiving. *Infant Mental Health Journal, Vol 17(3), 183-197.*

GEORGE, C., & WEST, M., & PETTEM, O. (1997). *Adult Attachment Projective.*

GEORGE, C., & SOLOMON, J. (1999). The development of caregiving: A comparison of attachment theory and psychoanalytic approaches to mothering. *Psychoanalytic-Inquiry, 19(4)*, 618-646.

GEORGE, C., & SOLOMON, J. (1999). Attachment and caregiving: The caregiving behavioral system. In P. R. Shaver, (Ed) & J. Cassidy (Ed). *Handbook of attachment: Theory, research, and clinical applications.* (pp. 649-670). New York, NY, US: Guilford Press.

GEORGE, C., & WEST, M. (1999). Developmental vs. social personality models of adult attachment and mental ill health. *British Journal of Medical Psychology, 72(3)*, 285-303.

GEORGE, C., & WEST, M. (2001). The development and preliminary validation of a new measure of adult attachment: The Adult Attachment Projective. *Attachment-and-Human-Development, 3(1)*, 30-61.

GEORGE, C., & WEST, MALCOLM. (2001). The development and preliminary validation of a new measure of adult attachment: The Adult Attachment Projective. *Attachment and Human-Development, 3(1)*, 30-61.

GLUECK, S., & GLUECK, E. (1950). *Unraveling Juvenile delinquency.* Oxford: Commonwealth Fund.

GRAVES, P. L., MEAD, L. A., & PEARSON, T. A. (1986), The Rorschach Interaction Scale as Potential Predictor of Cancer. *Psychosomatic Medicine, 48*, 549-563.

GREENBERG, J. R. & MITCHELL, S. A. (1983). *Object Relation in Psychoanalytic Theory*, Harvard University Press, Cambridge (Mass.). Trad. It. *Le Relazioni Oggettuali nella Teoria Psicoanalitica,* Il Mulino, Bologna (1986).

GRIFFIN, D., & BARTHOLOMEW, K. (1994). Models of the self and other: Fundamental dimensions underlying measures of adult attachment. *Journal of Personality and Social Psychology, 67*, 430-445.

HAJAL, F. & ROSEMBERG, E.B. (1991). The family life cycle in adoptive families. *American Journal of Orthopsychiatry, 61*, 78-85.

HANDLER, L., & MEYER, G. J. (1998). The importance of teaching and learning personality assessment. The LEA series in personality and clinical psychology. In M. J. Hilsenroth, (Ed) & L. Handler, (Ed). (1998). *Teaching and learning personality assessment.* (pp. 3-30). Mahwah, NJ, US: Lawrence Erlbaum Associates Publishers.

HARE, R.D., (1998). The Hare PCL-R: Some issues concerning its use and misuse. *Legal and Criminological Psychology. 3,* 99-119.

HARE, R.D., HARPUR, T.J., HAKSTIAN, A.R., FORTH, A.E., HART, S.D., & NEWMAN, J.P., (1990). The Revised Psychopathy Checklist: Descriptive statistics, reliability, and factor structure. *Psychological Assessment: A Journal of Consulting and Clinical Psychology, 2,* 338-341.

HARRIS, T. (2004). Implications of attachment theory for working in psychoanalytic psychotherapy. *International Forum of Psychoanalysis, 13,* 147-156.

HAZAN, C., & SHAVER, P. (1987). Romantic love conceptualized as an attachment process. *Journal of Personality and Social Psychology, 52(3),* 511-524.

HAZAN, C., & ZEIFMAN, D. (1999). *Pair bonds as attachments: Evaluating the evidence.* Shaver, P. R. (Ed); Cassidy, J. (Ed). (1999). *Handbook of attachment: Theory, research, and clinical applications.* (pp. 336-354). New York, NY, US: Guilford Press. XVII, 925 pp.

HESSE, E. (1996). Discourse, memory and the Adult Attachment Interview: A note with emphasis on the emerging Cannot Classify category. *Infant Mental Health Journal, 17,* 4-11.

HESSE, E. (1996). Discourse, memory, and the Adult Attachment Interview: A note with emphasis on the emerging cannot classify category. *Infant Mental Health Journal, 17(1),* 4-11.

HESSE, E. (1999). Second-generation effects of unresolved trauma in nonmaltreating parents: Dissociated, frightened, and threatening parental behavior. *Psychoanalytic Inquiry. Vol 19(4),* 481-540.

HILSENROTH, M.J., & BORNSTEIN, R.F. (2002). Interpersonal dependency and personality pathology: Variations in Rorschach Oral Dependency scores across Axis II disorders. *Journal of Personality Assessment, 75(3),* 478-491.

HOCHDORF, Z., LATZER, Y., CANETTI, L., & BACHAR, E. (2005). Attachment Styles and Attraction to Death: Diversities Among Eating Disorder Patients. *American Journal of Family Therapy, 33(3),* 237-252.

HOFFMAN, P. M. (2007).Attachment styles and use of defense mechanisms: A study of the Adult Attachment Projective and Cramer's Defense Mechanism Scale.

Dissertation-Abstracts-International:-Section-B:-The-Sciences-and-Engineering, 67(10-B), 6058.

HOLT H.K. (1968). A new method of investigating symptoms of dyslexia. *International Review of Applied Psychology, 17(1)*, 33-48.

HOOPES, J.L. (1982). *Prediction in child development: A longitudinal study of adoptive and non adoptive families*. New York: Child Welfare League of America.

HOPKINS, J., MARCUS, M., & CAMPBELL, S.B. (1984). Postpartum depression: A critical review. *Psychological Bulletin, 95(3)*, 498-515.

HOROWITZ, L. M., ROSENBERG, S. E., & BARTHOLOMEW, K. (1996). Interpersonal problems, attachment styles, and outcome in brief dynamic psychotherapy. *Journal of Consulting & Clinical Psychology, 61*, 549-560.

HOWARD, W. W. (1999). The utility of selected Rorschach indices of distress and attachment for differential diagnosis in a forensic setting. (inmates, antisocial personality disorder). *Dissertation Abstracts International: Section B: The Sciences and Engineering, 59(10 B)*, 5578.

HOWARD, S. (2005). The correlation of defensive responses between mothers and sons: An attachment perspective. *Dissertation Abstracts International: Section B: The Sciences and Engineering, 65(10-B)*, 5436.

INGLE, D. W. (2002). The pedophilic mind: Reconsidering pedophilia using the Rorschach Inkblot method. *Dissertation Abstracts International: Section B: The Sciences and Engineering, 62(11 B)*, 5377.

JACQUES, C.A. (2002). Disorganized attachment and its relationship to disordered thinking and emotional dysregulation. a study of adults with a history of childhood trauma, using the Adult Attachment Projective Test and the Rorschach Inkblot Test. *Dissertation Abstracts International: Section B: The Sciences and Engineering, 63(4-B)*, 2060.

JOHNSON, S. M., WHIFFEN, V. E. (2003). *Attachment processes in couple and family therapy*. New York: Guilford Press.

JOHNSTON, M. H., & HOLZMAN, P. S. (1979). *Assessing schizophrenic thinking* (Vol. 310). San Francisco: Jossey-Bass.

JONES, P. M. (2000). Measures of mental representation: The Adult Attachment Interview as a predictor of object relations on the Rorschach. *Dissertation Abstracts International: Section B: The Sciences and Engineering, 60(9 B)*, 4891.

KADUSHIN, A. (1964). Research in psychotherapy of significance to social casework: The "good" client, the "good" therapist," the "good" relationship. *Journal of the Hillside Hospital, 13(3-4)*, 221-243.

KADUSHIN, A. (1980). *Child welfare services* (3rd ed). New York: Macmillan.

KAPLAN N., GEORGE C., & MAIN M., (1984). *" The Adult Attachment Interview "unpublished manoscript.* University of Berkeley. California. U.S.A.

KASOFF, M. B. (2002). Interpersonal subtypes of generalized anxiety disorder: Derivation and differentiation in patterns of adult attachment and psychiatric comorbidity. *Dissertation Abstracts International:-Section-B: The Sciences and Engineering, 62(12-B)*, 5967.

KAYE, K. (1990). Acknowledgment or rejection of differences? In D. Brodzinsky & M. Schechter (eds.), The *psychology of adoption* (pp. 121-143). New York: Oxford University Press.

KIANG, L., & HARTER, S. (2006). Sociocultural values of appearance and attachment processes: An integrated model of eating disorder symptomatology. *Eating Behaviors, 7(2)*, 134-151.

KIRK, H. D. (1964). *Shared fate. New York*: The Free Press.

KLEIN, M. (1932). *The Psycho-Analysis of Children.*, London: Hogarth.

KOKALIARI, E. (2005). Review of Attachment theory and psychoanalysis. *Psychoanalytic Social Work, 12(2)*, 119-125.

KORLIN, D., EDMAN, G., & NYBACK, H. (2007). Reliability and validity of a Swedish version of the dissociative experiences scale (DES-II). *Nordic Journal of Psychiatry, 61(2)*, 126-142.

KRAUS, J. (1978). Family structure as a factor in the adjustment of adoptive children. *British Journal of Social Work*, 8, 327-337.

LERNER P.M. (1991). *Psychoanalytic theory and the Rorschach*. New York, Hillsdale: The Analytic Press.

LEVINSON, A., & FONAGY, P. (2004). Offending and Attachment: The Relationship between Interpersonal Awareness and Offending in a Prison Population with Psychiatric Disorder. *Canadian Journal of Psychoanalysis, 12(2)*, 225-251.

LEVY-SHIFF, R., BAR, O., HAR-EVEN, D. (1990). Psychological adjustment in adoptive parent-to-be, *American Journal of Orthopsychiatry, 60*, 258-267.

LEVY-SCHIFF, R., GOLDSCHMIDT , I., HAR-EVEN, D. (1991). Transition to parenthood in adoptive families, *Developmental Psychology, 27*, 131-140

LEVY, T. M., ORLANS, M. (2003). Creating and repairing attachments in biological, foster, and adoptive families. In S.M. Johnson & V. E. Whiffen (Eds.) *Attachment processes in couple and family therapy* (pp.165-190). New York: Guilford Press.

LEVY, K. N., MEEHAN, K. B., KELLY, K. M., REYNOSO, J. S., WEBER, M., CLARKIN, J. F., & KERNBERG, O. F. (2006). Change in Attachment Patterns and Reflective Function in a Randomized Control Trial of Transference-Focused Psychotherapy for Borderline Personality Disorder. *Journal of Consulting and Clinical Psychology, 74(6),* 1027-1040.

LEVY, K., CLARKIN, J. F., & KERNBERG, O. F. Das Adult Attachment Interview (AAI) als Veranderungsmass in der Behandlung von Borderline-Patienten / The Adult Attachment Interview (AAI) as a measure of change in treatments with borderline patients. *Personlichkeitsstorungen Theorie und Therapie, 8(4),* 244-250.

LEWIS, J. L. (2007). Using early recollections to predict attachment style of adults in outpatient psychotherapy. *Dissertation Abstracts International: Section B: The Sciences and Engineering, 68(5-B),* 3402.

LICHTENBERG, J. D. (1989). *Psychoanalysis and motivation.* Hillsdale, NJ: The Analytic Press.

LINGIARDI, V., & MADEDDU F. (2002). *I meccanismi di difesa. Teoria, valutazione, clinica.* Raffaello Cortina Editore, Milano.

LOFTIS, R. H. (1997). A comparison of delinquents and nondelinquents on Rorschach measures of object relationships and attachment: Implications for conduct disorder, antisocial personality disorder, and psychopathy. *Dissertation Abstracts International: Section B: The Sciences and Engineering, 58(5 B),* 2720.

LUBIN, B., LARSEN, R.M., MATARAZZO, J.D., & SEEVER, M. (1985). Psychological test usage patterns in five professional settings. *American-Psychologist, 40(7),* 857-861.

LYONS, R. K., & JACOBVITZ, D. (1999). Attachment disorganization: Unresolved loss, relational violence, and lapses in behavioral and attentional strategies. In P. R. Shaver, (Ed); J. Cassidy, (Ed). *Handbook of attachment: Theory, research, and clinical applications.* (pp. 520-554). New York, NY, US: Guilford Press.

MAGANA, A.B., GOLDSTEIN, M.J., KARNO, M., & MIKLOWITZ, D.J. (1986). A brief method for assessing expressed emotion in relatives of psychiatric patients. *Journal of Child Psychology and Psychiatry, 34(2),* 139-154.

MAIN, M., & GOLDWYN, R. (1984). Predicting rejection of her infant from mother's representation of her own experience: Implications for the abused-abusing intergenerational cycle. *Child Abuse and Neglect, 8(2),* 203-217.

MAIN, M., GOLDWYN, R. (1985-1986). *Adult attachment scoring and classification system. Unpublished scoring manual.* University of California: Berkeley.

MAIN, M., KAPLAN, N., & CASSIDY, J. (1985). Security in infancy, childhood, and adulthood: A move to the level of representation. *Monographs-of-the-Society-for-Research-in-Child-Development, 50(1-2),* 66-104.

MAIN, M., & Solomon, J. (1990). Procedures for identifying infants as disorganized/disoriented during the Ainsworth Strange Situation. The John D. and Catherine T. MacArthur Foundation series on mental health and development. In E. M. Cummings, (Ed); M. T. Greenberg, (Ed); D. Cicchetti (Ed). *Attachment in the preschool years: Theory, research, and intervention.* (pp. 121-160). Chicago, IL, US: University of Chicago Press.

MAIN, M. (1991). *Metacognitive knowledge, metacognitive monitoring, and singular (coherent) vs. multiple (incoherent) model of attachment: Findings and directions for future research.* New York: Tavistock / Routledge.

MAIN, M. (1995). *Discourse, prediction, and recent studies in attachment: Implications for psychoanalysis.* Emde, R. N. (Ed); Shapiro, T. (Ed). *Research in psychoanalysis: Process, development, outcome.* (pp. 209-244). Madison, CT, US: International Universities Press, Inc. VII, 447 pp.

MAIN, M. (1995). *Recent studies in attachment: Overview, with selected implications for clinical work.* Kerr, J. (Ed); Goldberg, S. (Ed); Muir, R. (Ed). *Attachment theory: Social, developmental, and clinical perspectives.* (pp. 407-474). Hillsdale, NJ, England: Analytic Press, Inc. XIII, 515 pp.

MAIN, M., & GOLDWIN, R. (1998). Adult *Attachment Scoring System. Manual in Draft: Version 6.3.* University of California: Berkeley.

MAIN, M., & HESSE, E. (1990). *Parents' unresolved traumatic experiences are related to infant disorganized attachment status: Is frightened and/or frightening parental behavior the linking mechanism?* Cummings, E. M. (Ed); Greenberg, M. T. (Ed); Cicchetti, D. (Ed). *Attachment in the preschool years: Theory, research, and intervention.* (pp. 161-182). Chicago, IL, US: University of Chicago Press. XIX, 507 pp.

MAIN, M., & SOLOMON, J. (1990). Procedures for identifying infants as disorganized/disoriented during the Ainsworth Strange Situation. *The John D. and Catherine T. MacArthur Foundation series on mental health and development.* Chicago: University of Chicago Press.

MAIN, M., KAPLAN, N., & CASSIDY, J. (1985). Security in infancy, childhood, and adulthood: A move to the level of representation. *Monographs of the Society for Research in Child Development, 50(1-2),* 66-104.

MARTIN AVELLAN, L. E., McGAULEY, G. (2005). Using the SWAP-200 in a personality-disordered forensic population: Is it valid, reliable and useful? *Criminal Behaviour and Mental Health,15(1)*, 28-45.

MATTLAR, C. E. (2004). The Rorschach Comprehensive System is Reliable, Valid, and Cost-Effective. In Andronikof, A. (Ed). *Rorschachiana XXVI: Yearbook of the International Rorschach Society.* (pp. 158-186). Ashland, OH, US: Hogrefe & Huber Publishers.

MAURICIO, A. M., TEIN, J. Y., & LOPEZ, F. G. (2007). Borderline and antisocial personality scores as mediators between attachment and intimate partner violence. *Violence and Victims, 22(2)*, 139-157.

MAZZARELLO, T. (2007). The intergenerational transmission of attachment and child externalizing behavior problems in a sample of adolescent mothers and their pre-school/early-school aged children. *Dissertation-Abstracts-International:-Section-B:-The-Sciences-and-Engineering, 68(3-B)*, 1962.

McBRIDE, C., ATKINSON, L., QUILTY, L. C., & BAGBY, R. M. (2006). Attachment as Moderator of Treatment Outcome in Major Depression: A Randomized Control Trial of Interpersonal Psychotherapy Versus Cognitive Behavior Therapy. *Journal of Consulting and Clinical Psychology, 74(6)*, 1041-1054.

McCARROLL, B. R. (1998). Caregiving disruptions and attachment in psychiatric inpatient adolescents. *Dissertation Abstracts International: Section B: The Sciences and Engineering,59(5 B)*, 2457.

McCARTHY, A.M. (1998). Paternal characteristics associated with disturbed father-daughter attachment and separation among women with eating disorder symptoms. *Dissertation Abstracts International: Section B: The Sciences and Engineering, 59(4-B)*, 1861.

MELOY, J R., & GACONO, C.B. (1998). *The internal world of the psychopath.* New York, NY: Guilford Press.

MELOY, J. R. (1992). *Violent attachments.* Lanham, MD: Jason Aronson.

MELOY, J.R., GACONO, C.B., & KENNEY, L. (1994). A Rorschach investigation of sexual homicide. *Journal of Personality Assessment, 62(1)*, 58-67.

MEYER, B., AJCHENBRENNER, M., & BOWLES, D. P. (2005). Sensory sensitivity, attachment experiences, and rejection responses among adults with borderline and avoidant features. *Journal of Personality Disorders, 19(6)*, 641-658.

MEYER, B., PILKONIS, P. A., & BEEVERS, C. G. (2004). What's in a (neutral) face? Personality disorders, attachment styles, and the appraisal of ambiguous social cues. *Journal of Personality Disorders, 18(4)*, 320-336.

MEYER, G. J. (1996). The Rorschach and MMPI: Toward a more scientifically differentiated understanding of cross-method assessment. *Journal-of-Personality-Assessment, 67(3),* 558-578.

MEYER, G. J., FINN, S. E., EYDE, L. D., KAY, G. G., MORELAND, K. L., DIES, R. R., EISMAN, E. J., KUBISZYN, T. W., & READ, G. M. (2001). Psychological testing and psychological assessment: A review of evidence and issues. *American-Psychologist, 56(2)* 128-165.

MEYER, G.J. (2001). Psychological testing and psychological assessment: A review of evidence and issues. *American Psychologist, 56(2),* 128-165.

MEYER, G.J., & ARCHER, R.P. (2001). The hard science of Rorschach research: What do we know and where do we go? *Psychological Assessment, 13(4),* 486-502.

MIKULINCER, M., & SHAVER, P. (2003). The Attachment Behavioral System in Adulthood: Activation, Psychodynamics, and Interpersonal Processes Zanna, M. P. (Ed). *Advances in experimental social psychology, 35,* 53-152.

MILLER, S. B. (1987). A comparison of methods of inquiry: Testing and interviewing contributions to the diagnostic process. *Bulletin of the Menninger Clinic, 51(6),* 505-518.

MINZENBERG, M. J., POOLE, J. H., & VINOGRADOV, S. (2006). Social-emotion recognition in borderline personality disorder. *Comprehensive Psychiatry, 47(6),* 468-474.

MORGAN, L., & VIGLIONE, D. J. (1992). Sexual disturbances, Rorschach sexual responses, and mediating factors. *Psychological Assessment, 4(4),* 530-536.

MURAS, A. (1996). Attachment style and its relationship to affect, social behavior, and object relations. *Dissertation Abstracts International: Section B: The Sciences and Engineering,* 56(10 B), 5777.

MURPHY P., & DONNA, M. (1996). An investigation of incarcerated females: Rorschach indices and psychopathy checklist scores. *Dissertation Abstracts International: Section B: The Sciences and Engineering, 56(1 B),* 0531.

NEUMANN, E., BIERHOFF, H. W. (2004). Ichbezogenheit versus Liebe in Paarbeziehungeri: Narzissmus im Zusammenhang mit Bindung und Liebesstilen / Egotism versus Love in Romantic Relationships: Narcissism Related to Attachment and Love Styles. *Zeitschrift fur Sozialpsychologie, 35(1),* 33-44.

NICKELL, A. D., WAUDBY, C. J., & TRULL, T.J. (2002). Attachment, parental bonding and borderline personality disorder features in young adults. *Journal of Personality Disorders, 16(2),* 148-159.

NOVICK, A. B. (1997). Self and other, mother and child: The role of maternal object relations, empathy, and attachment in the formation of object relations in the child. *Dissertation Abstracts International: Section B: The Sciences and Engineering, 58(6 B)*, 3323.

NOY-SHARAV, D. M. A. (2002). Good enough adoptive parenting – the adopted child and self object relations, *Clinical Social Work Journal*, 30 (1), 57-76.

O' BRIEN, M. L. (1987). Examining the dimensionality of pathological narcissism: Factor analysis and construct validity of the O'Brien Multiphasic Narcissism Inventory. *Psychological Reports, 61*, 499-510.

O' CONNOR, M., SIGMAN, M., & BRILL, N. (1987). Disorganization of attachment in relation to maternal alcohol consumption. *Journal of Consulting and Clinical Psychology, 55(6)*, 831-836.

ODIPO, C. O. (2002). Adult attachment classification and foster mothers' perceptions of their relationship with their at-risk foster children. *Dissertation-Abstracts-International-Section-A:-Humanities-and-Social-Sciences, 63(4-A)*, 1257.

OPD TASK FORCE (2001). *Diagnosi Psicodinamica Operazionalizzata. Presupposti e Applicazioni Cliniche.* (Ed. Italiana a cura di A. De Coro), Milano: Masson.

ORZOLEK-KRONNER, C. A. (2001). The relationship between attachment patterns and guilt in the function of eating disorder symptoms: Can symptoms be proximity-seeking? *Dissertation Abstracts International Section A: Humanities and Social Sciences, 61(11-A)*, 4551.

OZER, D. J. (1999). Four principles for personality assessment. In John, O. P. (Ed); Pervin, L. A. (Ed). *Handbook of personality: Theory and research* (2nd ed.). (pp. 671-686). New York, NY, US: Guilford Press.

PARKER, G., TUPLING, H., & BROWN, L. B. (1979). A parental bonding instrument. *British Journal of Medical Psychology, 52(1)*, 1-10.

PARKER, G., TUPLING, H., & BROWN, L. B. (1979). A Parental Bonding Instrument. *British Journal of Medical Psychology, 52*, 1-10.

PATRICK, M., HOBSON, R.P., CASTLE, D., HOWARD, R., ET ALL (1994). Personality disorder and the mental representation of early social experience. *Development and Psychopathology, 6(2)*, 375-388

PEARSON, J.L. (1994). Earned- and continuous-security in adult attachment: Relation to depressive symptomatology and parenting style. Cambridge University Press.

Penguin.

PERRY, W., & VIGLIONE, D. J. (1991). The Ego Impairment Index as a predictor of out-come in melancholic depressed patients treated with tricyclic antidepressants. *Journal of Personality Assessment, 56*, 487-501.

PERRY, W., & VIGLIONE, D.J. (1991). The Ego Impairment Index as a predictor of out-come in melancholic depressed patients treated with tricyclic antidepressants. *Journal of Personality Assessment, 56(3)*, 487-501.

PERRY, W., McDOUGALL, A., & VIGLIONE, D. J. JR (1995). A five year follow up on the temporal stability of the Ego Impairment Index. *Journal of Personality Assessment, 64(1)*, 112-118.

PINTO, A. F. (1999). A Rorschach study of object representations and attachment in male adolescents with disruptive behaviors. *Dissertation Abstracts International: Section B: The Sciences and Engineering, 59(9 B)*, 5105.

PIOTROWSKI, C., & KELLER, J.W. (1989). Psychological testing in outpatient mental health facilities: A national study. *Professional Psychology: Research and Practice*, 20(6), 423-425.

PIOTROWSKI, C., SHERRY, D., & KELLER, J.W. (1985). Psychodiagnostic test usage: A sur-vey of the Society for Personality Assessment. *Journal of Personality Assessment, 49(2)*, 115-119.

PIPP, S., EASTERBROOKS, M. A., & HARMON, R. (1992). The relation between attachment and knowledge of self and mother in one to three year old infants. *Child-Development, 63* 738-750.

POPPER, M. (2002). Narcissism and attachment patterns of personalized and social-ized charismatic leaders. *Journal of Social and Personal Relationships, 19(6)*, 797-809.

PRIEL, B., & BESSER, A, (2001) Bridging theap between attachment and object rela-tions theories: A study of the transition to motherhood. *British Journal of Medical Psychology, 74(Pt1)*, 85-100.

PRIEL, B., & BESSER, A. (2001). Bridging the gap between attachment and object rela-tions theories: A study of the transition to motherhood. *British Journal of Medical Psychology, 74(1)*, 85-100.

RADOJEVIC, V. (1992). Behavioral intervention with and without family support for rheumatoid arthritis. *Behavior Therapy, 23(1)*, 13-30.

RASKIN, R.N., & HALL, C. S. (1979). A narcissistic personality inventory. *Psychological Reports, 45(2)*, 590.

REID, R. R. (2001). Adult attachment and the Rorschach. *Dissertation Abstracts International: Section B: The Sciences and Engineering, 61(8 B)*, 4425.

REID, R. R. (2001). Adult attachment and the Rorschach. *Dissertation Abstracts International: Section B: The Sciences and Engineering, 61(8 B)*, 4425.

REID,-RHONDA-RENE (2001)Adult attachment and the Rorschach. Dissertation abstracts International: Section B: The Sciences and Engineering, 61(8-B), 4425

RHOLES, W. S., & SIMPSON, J. (2004). *Adult attachment: Theory, research, and clinical implications. Adult attachment: Theory, research, and clinical implications.* New York, NY, US: Guilford Publications. xiii, 481 pp.

RIGGS, S.A., PAULSON, A., TUNNELL, E., SAHL, G., ATKISON, H., & ROSS, C.A. (2007). Attachment, personality, and psychopathology among adult inpatients: Self-reported romantic attachment style versus Adult Attachment Interview states of mind. *Development and Psychopathology, 19(1)*, 263-291.

RITZLER, B.A., & ALTER, B. (1986). Rorschach teaching in APA-approved clinical graduate programs: Ten years later. *Journal of Personality Assessment, 50(1)*, 44-49.

RITZLER, B.A., & DEL GAUDIO, A.C. (1976). A survey of Rorschach teaching in APA-approved clinical graduate programs. *Journal of Personality Assessment, 40(5)*, 451-453.

RORSCHACH, H. (1921). *Psychodiagnostik.* Bern: Bircher.

ROSENSTEIN, D.S. (1993). Attachment, personality and psychopathology in adolescence. *Dissertation Abstracts International, 53(7-B)*, 3810.

ROSENSTEIN, D.S., & HOROWITZ, H.A. (1996). Adolescent attachment and psychopathology. *Journal of Consulting and Clinical Psychology, 64(2)*, 244-253.

ROSENTHAL, J. A., SCHMIDT, D., & CONNER, J. (1988). Predictors of special needs adoptions destruption: An exploratory study. *Children and Youth Services*, 10, 101-117.

ROTHMAN, P. D. (2004). The influence of the quality of adult attachment and degree of exposure to the World Trade Center Disaster on Post-Traumatic Stress symptoms in a college population. *Dissertation Abstracts International: Section B: The Sciences and Engineering, 64(8-B)*, 4060.

ROTHSTEIN, D. N. (1997). Object relations and attachment: A comparison of Rorschach responses and adult attachment classifications. *Dissertation Abstracts International: Section B: The Sciences and Engineering, 58(5 B)*, 2698.

RUSSEK, L. G., SCHWARTZ, G. E. (1997).feelings of parental caring predict health status in midlife: a 35-years follow-up of the Harvard Mastery of Stress Study. *Journal of Behavioural Medicine, 20,* 1-13.

SABLE, P. (2007). Accentuating the positive in adult attachments. *Attachment and Human Development, 9(4),* 361-374.

SACHSE, J., & STRAUSS, B. (2002). Bindungscharakteristika und behandlungserfolg nach stationarer psychodynamischer gruppenpsychotherapie / Attachment characteristics and psychotherapy outcome following inpatient psychodynamic group treatment. *Psychotherapie Psychosomatik Medizinische Psychologie, 52(3-4),* 134-140.

SAGI, A., VAN IJZENDOORN, M., SCHARF, M., NINA, K., TIRTSA J., & OFRA, M. (1994). Stability and Discriminant Validity of the adult Attachment interview: a Psychometric Study in Young Israeli Adults. *Developmental Psychology, 30(5),* 771-777.

SALCUNI, S., & LIS A. (2004). La richiesta di adozione: dimensione di personalità dei futuri genitori tramite il test di Rorschach. *Infanzia e Adolescenza, 2(3),* 137-146.

SAMEROFF, A. J., & EMDE, R. N. (1992). *Relationship disturbances in early childhood: A developmental approach.* New York, NY, US: Basic Books. x, 267 pp.

SANTONA, A., ZAVATTINI, G.C., DELOGU, A.M., CASTELLANO, R., PACE, C.S., & VISMARA, L. (2006). La transizione alla genitorialita attraverso l'adozione / Transition to Parenthood through Adoption. *Rassegna di Psicologia, 23(2),* 69-88.

SCHARFE, E. (2007). Cause or consequence?: Exploring causal links between attachment and depression. *Journal of Social and Clinical Psychology, 26,* 1048-1064.

SELBY, B. W. (2001). The relation of attachment, adjustment and narcissism to masculine gender role conflict. *Dissertation Abstracts International: Section B: The Sciences and Engineering, 61(9-B),* 5005.

SHAPIRO, C. H. (1988). *Infertility and pregnancy loss.* San Francisco: Jossey-Bass.

SHAVER, P. R., & FRALEY, R. C. (2000). Attachment theory and caregiving. *Psychological Inquiry, 11(2),* 109-114.

SHAVER, P. R., & MIKULINCER, M. (2002). Attachment-related psychodynamics. *Attachment and Human Development, 4(2),* 133-161.

SHAVER, P. R., & MIKULINCER, M. (2002). Dialogue on adult attachment: Diversity and integration. *Attachment and Human Development, 4(2),* 243-257.

SHAVER, P. R., BELSKY, J., & BRENNAN, K. A. (2000). The adult attachment interview and self-reports of romantic attachment: Associations across domains and methods. *Personal Relationships, 7(1),* 25-43.

SHOHAM-SALOMON, V., HANNAH, M. (1991). Client-treatment interaction in the study of differential change processes. *Journal of Consulting and Clinical Psychology,59(2),* 217-225.

SHOREY, H. S., & SNYDER, C. R. (2006). The Role of Adult Attachment Styles in Psychopathology and Psychotherapy Outcomes. *Review of General Psychology, 10(1),* 1-20.

SLADE, A. (1999). *Attachment theory and research: Implications for the theory and practice of individual psychotherapy with adults.* Shaver, P. R. (Ed); Cassidy, J. (Ed). *Handbook of attachment: Theory, research, and clinical applications.* (pp. 575-594). New York, NY, US: Guilford Press. XVII, 925 pp.

SLOAN, P., ARSENAULT, L., HILSENROTH, M., & HARVILL, L. (1995). Rorschach measures of posttraumatic stress in Persian Gulf War veterans. *Journal of Personality Assessment, 64(3),* 397-414.

SLOAN, P., ARSENAULT, L., HILSENROTH, M., HANDLER, L., & HARVILL, L. (1996). Rorschach measures of posttraumatic stress in Persian Gulf War veterans: A three year follow up study. *Journal of Personality Assessment, 66(1),* 54-64.

SMOLEWSKA, K., & DION, K. L. (2005). Narcissism and Adult Attachment: A Multivariate Approach. *Self and Identity, 4(1),* 59-68.

SOLANO, L., TORIELLO, A., BARNABA, L., ARA, R., & TAYLOR, G. J. (2000). Rorschach interaction patterns, alexithymia, and closeness to parents in psychotic and psychosomatic patients. *Journal of the American Academy of Psychoanalysis, 28(1),* 101-116.

SOLOMON, J., & GEORGE, C. (1996). Defining the caregiving system: Toward a theory of caregiving. *Infant-Mental-Health-Journal, 17(3),* 183-197.

SOLOMON, J., & GEORGE, C. (1996). Defining the caregiving system: Toward a theory of caregiving. *Infant-Mental-Health-Journal, 17(3),* 183-197.

SOLOMON, J., & GEORGE, C., & DE-JONG, A. (1995) Children classified as controlling at age six: Evidence of disorganized representational strategies and aggression at home and at school. *Development-and-Psychopathology, 7(3),* 447-463.

SOLOMON, J., & GEORGE, C. (1999). *Attachment disorganization.* New York, NY, US: Guilford Press. XXIII, 420 pp.

SOLOMON, J., & GEORGE, C. (1999).*The place of disorganization in attachment theory: Linking classic observations with contemporary findings.* George, C. (Ed);

Solomon, J. (Ed). *Attachment disorganization.* (pp. 3-32). New York, NY, US: Guilford Press. XXIII, 420 pp.

SROUFE, L. A. (1988). *The role of infant-caregiver attachment in development.* Nezworski, Teresa (Ed); Belsky, Jay (Ed). Clinical implications of attachment. (pp. 18-38). Hillsdale, NJ, England: Lawrence Erlbaum Associates, Inc. XVII, 440 pp.

SROUFE, L. A. (1986). Appraisal: Bowlby's contribution to psychoanalytic theory and developmental psychology—attachment, separation, loss. *Journal of Child Psychology and Psychiatry, 27(6),* 841-849.

SROUFE. J. W. (1991). Assessment of parent adolescent relationships: Implications for adolescent development. *Journal of Family Psychology,* 5, 21–45.

STANLEY, S. M. (2006). Attachment and prefrontal emotional reactivity: An EEG study of emotional processing in the context of attachment. *Dissertation-Abstracts-International:-Section-B:-The-Sciences-and-Engineering, 66(10-B),* 5261.

STECKLEY, P. L. (2006). An examination of the relationship between clients' attachment experiences, their internal working models of self and others, and therapists' empathy in the outcome of process-experiential and cognitive-behavioural therapies. *Dissertation Abstracts International Section A: Humanities and Social Sciences, Vol 67.*

STEELE, H., & STEELE, M. (1994). *Intergenerational patterns of attachment.* London, England: Jessica Kingsley Publishers.

STEELE, M., & BARADON, T. (1994). The Clinical Use of the Adult Attachment Interview in Parent-Infant Psychotherapy. *Infant Mental Health Journal, 25(4),* 284-299.

STEKETEE, G., & VAN NOPPEN, B. (2003). Family Approaches to Treatment for Obsessive Compulsive Disorder. *Journal of Family Psychotherapy, 14(4),* 55-71.

STRICKER, G., & GOLD, J.R. (1999). The Rorschach: Towards a nomothetically based, idiographically applicable, configurational model. *Psychological Assessment, 11, 240*-250.

STUBBE, D.E., ZAHNER, G.E., GOLDSTEIN, M.J., & LECKMAN, J.F. (1993). Diagnostic specificity of a brief measure of expressed emotion: A community study of children. *Journal of Child-Psychology and Psychiatry, Vol 34(2),* 139-154.

SULDO, S.M., & SANDBERG, D.A. (2000). Relationship between attachment styles and eating disorder symptomatology among college women. *Journal of College Student Psychotherapy, 15(1),* 59-73.

SWANN, W. (1997). The Trouble with change: Self-verification and allegiance to the self. *Psychological Science, 8,* 177–180.

SWEENEY, J. A., CLARKIN, J.F., & FITZGIBBON, M.L. (1987). Current practice of psychological assessment. Professional Psychology: Research and Practice, 18(4), 377-380.

TARGUM, S.D., DIBBLE, E.D., YOLANDE, B., & GERSHON, E.S. (1981). The Family Attitudes Questionnaire: Patients' and spouses' views of bipolar illness. Archives of General Psychiatry. 38(5), 562-568

TASCA, G. A., KOWAL, J., BALFOUR, L., RITCHIE, K., VIRLEY, B., & BISSADA, H. (2006). An attachment insecurity model of negative affect among women seeking treatment for an eating disorder. Eating Behaviors, 7(3), 252-257.

TASCA, G. A., RITCHIE, K., CONRAD, G., BALFOUR, L., GAYTON, J., LYBANON, V., & BISSADA, H. (2006). Attachment scales predict outcome in a randomized controlled trial of two group therapies for binge eating disorder: An aptitude by treatment interaction. Psychotherapy Research, 16(1), 106-121.

TASCA, G., BALFOUR, L., RITCHIE, K., & BISSADA, H. (2007). Change in attachment anxiety is associated with improved depression among women with binge eating disorder. Psychotherapy: Theory, Research, Practice, Training, 44(4), 423-433.

TASCA, G., BALFOUR, L., RITCHIE, K., & BISSADA, H. (2007). The Relationship Between Attachment Scales and Group Therapy Alliance Growth Differs by Treatment Type for Women With Binge-Eating Disorder. Group Dynamics: Theory, Research, and Practice, 11(1), 1-14.

Tessier, R. (1992). Mothers' experience of stress following the birth of a first child: Identification of stressors and coping resources. Journal of Applied Social Psychology, 22(17), 1319-1339.

TETI, D., GELFAND, D., MESSINGER, D., & ISABELLA, R. (1995). Maternal depression and the quality of early attachment: An examination of infants, preschoolers, and their mothers. Developmental Psychology, 31(3), 364-376.

TILUS, M. R. (2003). The roles of spirituality and adult romantic attachment in responses to exposure to trauma and the development of post-traumatic stress disorder in nonclinical military couples. Dissertation Abstracts International: Section B: The Sciences and Engineering, 64(1-B), 433.

TRACEY, T.J., & KOKOTOVIC, A.M. (1989). Factor structure of the Working Alliance Inventory. Psychological Assessment: A Journal of Consulting and Clinical Psychology, 1(3), 207-210.

TROXEL, W.M., CYRANOWSKI, J.M., HALL, M., FRANK, E., & BUYSSE, D.J. (2007). Attachment anxiety, relationship context, and sleep in women with recurrent major depression. Psychosomatic Medicine, 69, 692-699.

TURTON, P., MCGAULEY, G., MARIN-AVELLAN, L., & HUGHES, P. (2001). The Adult Attachment Interview: Rating and classification problems posed by non-normative samples. *Attachment and Human Development, 3(3)*, 284-303.

Urist, J. (1977). The Rorschach test and the assessment of object relations. *Journal of Personality Assessment,* 41, 3-9.

VAN IJZENDOORN, M. (1995). Adult attachment representations, parental responsiveness, and infant attachment: A meta-analysis on the predictive validity of the Adult Attachment Interview. *Psychological Bulletin, 117(3)*, 387-403.

VAN IJZENDOORN, M. H. (1995). Adult attachment representations, parental responsiveness and infant attachment: A meta-analysis on the predictive validity of the Adult Attachment Interview. *Psychological Bull.* 117(3), 387–403.

VAN IJZENDOORN, M.H., & KROONENBERG, P. M. (1988). Cross-cultural patterns of attachment: A meta-analysis of the strange situation. *Child Development, Vol 59(1)*, 147-156.

VAN IJZENDOORN, M.H., & BAKERMANS-KRANENBURG, M.J. (1996). Attachment representations in mothers, fathers, adolescents, and clinical groups: A meta-analytic search for normative data. *Journal of Consulting and Clinical Psychology, 64(1)*, 8-21.

VAN IJZENDOORN, M. H., & SAGI, A. (1999). *Cross-cultural patterns of attachment: Universal and contextual dimensions.* New York, NY: Guilford Press

VAN, HENRICUS, L., SCHOEVERS, R. A., KOOL, S., HENDRIKSEN, M., PEEN, J., & DEKKER, J. (2008). Does early response predict outcome in psychotherapy and combined therapy for major depression? *Journal of Affective Disorders, 105(1-3)*, 261-265.

VAN,-HENRICUS-L; SCHOEVERS,-ROBERT-A; KOOL,-SIMONE; HENDRIKSEN,-MARIELLE; PEEN,-JAAP; DEKKER,-JACK: Does early response predict outcome in psychotherapy and combined therapy for major depression? Journal-of-Affective-Disorders. Vol 105(1-3) Jan 2008, 261-265.

VAN-ECKE, Y., CHOPE, R. C., & EMMELKAMP, P. M. G. (2007). Immigrants and attachment status: Research findings with Dutch and Belgian immigrants in California. *Social-Behavior-and-Personality,33(7)*, 657-673.

VAN-IJZENDOORN, M. H., & BAKERMANS-KRANENBURG, M. J. (1996). Attachment representations in mothers, fathers, adolescents, and clinical groups: A meta-analytic search for normative data. *Journal-of-Consulting-and-Clinical-Psychology, l 64(1),* 8-21.

VAN-IJZENDOORN, M. H., & BAKERMANS-KRANENBURG, M. J. (1996). Attachment representations in mothers, fathers, adolescents, and clinical groups: A meta-analytic search for normative data. *Journal of Consulting and Clinical Psychology, 64(1),* 8-21.

VIGLIONE, D. J. (1999). A review of recent research addressing the utility of the Rorschach. *Psychological Assessment, 11,* 251-265.

VIGLIONE, D.J., & PERRY, W. (1991). A general model for psychological assessment and psychopathology applied to depression. British *Journal of-Projective Psychology, 36(1),* 1-16.

VOSS, K. (2001). Understanding adolescent antisocial behaviour from attachment theory and coercion theory perspectives. *Dissertation Abstracts International: Section B: The Sciences and Engineering, 61(12-B),* 6723.

VOSTANIS, P., NICHOLLS, J., & HARRINGTON, R. (1994). Maternal expressed emotion in conduct and emotional disorders of childhood. *Journal of Child Psychology and Psychiatry, 34(2),* 139-154.

WADDINGTON, C. (1957). *The strategy of the genes.* London: George Unwin & Unwin.

WARD, A., RAMSAY, R., TURNBULL, S., STEELE, M., STEELE, H., & TREASURE, J. (2001). Attachment in anorexia nervosa: A transgenerational perspective. *British Journal of Medical Psychology, 74(4),* 497-505.

WARD, M. J., BOTYANSKI, N. C., PLUNKET, S. W., AND CARLSON, E. A. (1991). *The concurrent validity of the AAI for adolescent mothers.* Symposium presented at the biennial meeting of the Society for Research in Child Development. Seattle, WA.

WARD, M.J., LEE, S. S., & POLAN, H. J. (2006). Attachment and psychopathology in a community sample. *Attachment and Human Development, 8(4),* 327-340.

WARREN, S., HUSTON, L., EGELAND, B., & SROUFE, A. (1997). Child and adolescent anxiety disorders and early attachment. *Journal of the American Academy of Child and Adolescent Psychiatry, 36(5),* 637-644.

WATERS, E., & POSADA, G. (1993). Is attachment theory ready to contribute to our understanding of disruptive behavior problems?. *Development-and-Psychopathology, (1-2),* 215-224.

WATERS, E., CROWELL, J., TREBOUX, D., O' CONNOR, E., POSADA, G., & GOLBY, B. (1993). *Discriminant validity of the Adult Attachment Interview.* Poster presented at the 60th Meeting of the Society for Research in Child Development, New Orleans, LA.

WEBER, C. A. (1991). Analysis of attachment through texture, human movement and human content Rorschach variables in inpatient conduct disordered and dysthymic adolescents. *Dissertation Abstracts International, 51(9 A)*, 3024.

WEBER, C. A., MELOY, J. R., & GACONO, C. B. (1992). A Rorschach study of attachment and anxiety in inpatient conduct disordered and dysthymic adolescents. *Journal of Personality Assessment, 58(1)*, 16-26.

WEINER, I. B., & Exner, J. E. (1991). Rorschach changes in long-term and short-term psychotherapy. *Journal-of-Personality-Assessment, 56(3)*, 453-465.

WEINER, I. B. (1998). *Principles of Rorschach interpretation*. Mahwah, NJ: Lawrence Erlbaum Associates, Inc.

WEINER, I.B. (2001). Advancing the science of psychological assessment: The Rorschach Inkblot Method as exemplar. *Psychological Assessment, 13*, 423-432.

WEISS, R. J. (1982). Understanding moral thought: Effects on moral reasoning and decision making. *Developmental-Psychology, 18(6)*, 852-861.

WEISS, S., (2002). Maternal Expressed Emotion as a predictor of emotional and behavioral problems in low birth weight children. *Issues in Mental Health Nursing, 23(6)*, 649.

WELLMAN, P. (1990). A review of the physiological bases of the anorexic action of phenylpropanolamine (d,l-norephedrine). *Neuroscience and Biobehavioral Reviews, 14(3)*, 339-355.

WEST, M., & GEORGE, C. (2002). Attachment and dysthymia: The contributions of pre-occupied attachment and agency of self to depression in women. *Attachment-and-Human-Development, 4(3)*, 278-293.

WEST, M., & SHELDON-KELLER, A. E. (1994). *Patterns of relating: An adult attachment perspective*. New York, NY, US: Guilford Press. xii, 210 pp.

WEST, M., & GEORGE, C. (1999). Abuse and violence in intimate adult relationships: New perspectives from attachment theory. *Attachment and Human Development, 1(2)*, 137-156.

WEST, M., & SHELDON-KELLER, A. (1994). *Patterns of relating: An adult attachment perspective. Patterns of relating: An adult attachment perspective*. New York, NY, US: Guilford Press. xii, 210 pp.

WINNICOTT, D. (1958). *Dalla pediatria alla psicoanalisi*. Tr. It. Martinelli, Firenze 1975.

WINNICOTT, D. W. (1960). The theory of parent-infant relationship. *International Journal of Psychoanalysis, 41*, 585-595.

YOUNG, J. (1964). Memory mechanisms of the brain. *Journal-of-Mental-Science, 108,* 119-133.

ZAKALIK, R.A., & WEI, M. (2006). Adult Attachment, Perceived Discrimination Based on Sexual Orientation, and Depression in Gay Males: Examining the Mediation and Moderation Effects. *Journal of Counseling Psychology,* 53, 302-313.

ZEANAH, C.H., & BARTON, M. L. (1989). Introduction: Internal representations and parentnfant relationships. *Infant Mental Health Journal, 10(3),* 135-141.

ZUELLIG, A. R. (2003). A comparison of the effect of three therapies on generalized anxiety disordered adults' self-reported internal working models of attachment. *Dissertation Abstracts International: Section B: The Sciences and Engineering, 63(9-B),* 4392.